THE WORK IS YOURS

The Life of
Saint John Baptist de La Salle

Saint John Baptist de La Salle, detail of an engraving by J. B. Scotin of a painting by P. Léger printed in the biography of De La Salle by J. B. Blain in 1733; reverse photo by Emile Rousset, FSC.

THE WORK IS YOURS

The Life of
Saint John Baptist de La Salle

by
Luke Salm, FSC

1989
Christian Brothers Publications
Romeoville, Illinois

BROTHER LUKE SALM, a Doctor of Theology, is Professor of Religious Studies at Manhattan College in New York City and a past president of the Catholic Theological Society of America. An elected delegate to the 39th, 40th, and 41st General Chapters of the De La Salle Brothers, Brother Luke is currently engaged in making available to a wider public recent scholarly research on the life of Saint John Baptist de La Salle and the early history of the Brothers' Institute. Already published are his *Beginnings: De La Salle and His Brothers* (1980), *Encounters: De La Salle at Parmenie* (1983), and *John Baptist de La Salle: The Formative Years* (1989). Brother Luke has also authored biographies of Brothers Miguel, Benilde, Mutien-Marie, Scubilion, and Arnold.

The etching on page 23 is of the Sorbonne, from *Views of France and Italy,* by Israel Silvestre and various artists, 1621–1691. The National Gallery of Art, Washington, D.C. Gift of Robert H. Thayer. Used with permission of the National Gallery.

Published by Christian Brothers Publications
100 De La Salle Drive, Romeoville IL 60441-1896

Printed in the United States of America

Library of Congress catalog card number 89-62641
ISBN 0-9623279-1-3

Cover: Mural by Fabian Zaccone in the chapel of De La Salle and his Brothers at Manhattan College, New York City.

Contents

List of Illustrations

Preface

More than thirty years have passed since the appearance in 1957 of Brother Clair Battersby's life of Saint John Baptist de La Salle, the most enduring biography of the Founder of the Institute of the Brothers of the Christian Schools to be written in English. That landmark volume is now out of print. So also are the earlier studies of Martin Dempsey and Edward Fitzpatrick. In the meantime, the results of intensive research in the field of Lasallian studies have shed new light on many aspects of the life and times of De La Salle. Now seems to be the time for a new biography in English.

There are other reasons as well. Ever since Vatican Council II, the Institute of the Brothers has undergone radical change in its policies and structure. In the process there has developed among the Brothers unprecedented diversity in dress, lifestyle, and ministries. In that situation, the person and the charism of the Founder have assumed a new importance as the strongest bond of unity for the Brothers. Furthermore, the recent emphasis on the Lasallian family has led the Brothers to realize that they share the tradition inherited from the Founder with their colleagues and associates in the ministry of education. This has generated a fresh interest in the vision and achievement of De La Salle that extends beyond the members of the Institute. More and more people are anxious to learn just who was that "La Salle" or "De La Salle" after whom their schools are named.

These considerations have determined to a great extent the style and the format of the work that follows. Although it reflects many of the most recent findings in Lasallian studies, the book makes no pretentions to high scholarship. Footnotes have been eliminated altogether so as not to impede the flow of the narrative. Since most of the source material is in French, there seems to be little purpose in burdening the text with references not immediately accessible to most of those for whom the book is intended. This approach points out a further need, that is, for a fully elaborated and documented biography of De La Salle in English that will meet the highest standards of historical and interpretative scholarship. But that is a project for the future.

Since, however, a good bit of the material in this biography is appearing in English for the first time, and since some of it amplifies or even contradicts traditionally held notions about events and their significance in the life of the Founder, it is appropriate to give some assurance that the narrative has not been fabricated out of the author's imagination or prejudice. The remainder of this preface, then, will constitute a sort of extended footnote, indicating in a general way the sources for the various sections of this present study and where they may be found. The casual reader might want to skip over this section, for the time being at least, and proceed at once to the Prologue in order to be introduced to a young priest wondering what it was that God was leading him into.

The Prologue is an imaginative meditation intended to draw the reader immediately into the life drama of the man who was John Baptist de La Salle, a real human being facing difficult decisions. Today he would be called "Father De La Salle." It is an anachronism to name him "Saint La Salle," or to think of him that way, as many Brothers do, as if he came into the world endowed with canonizable sanctity from the day he was born. Pious and devout as he no doubt was all through his life, the use of the title "saint" is appropriate only in reference to his life after death. No, he was John Baptist (in French the name is hyphenated), son of Mr. and Mrs. De La Salle.

The Prologue situates the decision to bring the teachers to his table on Easter in 1680. That is an educated guess. The event is historical; the year is accurate; the date is possible and even probable, despite some authors who prefer to locate it in June. This author is indebted to Brother Michel Sauvage and a talk he delivered in Rome in 1984 for suggesting Easter as the critical date, and for many other insights, a debt that is here gratefully acknowledged. In any case, the important thing in the Prologue is not the date but the decisive character of this step as De La Salle was becoming increasingly involved in a process he could not completely control and the outcome of which he could not possibly foresee.

The chapters dealing with the Founder's family and education are drawn for the most part, and sometimes paraphrased, from the volumes of the *Cahiers lasalliens* authored by Brother Léon Aroz, especially Volume 41 II, entitled *Les années d'imprégnation*. There is in these early chapters a good bit of material that is not found in the biographies hitherto available in English. A more fully developed treatment of this material can be found in English in the author's recent *John Baptist de La Salle: The Formative Years*, part of the series known as Lasallian Publications.

The guide, model, and principal source for the narrative covering the years from 1679, when De La Salle first became involved
with the schoolmasters of Nyel, until his death in 1719 has, for the
most part, been the three-volume biography of Blain. Canon Jean-
Baptiste Blain was the ecclesiastical superior, that is, the liaison with
the archdiocesan authorities, for the Brothers in Rouen during the
last years of De La Salle's life and for several years after his death.
Blain had been commissioned by Brother Timothée, the second
Superior General after the Founder, to write the official biography,
necessary if ever there would be a hope of canonization. Blain thus
had at his disposal the Founder's personal written memoirs as well
as the notes and recollections that had been solicited from the
Brothers who knew him. He also had the manuscript of a previous,
unpublished attempt by Brother Bernard and copies of the first
version of a biography, written independently and without the
knowledge of the Brothers, by the Founder's nephew, Dom Elie
Maillefer.

Blain's completed work was published in 1733. It comprises
two quarto volumes of about 500 closely printed pages each, divided into four sections or "books." The first three books are the
biography proper; the fourth, entitled "Spirit and Virtues," is clearly
an early attempt to gather the evidence for holiness of life that might
someday be required in the formal canonization process. An anastatic
reproduction of the first French edition has been published in the
Cahiers lasalliens, Volumes 7 and 8.

Although Blain's work has been the basis for all the others
published since, the fourth book on the "Spirit and Virtues" was
for years the only section that had been translated into English, ostensibly for the spiritual reading of the candidates in the Brothers'
novitiates. The biography as such became available in English for
the first time only recently in the translation by Brother Richard
Arnandez, published in a limited offset edition by the Christian
Brothers Conference. For all practical purposes Blain's biography
remains virtually unknown to those who never had the occasion to
read it in the original French.

Blain is not easy to read. He indulges in extensive moralizing
and flights of pious rhetoric; he is utterly uninhibited in interpreting
the designs of divine Providence; like an old fashioned western
movie, his narrative is all black and white, with De La Salle and
his Brothers as the heroes and their enemies the villains; in short,

he uses all the techniques that are characteristic of an older school of hagiography. On the other hand, he had the written sources at hand and often quotes them verbatim; he can tell a good story with an eye for context and significant detail; the narrative portions of his work constitute high drama. The author of the present biography has tried to preserve some of the intensity of Blain that more somber biographers have chosen to leave aside.

At times the temptation to quote Blain directly, to let him "tell it in his own words," proved too strong to resist. In those cases the author has made free use of the Arnandez translation, with occasional modifications for clarity or emphasis. It seemed pretentious and unnecessary to supply page references. For those who have access to the text of Blain, the context of the quotations cited here is sufficient to guide the inquisitive reader to the appropriate place in any French or English edition.

Blain cannot be used as a unique source in isolation from the other authors contemporary with the Founder. The earliest of these was Brother Bernard, who was only in his early twenties when he was assigned by Brother Timothée, then Superior General, to undertake a biography of the Founder based on the available documents and the written notes of the Brothers. The poor Brother proved unequal to the task, and his work was deemed by the Superior to be unsuitable for publication. Only 86 manuscript pages have survived, covering the period up to the year 1688. The manuscript has one valuable aspect. It had been sent for comment to Jean-Louis de La Salle, the Founder's brother, who took exception to certain passages, crossed them out, and added some marginal notes of his own. A photographic copy of the entire manuscript, with a printed transcription, has been published in *Cahiers lasalliens,* Volume 4. An English translation by Brother William Quinn is scheduled for publication in the near future.

While Brother Bernard was still working on his biography, the Founder's nephew, Dom Elie (François) Maillefer, without the knowledge of the Brothers, had undertaken to write his own version of the Founder's life, a work he completed in 1723. His stated purpose was to edify. For that reason he was careful to sidestep controversial issues, such as the tensions between John Baptist and the rest of the De La Salle family, the difficulties with ecclesiastical authorities, and the crisis over Jansenism. Since Dom Maillefer himself was known for his Jansenist sympathies, the Brothers were reluctant to publish his manuscript once they learned that it was available. But one of the Brothers borrowed it and had several copies made, two of which have survived.

When Blain was commissioned to write the official biography, he was given a copy of Maillefer's work and made extensive use of it without acknowledging the source. As soon as Blain's work appeared in 1733, Maillefer was so enraged that he resolutely set about to produce a second version of his own, which he completed in 1740. It is this version that is commonly cited by subsequent biographers. Although Maillefer complains bitterly in his introduction about Blain's use of his material, he himself does not scruple to make adjustments in his revision on the basis of what Blain had published.

The original manuscript of Maillefer's 1740 text has been preserved in the municipal library of Reims. Both the 1723 and the 1740 Maillefer texts have been published in *Cahiers lasalliens*, Volume 6. An English translation by Brother William Quinn appeared in 1963, and was reprinted in 1980 for the tercentenary of the foundation of the Institute. That celebration was also the occasion for a new French edition, with a valuable introduction and footnotes provided by the late Brother Maurice-Auguste Hermans.

Maillefer is different from Blain. Although he too has a point of view and is not beyond moralizing, his style is more direct. His work is relatively short and easy to read. Although there is an interdependence between the two, they often disagree on precise dates and the sequence of events, neither of which seems to have been a matter of concern for the typical hagiographers of the time. As a result, the modern biographer has the task of making comparisons and, in the absence of outside documentary evidence, simply opting for one or another of the available solutions.

If Blain, corrected by Bernard and Maillefer, has been the guide or the model for the narrative sections of this present work, there are other sources now available to fill in the background material. The section in Chapter IV, for example, on the social and educational situation in seventeenth-century France is heavily indebted to the published and unpublished work of Brothers Yves Poutet and Jean Pungier, especially in the notes they have prepared for the use of the renewal program held annually at the generalate of the Brothers in Rome.

Blain and Maillefer are sometimes incomplete on the factual details concerning the legal battles in which the Founder was engaged, as well as the negotiations he conducted with the sponsors of the schools in various cities throughout France. Research by many biographers, beginning in the nineteenth century with authors such as Lucard, Ravelet, and Guibert, has brought to light a good deal of documentary material relative to the expansion of the Institute during the Founder's lifetime. Most of this material has been made available in the first volume of Georges Rigault's monumental history of the Institute, published in Paris in the 1930's. More recently, Brother Yves Poutet, in Volume II of his *Le XVIIième siècle et les origines lasalliennes,* published in Rennes in 1970, has described and documented the negotiations and conflicts with both civil and ecclesiastical authorities in each of the centers where the Brothers had schools. Extensive use has been made of both Rigault and Poutet in this present work.

The period in the life of De La Salle that is fraught with the greatest problems, concerning both the historical facts and their interpretation, covers the years 1711 to 1714, during which time the Founder made two journeys to the South of France. Ever since the acquisition by the Institute of the property at Parménie, much discussion has centered around the length of the Founder's stay and the significance of Sister Louise in his decision to accept the command of the Brothers to return and resume the government of the Institute. A discussion of these questions can be found in Brother Leo Burkhard's doctoral dissertation, which has been partially translated and expanded by this author, and published by the Christian Brothers Conference under the title *Encounters: De La Salle at Parmenie.*

The most recent full length and documented biography of De La Salle, authored by Brother Saturnino Gallego, was published in Spanish in 1986 under the title *San Juan Bautista De La Salle.* Even for those who do not easily read Spanish, this work is of great value. It has served this author as a means of controlling bibliography and source materials on disputed questions.

Ever since Vatican Council II urged religious institutes to undertake a program of renewal based on the Gospel, the charism of their Founder, and the signs of the times, there has been a growing interest among the Brothers at every level to try to recapture the vision and to define the characteristic spirituality of John Baptist de La Salle. For this purpose, the Founder's own writings are fundamental. All of these have been published in the original French in the *Cahiers lasalliens*.

English-speaking Lasallians have been indebted for years to the pioneering translations by Brother Clair Battersby of the *Meditations* and a volume of the Founder's letters and other documents written in his own hand. In 1975 Brother Augustine Loes produced a new translation of the *Meditations for the Time of Retreat*. More recently, there has been published a new and complete edition of the letters of De La Salle, translated with introduction and commentary by Brother Colman Malloy, and with significant editorial work and additional commentary by Brother Augustine Loes. This is the first in the Lasallian Publications series that will eventually provide translations into English of all the Founder's writings.

Fresh insight into the progressive character of De La Salle's spiritual development has been set forth in the two-volume doctoral dissertation of Brother Miguel Campos on what he calls the Founder's *itinéraire évangélique*. This has been published in Volumes 45 and 46 of the *Cahiers lasalliens*. The principal themes of this work have been summarized in English by Campos himself in the 44-page introduction to the Loes translation of the retreat meditations.

A more extensive adaptation into English of the first volume of the Campos work has been authored by Brother Edwin Bannon. Originally circulated in successive issues of the newsletter of the London province of the Brothers under the title *Lasallian Origins*, Bannon's work has recently appeared in book form under the title *De La Salle: A Founder as Pilgrim*. For those who already have some acquaintance with the life of De La Salle, there is nothing presently available in English that explores in such depth the spiritual journey of the Founder as it unfolded in the course of his personal history. A more specialized study of the spirituality of De La Salle by Brothers Miguel Campos and Michel Sauvage had earlier appeared in English under the title *Announcing the Gospel to the Poor*.

There is, then, enough source material to supply the reader who finds the present study inadequate with leads to follow up on some of the issues that can be treated only briefly in a popular presentation such as this. In one way or another, whatever value this work has is due to the relentless scholarly research and publication of the authors cited in the preceding paragraphs.

Not all of the resources tapped in the production of this book are to be found in the printed word. Many persons, too, as persons, have contributed time and effort to the enterprise. Thanks are due to Brother Brendan Hayden and his staff at Romeoville, Illinois. This is the last publication in which Brother Brendan will be involved in his capacity as Director of Christian Brothers Publications. We wish him well in his new ministry and are grateful for his efforts to hand the manuscript of this work, all but ready to go to press, over to his successor. A special word of gratitude goes to that successor, Brother Paul Grass, Regional Coordinator, for his discerning eye and steady hand in the final stage of the editorial process. The press as always is Saint Mary's Press in Winona, Minnesota. Thanks once again to Brother Damian Steger and his staff for the exceptionally high quality of their work.

The author wishes to thank in a special way, or perhaps to blame, Brother Joseph Schmidt, Secretary of Formation in the United States/Toronto Region of the Brothers, for suggesting the project in the first place, as also for a careful and critical reading of the manuscript. We all need challenges, this author more than most, and Brother Joseph is the man to issue them. The other indispensable critic, ever dependable to keep in line the author's tendency to exaggerate or to improvise, has been Brother Augustine Loes. For which, much thanks, even when it hurts. If this triumvirate ever makes it inside the pearly gates, it will be most exciting to find out on so many issues which of us was right. Thanks, finally, to the readers of the Preface who have come this far. Now it is time to join those who skipped these pages. Pass now, please, to the Prologue and meet John Baptist de La Salle.

Luke Salm, FSC
Manhattan College
April 30, 1988

THE WORK IS YOURS

The Life of
Saint John Baptist de La Salle

Prologue

The year was 1680. It was Easter Sunday in Reims. Lent was over and a wealthy 29-year-old priest was ready to put his Lenten resolution to the test. John Baptist de La Salle—that was his name—knew full well that this resolve might involve a personal crucifixion, but how else could he fittingly celebrate the resurrection of the Lord? Or how, indeed, celebrate the anniversary of his own ordination two years earlier? Yes, he had to go through with it. The prayer and fasting of the long Lenten observance had made it clear what God was asking him to do.

In what strange and unlikely guises God speaks to us, he reflected. Who would have thought even a year ago that he would ever become involved in the business of establishing schools? But now one thing was leading to another. Those bedraggled and nondescript schoolteachers in the house across the street that he had rented for them were getting out of hand. Their leader, Adrien Nyel, was away most of the time and he wasn't very good at controlling them anyway. They needed more supervision, more discipline, more refinement. Above all, they needed a spiritual vision. Otherwise they could never be effective in educating the deprived lads who came to the schools. Yes, he would invite the teachers into his own home for meals. It was high time that they learned some manners. They might even be converted in the process.

Ever since the death of his parents almost ten years earlier, Father De La Salle had presided over an orderly household, providing for three of his younger brothers a refined and respectable atmosphere in which they could grow up in a manner befitting their upper-middle-class status. Sometimes there were interesting guests at the family table. Father De La Salle regularly invited his priest friends to come for days at a time to pray, to study, and to share together their priestly concerns. Adrien Nyel himself, who looked and dressed something like a priest, had stayed with them while plans were being laid to open the first schools for poor boys.

But these schoolteachers were something else. Barely literate themselves, they were uneducated, uncouth, unkempt, and often unclean. It was not a pleasant prospect to think of inviting them to sit at table with himself and his brothers. De La Salle also knew that there would be hell to pay with the rest of the family when they got wind of it. But he had no choice. It was evidently God's will that the schools should succeed. It was little enough, De La Salle reflected, that he was being asked to do. Once the enterprise got off the ground and the teachers could take care of themselves, he would be done with them. Then life in the mansion on the Rue Sainte Marguerite could return to normal.

But it was not to be that way. The hand of divine Providence was opening only one door at a time. Reflecting on it years later, De La Salle would express his experience in these words: "God, who guides all things with wisdom and serenity and whose way it is not to force the inclinations of persons, willed to commit me entirely to the development of the schools. He did this in an imperceptible way and over a long period of time so that one commitment led to another in a way that I did not foresee in the beginning."

The sudden presence of these schoolteachers in the De La Salle home did indeed send shockwaves throughout the whole family and the social milieu in which they lived. It provoked, in effect, a direct confrontation between two entirely different social worlds. There was the insecure world of the schoolmasters, caught in the struggle for survival without resources, without status, without even a mar-ketable skill, living by their wits, cunning, devious, and despicable, so much so that De La Salle himself considered their status beneath that of his own valet. In contrast there was the world of the De La Salles, comfortable, secure, refined and dignified, lacking nothing, pillars of the church and society, charitable and generous to the poor, of course, but from a distance and over a gap that it was unthinkable to try to bridge.

The decision to go through with his resolution to invite the teachers to his table would also have profound consequences for Father De La Salle deep within the very core of his being. It was a bold and significant first step that would bring him personally face to face with the world of the poor. There he would experience within himself the cry of the poor in the concrete circumstances of their misery, their need, so far from salvation did they seem to be, to hear the good news of the Gospel. In that cry, the young priest would hear the voice of God challenging him to begin the work of his own conversion to live the Gospel. It was the beginning of a process that would bring him along a road that he had neither the intention, the desire, nor the courage to travel by himself.

Follow along that road, he did. By the time of De La Salle's death some 40 years later, the Institute of the Brothers of the Christian Schools that grew out of the motley crew that came to Easter dinner in 1680 would be firmly established in the major cities in France from Calais on the English Channel to Marseille on the Mediterranean Sea. In 1980, some 10,000 Brothers teaching in schools in every part of the world would celebrate, together with their students, colleagues, and friends, the tercentenary of the occasion when John Baptist de La Salle took the first step toward accomplishing the work that the Lord wanted him to do. That was how he himself would come to describe it: *Domine, opus tuum* — Lord, the work is yours.

1

Family and Education
(1651–1669)

John Baptist de La Salle was born in Reims on April 30, 1651. His parents were Louis de La Salle, a magistrate of the presidial court at Reims, and Nicole Moët, the daughter of the Seigneur de Brouillet. They had been married in August 1650; he was 25 years old at the time, she was 17. Altogether they had 11 children in 20 years of married life. Four of the De La Salle children died in infancy. In addition to John Baptist, the oldest, there survived two girls, Marie and Rose-Marie, and four boys, Jacques-Joseph, Jean-Louis, Pierre, and Jean-Remy.

Ancestry

The legendary ancestor of the De La Salle family was Johan Sala, a Catalonian knight in the service of Alfonso the Chaste, King of Oviedo in Spain. Johan died in the year 818 in the war against the Moors, his legs broken in battle. There is a legend, originating only in the nineteenth century, that ascribes the origin of the three broken chevrons in the family coat of arms to this incident.

During the tenth century Armand Sala, a putative descendant of Johan, built a castle for his family, which thereafter was known by the name De La Sala. In the twelfth century the De La Sala knights were dispersed widely throughout France, serving in the armies of the various local princes. In this way the name assumed its French form of De La Salle. Under these circumstances it is not surprising that the name became rather common throughout France. There is no genealogical evidence, however, to connect any of the various families named De La Salle to the original Sala family.

The name De La Salle surfaces again in the fourteenth century with Bernard de La Salle, a captain of Aquitaine, who had only one son, a bastard, who left no heirs. Bernard's brother, Hortingo de La Salle, fought on both sides of the struggle between the Italians and the Avignon papacy. He was rewarded in 1376 with a castle in Aougny in northern France. It is possible that the De La Salle family of Reims may be among his descendants, but there is no historical evidence to prove it.

The De La Salle family of Reims always traced its ancestry to Menault de La Salle, a cloth merchant who lived in Soissons in the late fifteenth century. His grandson, Lancelot de La Salle II, moved the family to Reims in 1561. Louis de La Salle, the father of John Baptist, was the youngest of the six surviving children of Lancelot de La Salle III and his wife, Barbara Coquebert.

Thus, despite the claims of the early and more recent biographers, the De La Salle family did not belong to the nobility. They were rather wealthy members of the upper bourgeoisie and some of them, including the father of John Baptist, married women of noble rank. These women, however, lost all claim to noble rank once they were married to a bourgeois.

During the nineteenth century, as the process leading to the canonization of John Baptist de La Salle was moving forward, there was an attempt on the part of two other families named De La Salle to claim relationship. The De La Salle family of Rochemaure in the Auvergne boasted a distinguished prelate named John Baptist de La Salle, who lived from 1723 until 1787. The son of Count Joseph de La Salle of Rochemaure, he had been vicar-general of the diocese of Vienne. When Pope Leo XIII conferred a noble title on Felix de La Salle of Rochemaure in 1899, the pope erroneously referred to the new papal duke as a member of the same "house of De La Salle" as the Founder of the Brothers who was about to be canonized the following year. There is no evidence, however, of any direct connection between the two families.

Then there was François de La Salle du Change, a priest who lived from 1775 until 1874. He was an historian and archivist as well, belonging to the De La Salle family of Périgueux. In 1859 he wrote to one of the Rochemaure family: "You ought to know that the Founder of this interesting Institute was Father De La Salle, one of our ancestors (sic!) . . . a fact verified by several letters from the superiors of that order." Whatever documents Father François had in his possession were later lost in a fire. In any case it seems certain that both the superiors of the Brothers and the various De La Salle families were finding connections to noble origins and to the Founder where there was no solid basis in historical fact.

Brother Clair Battersby, in his 1957 biography, claims that the family of the Founder belonged to the "nobility of the robe," as distinct from the hereditary nobility derived from knighthood, the "nobility of the sword." It is true that the judges in the courts of Paris were given noble titles on this basis. The magistrates in Reims, however, such as Louis de La Salle, were merely members of a provincial court with limited jurisdiction and not thereby ranked among the nobility. Furthermore, the De La Salle name does not appear in the contemporary lists of those families entitled to be ranked with the "nobility of the robe."

Nobility, therefore, is not essential to understanding the privileged circumstances in which John Baptist de La Salle grew up. At the time of his birth, his father and mother shared the spacious mansion known as La Cloche with the paternal grandparents and the family of his only paternal uncle, Simon de La Salle d'Etang. Lancelot de La Salle, the grandfather, died the year John Baptist was born; the grandmother, Barbara Coquebert, died two years later. By a codicil in her will she provided that the rooms in the house would be shared by the families of her two sons, Simon and Louis, the father of John Baptist. As the family of Louis de La Salle grew, he was able to buy from his brother Simon the exclusive rights to the spacious mansion.

Childhood

The maternal grandparents, Jean Moët and Perrette Lespagnol, had a much greater influence on the young John Baptist. They were the godparents at his baptism. The baptism took place in the church of Saint Hilary, the parish where the Moët townhouse was located. For this reason it is possible that John Baptist may have been born in the Moët house. It was not uncommon for a young wife to go to the home of her own mother for the birth of her first child. Besides, three De La Salle families were sharing the facilities of La Cloche at the time Nicole was ready to give birth. If the boy had been born at La Cloche, he would more likely have been baptized in the old Saint Peter's, the parish where the De La Salle mansion was located.

Whatever the house in which he was born, it is certain that for the first 13 years of his life, John Baptist de La Salle grew up in the La Cloche mansion, nurtured by the loving care of his parents and by frequent visits from his maternal grandparents. Jean Moët had a great affection for his grandson, and no doubt brought him

Courtyard of the Hôtel de la Cloche, nineteenth-century engraving

from time to time to visit the vineyards and play in the open fields of the Brouillet estate. As the local Seigneur, Jean Moët had a special bench in the chapel of the estate where he could show the boy off to the townsfolk of a Sunday morning. He himself loved to say the divine office of the Church, and is said to have taught John Baptist how to follow the complicated rubrics of the breviary. Perrette Lespagnol Moët, the grandmother, was likewise a source of guidance and support up until the time of her death in 1691.

During the 13 years the family lived in the La Cloche house, John Baptist learned to share his experiences and diversions with his sisters and his younger brother as they grew older: Marie, who was born in l654, Rose-Marie in 1656, and Jacques-Joseph in 1659. To add to the variety, there were living in the neighborhood cousins galore, with the names of De La Salle, Moët, Lespagnol, and Coquebert, swelling the ranks of the extended family. There was sorrow to be shared, too, with the deaths in infancy of Remy born in 1652, Marie-Anne born in 1658, and the first to be named Jean-Louis, who was born in 1663.

Only a few blocks away from La Cloche was the praesidium where Louis de La Salle functioned as a magistrate. It is likely that he took his oldest son to his office or to the court on occasion to try to interest him in the law. In the rather prosperous neighborhood there were other places that might arouse the curiosity of a young boy, such as the two busy marketplaces, one named for the cloth merchants and the other for the wheat dealers, or the sumptuous mansions, many of which belonged to the relatives of the De La Salles.

To this day one can stand in front of La Cloche and look down the street to see the flying buttresses supporting the apse of the Reims cathedral. The young John Baptist had only to look out the window to see the colorful processions pass along the Rue de l'Arbalète on the way to the cathedral. That was the customary route for the bridal processions in important weddings as well as for the processions of vested ecclesiastics on major feasts.

Since John Baptist was only three years old at the time, it is not likely that he would have remembered the occasion when Reims was the scene of the coronation of King Louis XIV, whose reign as the "Sun King" (1654 to 1715) would roughly parallel the life span of John Baptist himself (1651 to 1719). He certainly would have witnessed the processions in honor of Saint Remy after the pestilence of 1659 and the bonfires celebrating the treaty of the Pyrénées later that same year.

As respected members of the upper middle class, the De La Salle family and their relatives were active in the social life of Reims. Household routine was governed by the rules of correct and conventional social behavior. Music and the arts were held in esteem. There was a well stocked library and the books were read. We can gather from problems in adjustment that John Baptist experienced later on, that the food at home was of high quality and that the family dressed in the latest fashion. There were servants, though not many full-time, to spare the children from having to do menial or disagreeable chores.

As a child, John Baptist seems to have been bored by the cultural soirées that were frequently held in the De La Salle mansion. It is told that on one occasion he ran to his grandmother to ask her to read to him stories from the lives of the saints as an alternate diversion. Musical performances in particular, a favorite form of entertainment that the father provided for his guests, were not to the liking of his young son. The early biographers attribute this conduct to precocious sanctity; on the other hand, such attitudes are not uncommon in boys of that age.

There can be no doubt, however, that things religious had a special attraction for John Baptist from his earliest youth. The first biographers, who had the sources at their disposal, speak of the delight he took in attending church services, his fascination with the ceremonies, the games he devised to imitate them at home, the penetrating questions he asked about the meaning of all that he experienced or was taught about his religion.

Not all of this can be interpreted as a superficial religiosity. Surrounded by love and endowed with a trusting spirit, the young De La Salle developed a natural sensitivity to the needs of others. This emerged in later life in what the biographers could call "the natural goodness" of his "upright heart."

The elementary education of the De La Salle children began at home and was entrusted to private tutors. John Baptist would have learned to read and spell from Latin texts as was the custom. He was ten years old when, on October 10, 1661, after four years with the tutors, John Baptist de La Salle was enrolled in the sixth class of the Collège des Bons-Enfants in Reims.

The Collège des Bons-Enfants had been founded in the ninth century as an adjunct to the cathedral school, and so fell under the direction of the cathedral chapter of canons and the archbishop of Reims. It was originally intended for the education of poor students, the *bons enfants de la miséricorde,* as they were called, especially those who might be contemplating an ecclesiastical career. When the University of Reims was formally established by papal and royal decrees in 1545, the college was absorbed into the university as the school of liberal arts.

The classes in the college were numbered in descending order, beginning with the tenth grade for the untutored beginners. The sixth grade, where De La Salle entered the system, and the fifth, were devoted to mastering the rules of Latin grammar with readings from the easier Latin authors: the plays of Terence, Cicero's letters, and Virgil's *Eclogues*. Greek grammar would be introduced in grades four and three, along with readings in the more difficult Latin authors. In the second and first grades the emphasis was on rhetoric, with readings from the orators and rhetoricians in both Latin and Greek. This program prepared the students for the two years of philosophy that followed, meriting for those who succeeded the degree of Master of Arts.

As may be inferred from this outline of the curriculum of the Collège des Bons-Enfants, there was little room for the study of contemporary authors. In fact, the statutes explicitly forbade the introduction of any recent works or any that might be considered suspect. The theory was that the student "ought to drink at the font of knowledge that is fed from only the purest springs."

Likewise, the prescribed curriculum made no provision for the study of either geography or history. Whatever the students learned about these subjects would have come indirectly through the study of the ancient historians or, perhaps, through the historical passages of the Bible. The contemporary world was avoided as a fit subject for serious study. As far as the masterpieces of French literature were concerned, there was no place for them either. On this basis, none of the great writers of the time would have penetrated the Bons-Enfants: not the Pléiade, not Montaigne, Malherbe, Corneille, Racine, La Fontaine, or Molière, and certainly not Rabelais.

This does not necessarily mean that John Baptist de La Salle grew up totally ignorant of the subjects that did not form part of the curriculum of the college. His father, Louis de La Salle, was an accomplished humanist: most of his bourgeois friends and relations were involved in politics, and some of them had travelled widely. It might be supposed that the men of the family would have discussed the literary and political movements of the time in the presence of the younger generation of De La Salles.

Among his contemporaries enrolled in the Collège des Bons-Enfants, John Baptist would have found many of his young relatives. There were others related to the De La Salle family whose parents preferred the rival college of the Jesuits, which had been opened in Reims some 50 years earlier. The Jesuit college had a reputation for being rather more innovative in its educational methods and a challenge to the staid and traditional Bons-Enfants. All through the seventeenth century, the precise relationship of the Jesuit college to the University of Reims and its privileges was the subject of a bitter dispute. It is tempting, nonetheless, to speculate on what influence a Jesuit undergraduate education might have had on John Baptist de La Salle.

In any case, the student body was exclusively male, as was also the teaching and administrative staff. According to the statutes of the university, women were not to be admitted, even in the role of servants. Although there was little or no tuition to be paid, with only minimal gratuities required from time to time, the children of the artisans and the poor were for all practical purposes excluded. They could not even afford the examination fees or the cost of books and school supplies.

In the social climate of the time, such students would have been out of place and totally unwelcome by reason of their dress, their manner of speech, and their patterns of behavior. Furthermore, the duration of the course of study and the subject matter of the curriculum were far removed from the situation of the poor families who were forced to send their children out to work at an early age. From his earliest years, John Baptist de La Salle learned from experience to take this sort of social segregation for granted.

Clerical Tonsure

Toward the end of his first year at the college, on March 11, 1662, John Baptist de La Salle received the clerical tonsure. This ceremony, which consisted in a ritual clipping of hair from the crown of the head in the style of the ancient monks, marked the formal entrance of a candidate for the priesthood into the clerical state. The tonsure was conferred at the invitation of Father Pierre Dozet, a cousin of De La Salle. He was vicar-general of the Reims archdiocese at the time, and chancellor of the university as well. It is likely that he wanted to direct his talented young cousin toward the priesthood at an early age.

John Baptist was not quite 11 years old when he was tonsured. It was not uncommon at the time to give the tonsure to boys that young. For one thing it made them eligible for ecclesiastical benefices without committing them irrevocably to the obligations associated with Holy Orders. The early biographers insist, however, that for John Baptist, young as he was, this was a conscious choice that signaled his determination to follow in the vocation to which he felt God was calling him. The parents, too, in approving this step, consciously sacrificed any hopes they may have had that their eldest son would follow his father in a career at law.

After the ceremony, John Baptist de La Salle, now tonsured and in some sense set apart from his companions, returned to complete his first full school year at the Bons-Enfants. He continued as before to live at home with his parents, but now he would come to school wearing the black ecclesiastical cassock. There were of course other young ecclesiastics in his classes dressed in the same style. Although clerics were allowed to let their hair grow back normally, the regulations forbade flamboyant hairstyles. This might have been a problem for John Baptist, if indeed the regulation was enforced, since his chestnut brown hair tended to fall loosely in abundant curls.

Meanwhile De La Salle continued in the prescribed course of classical studies at the college. His early biographers are at pains to point out that he was a good student, that he was respected by his teachers and his fellow students, that he made remarkable progress in a short time. Whether this is based on hard evidence, or whether it comes from hindsight and admiration for their subject, is not always clear.

A printed program from April 1663 indicates that John Baptist had a secondary role in a school play dealing with the martyrdom of Saint Timothy. From the year 1665 a document has survived listing the winners at the annual distribution of prizes in April of that year. On that occasion John Baptist de La Salle was awarded a second prize in elocution and an honorable mention in extempore declamation.

Between these two documented events, another change occurred in the life of the De La Salle family. By that time the La Cloche mansion was becoming inadequate to accommodate comfortably the growing numbers. In May 1664, Louis de La Salle moved the family from La Cloche to a mansion he had just purchased on the Rue Sainte Marguerite. The house was diagonally across from the apse of the cathedral, but located in the parish of Saint Symphorien, a block away in the opposite direction. At the time, Nicole Moët de La Salle was expecting her eighth child; four of her children were still living.

During the years in the house on the Rue Sainte Marguerite, four more children were born to Louis and Nicole de La Salle. All but one of them would live to maturity. In December of 1664, Jean-Louis was born and given the name of his brother who had died as an infant the year before. There followed Pierre, born in 1666; Simon, born in 1667, who died two years later; and finally Jean-Remy, born in 1670. Jean-Louis would eventually become a priest, Pierre a lawyer, and Jean-Remy, after a varied career and a succession of marital troubles, was to die in a mental institution.

Canon of the Cathedral Chapter

Toward the end of 1666 Pierre Dozet decided to resign his benefice as a canon of the cathedral of Reims in favor of his young cousin, John Baptist de La Salle. The formal ceremony of investiture took place on January 7, 1667. For John Baptist, not yet 16 years old, it was a distinct honor to enter the company of the cathedral chapter of Reims which numbered among its alumni three popes, 23 cardinals, more than 30 bishops and, most distinguished of all perhaps, Saint Bruno, who had resigned the office in the year 1084 to found his order of hermits in the Chartreuse mountains near Grenoble.

In accepting this office, John Baptist assumed both the privileges and the duties of a canon of the cathedral and a member of the cathedral chapter. The duties were related principally to public prayer, especially the daily chanting in the cathedral choir of the liturgy of the hours and the capitular celebration of the Eucharist. The canons always had a place of honor in the solemn liturgies and processions that marked the great feasts of the church year. In addition to these liturgical offices there were regular meetings of the chapter to attend to its internal affairs and to serve, when asked, as an advisory group to the archbishop.

The position of canon was not without its rewards. Each canon was assigned a house adjacent to the cathedral. If he did not occupy it himself, as in the case of De La Salle, he could rent the lodgings to some suitable client. There was a fixed stipend for participation in each of the liturgical services that added up in the course of a year to a considerable sum. Above all, there were the dignity and prestige attached to the office, prelatial robes trimmed in ermine, and privileged seating at all the ecclesiastical and civic ceremonies.

It could not have been easy in the stratified society of the time for a young canon to accept without some sense of self-importance the honors that came from his new dignity. On the other hand, the regulations of the chapter imposed a rather rigid discipline on the younger canons who were not priests. They were expected to pay special deference to the priest-canons, to be zealous in their studies and modest in their behavior. Although the canons attending the university were exempt from attendance at choir and meetings on school days, they were strictly bound to the long liturgical offices that occupied the greater part of the day on Sundays and feasts.

Master of Arts

It was in these circumstances that John Baptist completed the standard program in classical studies in the summer of 1667. Day in and day out, week after week for the six years between 1661 and 1667 he had recited the rules of grammar, prepared the required exercises in composition and elocution, mastered the Greek and Latin authors, and engaged in public demonstrations of rhetorical skill.

His written style would always bear the stamp of these mental gymnastics: not much lyricism, but always the correct phrase, accurately expressed, logical and precise, yet often marked by austerity and a certain heaviness. Although his extensive study of the Greek and Latin classics must have helped to form his intelligence, there is little explicit reference to them in his later writings. While these were always laced with extensive quotations from Scripture and the Fathers of the Church, scholars have been unable to trace more than a handful of allusions to classical authors.

With all of these advantages and disadvantages, the 16-year-old Canon De La Salle began the traditional two-year course in philosophy in October 1667. The first year was devoted to the study of logic in the morning and ethics in the afternoon. The principal source for the logic course was Aristotle's *Organon,* dealing with logical categories, hermeneutics, prior and posterior analytics, exercises in dialectics, and refutation of sophisms. The ethics course was devoted to the study of Aristotle's *Nicomachean Ethics,* with an examination of the meaning of the human life as human, the intellectual and moral virtues, and contemplation by participation in the divine intelligence as the greatest human happiness.

The routine of the first year of philosophy was interrupted briefly when, on March 17, 1668, John Baptist de La Salle took the four minor ecclesiastical orders of porter, lector, exorcist, and acolyte. This important step was significant for his status as canon and a sign of his determination to move forward in his vocation to the priesthood. Then, just before the new school year was to begin, his father's cousin, Pierre Dozet, who only two years earlier had resigned his canonry in favor of John Baptist, died in Reims on October 3, 1668.

The second year of the philosophy course was particularly heavy. The morning was devoted to the study of Aristotle's *Physics,* the afternoon to the same philosopher's *Metaphysics.* At the end of the school year, on July 9, 1669, John Baptist de La Salle presented himself for the final examination. The examination was oral and conducted entirely in Latin over two sessions. The first was devoted to logic and ethics, the second covered the entire field of philosophy. De La Salle passed with the highest honors. The diploma, dated July 10, 1669, conferring the degree of Master of Arts, *summa cum laude,* is preserved in the archives of the Brothers' generalate in Rome.

In this way the career of John Baptist de La Salle at the Collège des Bons-Enfants came to an end. At the age of 18, a canon of the cathedral of Reims in minor orders with a Master of Arts degree, he was considered equipped to pursue advanced studies and a distinguished career based on the solid foundation that had been laid during his eight years at the college. It was time now to turn his attention to the specialized studies required to respond to his vocation to the priesthood.

2

Theology and the Priesthood
(1669–1680)

First Year Theology at Reims

With the degree of Master of Arts, John Baptist de La Salle was eligible at the age of 18 to enter any of the advanced programs in the university leading to the doctorate, whether in letters, theology, medicine, or law. Long since committed to his vocation to the priesthood, De La Salle, not surprisingly, enrolled in the school (or "faculty") of theology.

Contrary to the impression given by the early biographers that De La Salle began his theological study in Paris, documents survive to show that he was enrolled in the first-year theology courses at the University of Reims during the academic year beginning on October 18, the feast of Saint Luke, in 1669.

The theology courses at Reims were offered in two centers by two professors: Michel de Blanzy lectured at Saint Patrick's Hall in the morning; Daniel Egan taught his course in the Abbey of Saint Denis in the afternoon. De Blanzy, a native of Soissons, was a distinguished priest, canon, and scholar with a taste for the comfortable lifestyle which his extensive income made possible. Egan, a fugitive from persecution in his native Ireland, was also a priest, canon, and scholar, but known rather to prefer the simple life, the solitude of his study, and his professional contacts with his students. Much of Egan's income was devoted to providing the means for young Irishmen interested in the priesthood to come to Reims to study.

In the morning sessions, De Blanzy taught the traditional scholastic tract on God and creation. The *Book of Sentences* of Peter Lombard served as a text. In the afternoon, Egan presided over a series of practical exercises in theological disputation. There was also a basic course in Sacred Scripture "as interpreted by the Fathers of the Church," but it is not clear which of the two professors taught this course.

The students were expected to master this material in all of its complicated detail. The emphasis was on memory and technique rather than on personal conviction, and not at all on critical or creative independent thought. There is no doubt that this training left its mark on John Baptist de La Salle. All his life he displayed a prodigious memory for the texts of Sacred Scripture and the Fathers, but this was coupled with a firm resistance to theological innovation. There are documents attesting to the fact that De La Salle followed and successfully completed these first-year theology courses at Reims.

In the normal course of events, De La Salle would have continued to follow at Reims the remainder of the course leading to the degree of Bachelor of Theology. During the academic year 1669–1670, however, his first in the school of theology, a dispute arose between the professors of the faculty and the administration of the University of Reims.

The trouble had its origin in 1668 with the retirement of Pierre Dozet as Chancellor of the University, a position he had held for fifty years along with all his other titles. Appointed to succeed him was a priest named Louis-Eléonor Tristan who, unfortunately, had only a bachelor's degree in theology. This did not sit well with the professors, all of whom had doctorates or licentiates. How, they asked, could a chancellor with only a bachelor's degree preside over examinations for the higher degrees which he himself did not have?

The professors brought suit before the presidial court of Reims, which was able to calm things down during the fall term. In the spring of 1670, when the chancellor insisted on holding the examinations as usual, the professors immediately declared them null. The case again was brought to court, and the judgment went against the professors. A later appeal to the parliament in Paris failed and Tristan was eventually confirmed in the office of chancellor.

Although it is not known exactly how the students were affected by all of this controversy in the day-to-day classes, it is easy to imagine the confusion that must have resulted once the procedures for the examinations, as well as their validity, were called into question. The situation must have been especially painful for De La Salle, since at the time both his father and his grandfather were members of the Reims court that was charged by law to protect the privileges of the administration of the university.

The dispute was in its initial stages when John Baptist de La Salle was first enrolled in the faculty of theology at Reims in the fall of 1669. The option for Reims rather than Paris on the part of the son of Louis de La Salle might have been intended as support for Chancellor Tristan and a gesture of reconciliation. By the end of that academic year, however, the situation had worsened considerably. This may have been the reason why, after one year of theological study at Reims, John Baptist de La Salle left Reims for Paris in October 1670, where he enrolled in the Seminary of Saint Sulpice.

The Seminary of Saint Sulpice

The seminary in Paris as De La Salle knew it was under the direction of the priests of the Society of Saint Sulpice, which had been founded a generation earlier by Jean-Jacques Olier. In the course of a long spiritual odyssey, Father Olier had come under the influence of Charles de Condren, who trained him in the principles of the French school of spirituality that had originated with Cardinal Bérulle earlier in the seventeenth century.

The spirituality of this school was dominantly Christocentric, focusing on the total self-abnegation of the divine Word in the mystery of the Incarnation and manifest in the successive events in the life of Christ. Meditation on the "mystery" element of these events was considered an important means to cultivate this internal attitude of personal nothingness which, at the same time, was the promise and the condition of deep personal union with God.

Convinced of the need for a well-trained clergy, Olier founded his first small seminary at Vaugirard in 1641. His appointment as pastor of Saint Sulpice in 1646 was the occasion for establishing the seminary and founding the Society in the parish from which it took its name. The goal was to produce priests committed to a life of self-sacrifice and self-discipline, zeal for the salvation of souls, especially the poor, and exactitude in living up to the demands of the clerical state.

With this in view, seminary discipline was exceptionally strict. It was early to bed (night prayer at 8:00 P.M.) and early to rise (5:00 A.M.). There were the customary spiritual exercises: vocal prayer and meditation, daily Mass, the divine office for those obliged to it (the rosary in common for the others), and spiritual reading. Silence was imposed and strictly observed, even during meals, when the seminarians took turns reading aloud. All were expected to be serious and modest in their external behavior, and nothing was to be done without permission.

The fees at the seminary were relatively high, so much so that only wealthy clerics could afford to go there. A successful sojourn at Saint Sulpice set the young cleric apart and was practically a guarantee of high ecclesiastical preference afterwards. Despite the elite quality of the clientele, professors and students alike were required to maintain a simple lifestyle in common and to observe exactly every last detail of the seminary regulations.

As part of their preparation for pastoral work the seminarians were given the opportunity to teach catechism in the various centers located throughout the large parish that embraced some of the poorest neighborhoods in the Paris of that time. The seminarians were prepared carefully for this ministry by one of the priests of the faculty who supervised both the content and the method of instruction. The seminarians usually worked in pairs: one would explain the lesson of the day while the other tried to keep the children quiet and orderly. The records show that these sessions were popular among the young people of the parish and were well attended.

Although it may be presumed that De La Salle took part in this program, there is no evidence that in his seminary years he ever thought of the catechetical ministry as a vocation in itself. More than likely, at that time, to him it was just one more aspect of seminary life, challenging and agreeable, perhaps, but only a passing phase in his formation for the priesthood. It may have also provided some more direct contact with the poor than he had been used to, arousing his sympathy and charitable feelings, but certainly no thought that he might some day become one of them.

Of all the Sulpicians on the faculty of the seminary at the time, the one who had the greatest influence on John Baptist de La Salle was Father Louis Tronson. He was the senior spiritual director of the seminary, and quite possibly De La Salle was assigned to his charge. He would eventually become Superior General of the Sulpicians, the second after Father Olier to hold that office.

Whether or not Tronson was actually the spiritual director of De La Salle, his influence would have been considerable. He regularly addressed the assembled seminarians in conferences that were reputed to evoke a positive response from his hearers. His contemporaries described him as a lovable priest who gave wise advice, whose demeanor was calm, and whose conversation was charming. His portrait shows that he was rather chubby with a fatherly look in his eye.

Tronson wrote extensive treatises on various aspects of seminary life, including a manual for seminarians and a series of meditations. These were considered classics in their own time and were later published. In the tradition of Olier, the emphasis was on meditation, spiritual reading, daily examination of conscience on a particular subject, and openness to the spiritual director. The need for serious study, especially of theology and Scripture, found a place in Tronson's exhortations. One of his favorite maxims was: "Learning without piety produces a proud cleric; piety without learning produces a useless one."

Some aspects of the spiritual doctrine of Tronson might strike the modern reader as rather severe. In his treatise on obedience he devotes 17 chapters to the importance of submitting to even the smallest details of the seminary regulations. In the manual he prepared for the seminarians, there is a notable mistrust of the body and its functions: eating, drinking, and sleeping are considered animal actions that ought to be minimized as much as possible.

Among the other priests on the staff of the seminary who would play a part in the subsequent history of De La Salle, there were two who would later become pastors of the parish of Saint Sulpice, Father Claude de La Barmondière and Father Henri Baudrand. Then there was Jean-Jacques Baüyn, a convert from Calvinism and not yet a Sulpician when De La Salle was at the seminary. Once converted, Baüyn became noted for his extraordinary spiritual gifts, his austerity of life, and his deep humility and charity. He would one day serve as De La Salle's spiritual director during a difficult period when the two of them were neighbors in the suburb of Paris known as Vaugirard.

Two of the students living at Saint Sulpice while De La Salle was there would eventually play a part in the foundation of the Institute of the Brothers. Paul Godet des Marais, upon becoming Bishop of Chartres in 1692, would be the first bishop to invite the Brothers into his diocese. It was to him that De La Salle would address his policy statement on the teaching of Latin. Later still, Guillaume de Mérez, a fellow seminarian, would invite the Brothers to Alès in 1707 in his capacity as vicar-general of the diocese.

Theological Studies at the Sorbonne

While the training in spirituality for candidates aspiring to the priesthood was provided at the Seminary of Saint Sulpice, the courses in academic theology leading to advanced degrees were given at the Sorbonne, which originated in the thirteenth century and eventually became the School of Theology in the University of Paris. The professors and graduates, known as the "Doctors of the Sorbonne," were a powerful influence in French political and ecclesiastical life.

De La Salle's association with the Sorbonne was simply in his capacity as a student of theology. He was not part of the "college" of the Sorbonne since he did not reside there, but at Saint Sulpice, a 15-minute walk away. The theology classes were held in buildings which had been renovated in 1627 by Cardinal Richelieu, whose tomb can still be seen in what was once the sanctuary of the college chapel. Whether De La Salle might have eventually joined the prestigious "Company of the Sorbonne" remains problematic since he had to leave Paris before obtaining any academic degrees from that university.

De La Salle came to the Sorbonne from Reims armed with the prerequisite Master of Arts degree plus a full year of theology. He needed two more years of theology, with only two courses required in each year in either dogma, moral theology, or Sacred Scripture.

The Sorbonne

De La Salle opted for the dogma cycle. Then there would be two more years of advanced philosophy in order to meet the five-year requirement for the Bachelor of Theology degree.

The theology courses at the Sorbonne were then being taught by two distinguished scholars and doctors of theology with the title (and the revenue) of "royal professors," Father Jacques Despériers and Father Guillaume de Lestocq. They were much involved in the theological controversies at the time. Both were staunch defenders of the Roman, and the royal, opposition to the rigors of Jansenism; both shunned what were considered the dangerous novelties in the philosophy of Descartes; both opposed the Gallican claims of the French church against the papacy, but there is some suspicion that De Lestocq at least was not so strongly Roman on this issue as his public stance would indicate.

During his first year in Paris, his second year of theology, John Baptist de La Salle followed the course of Despériers on the Incarnation and the course of De Lestocq on the Triune God. During the following year he took the course of Despériers on the Sacraments in General and Baptism, and that of De Lestocq on Grace. The certificates attesting to his attendance at these courses have been preserved in the archives of the Brothers' generalate in Rome.

The courses followed the "thesis method" traditional in scholastic theology. A statement of doctrine dealing with the subject matter would be presented as a thesis, then defended by *a priori* citations from Scripture, the Councils, and Fathers of the Church. Opposing views of heretics and dissident theologians would be refuted and, finally, an analysis would prove that the doctrine of the thesis was based on sound theological reasoning. The content and the methodology were not much different from what was customary before and since in Catholic seminary courses, at least until Vatican II.

By the very fact of having attended the Sorbonne, De La Salle became associated with a distinguished group of prelates and ecclesiastics who had shared the same experience. Among those who preceded him at the Sorbonne was Charles-Maurice Le Tellier who, as Archbishop of Reims, would ordain him to the priesthood. Among the doctoral candidates during De La Salle's student days were François de Harlay de Champvallon and Louis-Antoine de Noailles, who would be successively Archbishops of Paris during the difficult years when the Institute of the Brothers had to struggle to survive.

Interruption

John Baptist de La Salle was in the final weeks of his first year at the seminary in Paris when he learned of the death of his mother in July 1671. Less than nine months later, during the Holy Week retreat at the seminary, word came that his father had died on April 9. After only 18 months at Saint Sulpice De La Salle had to leave the seminary for good in order to attend to family affairs back in Reims. He arrived home just before his twenty-first birthday in April 1672.

A complex set of responsibilities awaited the young canon. As executor of his father's will he had to provide for the equitable distribution of the family inheritance, collect and manage the revenue from his father's property holdings and investments, and assume his own role as head of the household. Although himself legally a minor — the age of majority at the time was 25 — he became the legal guardian of his four brothers and two sisters.

It might easily be presumed that under these circumstances De La Salle would have struggled through a crisis in his vocation to the priesthood. Man of faith that he was, he might well have been inclined to interpret these events as a sign that God was directing him along another path. But he had also learned in the months at Saint Sulpice not to trust his own judgment in such matters. Accordingly he looked about for a spiritual director to guide him through this difficult time.

He found such a one in the person of Father Nicolas Roland, a man ten years older than himself and a fellow canon in the cathedral chapter of Reims. In order to keep open the option of the priesthood, Roland suggested that he enroll at once in the University of Reims to complete the theology courses that he had begun the previous autumn in Paris. Then, as Pentecost approached, and supported in overcoming his hesitation by Roland's advice, De La Salle decided to present himself for ordination to the subdiaconate. The ceremony took place at Cambrai in the chapel of the archbishop on the eve of Trinity Sunday, June 11, 1672.

At the same time there were problems at home to be taken care of. Shortly after the ordination of John Baptist as subdeacon, Marie, the older of his two sisters, went to live with the maternal grandmother, Perrette Lespagnol Moët. She took with her their youngest brother, Jean-Remy, who was just two years old. The younger sister, Rose-Marie, had already entered the convent of the Canonesses of Saint Augustine in Reims shortly before the father's death. This left John Baptist with only three of his younger brothers to care for in the house on the Rue Sainte Marguerite: Jacques-Joseph, who was 13 years old; Jean-Louis, who was eight, and Pierre, who was six.

Theological Degrees and Ordinations

During the academic year 1672–1673, De La Salle put aside his theological studies to take care of his brothers and to manage his father's estate. By the fall of 1673 family affairs seemed to be well enough in hand for him to resume his university studies while continuing to live at home. In addition to the three years of theology already completed, there yet remained two more years of advanced philosophy required for the degree of Bachelor of Theology, which De La Salle was awarded by the University of Reims in August 1675.

De La Salle might have terminated his theological studies at this point since he had already completed more than was required for ordination to the priesthood. There was, however, much prestige attached to the advanced degrees in theology since they considerably enhanced the prospects for promotion to high ecclesiastical rank. It is reasonable to suppose that at this time De La Salle might have envisioned such a career for himself. In any case, in January 1676, he began the two-year course that would lead to the conferral of the licentiate in theology in 1678.

The year 1676 also saw De La Salle involved in some non-academic affairs that would be significant for his future life as a priest. Early in that year it became known that Father André Clocquet wanted to resign as pastor of the old Saint Peter's church in Reims to devote himself to prayer and study. Nicolas Roland, De La Salle's spiritual director, sensed that here was an opportunity to point his young protégé toward a more apostolic ministry. The fact that De La Salle was only a subdeacon at the time was no obstacle. There was precedent for clerics in minor orders to be appointed pastors. They would then engage an ordained priest to supply the required sacramental ministry.

For De La Salle even to consider such an offer involved a real sacrifice since it meant that he would have to resign his office as canon and, of course, the revenue attached thereto. But consider it he did, and he even went so far as to sign an agreement to that effect, convinced that in following the advice of his director he was doing the will of God.

When word of the proposed plan leaked out, the reaction of the De La Salle family was negative and intense. John Baptist, still anxious to discern the will of God in such crises, decided to consult with his archbishop, Charles-Maurice Le Tellier, who was in Paris at the court, where he was accustomed to spend a good part of his time. De La Salle probably expected that the archbishop would approve, especially since he was following the advice of his spiritual director and acting from the loftiest motives in his willingness to renounce his canonry.

Influenced perhaps by the family, the archbishop commanded the zealous young subdeacon to abandon the project at once and not even to think about it any further. As it turned out, Father Clocquet himself had second thoughts about the whole affair and took steps to have the signed agreement nullified. De La Salle later on admitted that all along he felt that an inner voice was telling him that God did not want him to be a parish priest.

While in Paris, either on the occasion of his visit to Le Tellier or shortly thereafter, John Baptist de La Salle was ordained a deacon on the eve of Passion Sunday, March 21, 1676. The ceremony was performed by a Capuchin bishop in the chapel of the Archbishop of Paris, François de Harlay de Champvallon.

On April 30 of that same year, 1676, John Baptist de La Salle arrived at his legal majority. At the same time he decided to relinquish the guardianship of his younger brothers to Nicolas Lespagnol, a cousin of his maternal grandmother. Before doing so, he was required to render to the bailiff of Reims a detailed account of how he had managed the family finances during the previous four years. The discovery of this document in the municipal archives of Reims in 1964 by Brother Léon Aroz has given new insights into the character of De La Salle, the meticulous care and administrative acumen that he brought to this responsibility he had inherited from his father.

The reason for De La Salle's decision to cede to his older cousin the care of his younger brothers was, no doubt, the pressure of academic work in preparation for the licentiate degree in theology.

So far as can be ascertained from the sources, this program did not involve extensive course work, but rather preparation through personal study to defend in a series of oral examinations a number of theses covering the whole field of theology. The final public examination took place on January 26, 1678. De La Salle, along with four other candidates, succeeded in convincing the jury composed of several doctors of theology as to his mastery of the field. The degree of License in Sacred Theology (STL) was formally conferred on the Monday before Ash Wednesday in 1678.

Thus John Baptist de La Salle began the season of Lent in 1678 as a canon and a deacon with the licentiate in theology. On the last day of Lent in that year, Holy Saturday, April 9, 1678, he was ordained to the priesthood. The ceremony took place in the palace of the Archbishop of Reims, with Charles-Maurice Le Tellier himself as the ordaining prelate. The next day, Easter Sunday, Father De La Salle celebrated his first Mass before a small gathering of relatives and friends in the Lady Chapel of the Reims cathedral.

After his ordination to the priesthood, there remained the question of whether or not De La Salle would pursue the degree of Doctor of Theology. At the time, it was customary to take the examinations for the doctorate soon after the licentiate; ability to pay the high fees was more at issue than any additional study or research. There was no requirement of a written or published thesis such as is the almost universal practice today. It was simply a question of another series of oral examinations covering much the same theological ground as for the licentiate.

In this matter, as in so many others, De La Salle did not follow the usual pattern. In the beginning he hesitated. Whether through humility and modesty, lack of funds, his initial involvement with the schoolteachers, or simply in obedience to his spiritual directors, De La Salle did not present himself for the doctoral examinations for another two years. Finally in 1680 he was awarded the degree of Doctor of Theology in a formal ceremony in Saint Patrick's Hall at the University of Reims.

Early Years in the Priesthood

The human joy and spiritual elation that De La Salle must have experienced at his ordination and first Mass at Easter of 1678 was soon tempered by the untimely death on April 27 of Nicolas Roland, his spiritual director. Just before he died Roland had appointed De La Salle, not quite 27 years old, and Nicolas Rogier, fellow canons, to be the executors of his will. In this capacity De La Salle was suddenly faced with the complicated negotiations that Roland had begun, to secure legal recognition for a community of Sisters he had established for the education of poor girls.

Helped in large measure by the support and influence of Archbishop Le Tellier, De La Salle was able to convince the civic and religious leaders in Reims to endorse the petition to the king for letters patent, equivalent to legal incorporation, for the Sisters of the Holy Child Jesus, as they were called. Less than a year later, in February 1679, the document arrived bearing the signature of Louis XIV and the royal seal, thus assuring permanence to the community of Sisters and their apostolic work. To this day the Sisters consider De La Salle, together with Roland, as a co-founder of their Institute.

De La Salle's contact with the Sisters did not end with the granting of the letters patent. He frequently said Mass for them and otherwise provided for their spiritual needs. In addition, although the Sisters now had legal control over their own finances, De La Salle continued to advise them in this and other temporal matters which had been his responsibility as executor of Roland's will.

It would be in connection with some such matters of business, usually conducted in the convent parlor, that the Sister Superior, Françoise Duval, would have the opportunity to introduce De La Salle to Adrien Nyel, just arrived from Rouen. That was an encounter destined to change the entire course of De La Salle's life.

Along with his service to the Sisters of the Child Jesus, De La Salle fell into the routine of priestly ministry, such as any newly ordained priest might do today. Central to this ministry would be the daily celebration of the Eucharist. The special devotion and seriousness with which he said the Mass attracted people, and many of them waited afterwards to speak to him of their spiritual needs and problems.

No small part of De La Salle's daily routine would be occupied with his duties as a canon, which could require as much as five or six hours a day in attendance at the cathedral. He had the required authorization of the archbishop to hear confessions. It seems that in this regard he had a special gift for dealing with hardened sinners who had for a long time abandoned the practice of their religion. On at least one occasion he was formally designated to receive a non-Catholic woman from another diocese into the Catholic Church.

During the summer of 1679 De La Salle became involved in an incident that created something of a sensation and a scandal in the close-knit ecclesiastical circles of Reims. One of the canons of the cathedral, César Thuret by name, had apparently been living in concubinage with a servant girl for some time when De La Salle formally denounced him before the chapter. Thuret vehemently denied the charge, and a committee was appointed to investigate.

Meanwhile De La Salle himself became the target of gossip and abuse. Who was this young priest, daring to bring into the open a scandal that could only harm the reputation of the cathedral and its chapter? Popular or not, the investigation was thorough and lasted several months.

The delinquent canon was eventually found guilty on the basis of the testimony of several witnesses, including the girl herself, who was persuaded to testify against him. Assigned to a year of penance and deprived of his privileges as a canon, Thuret left Reims and accepted title to the chapel of Saint Gervais in the village of Guise. One author remarked that, rather than change his life, he changed only his residence.

Another aspect of De La Salle's daily routine ought to be mentioned in connection with this period in his life. Little by little he managed to turn the family residence on the Rue Sainte Marguerite into a religious center where some of his fellow priests could gather for longer or shorter periods to discuss common problems, to pray together, and to share a community experience. This provided not only some continuity with De La Salle's formative years in the priesthood, but also a setting for the radical change that was soon to come.

3

Beginnings in Reims
(1679–1688)

We go back to the spring of 1679. At the age of 28, John Baptist de La Salle was settling gradually into the routine and the lifestyle of a pious and zealous but rather comfortable and respected young priest. All the signs, internal and external, pointed to a brilliant career in the Church, with the promise of high ecclesiastical offices and dignities for which his family background and his university education had prepared him.

However, the chance encounter with Adrien Nyel at the door of the Sisters of the Child Jesus in Reims was to set his life's course in a totally new direction. De La Salle had never before met this man, but once the two of them had been admitted to the convent parlor, they were introduced to each other by the Sister Superior, Françoise Duval.

Adrien Nyel

Nyel, a zealous layman in his early 50s, had been sent from Rouen by Madame Maillefer, herself a native of Reims with connections by marriage to the De La Salle family. This fortunate meeting gave Nyel an opportunity to explain the purpose of his mission to the young and influential canon of Reims.

For some time now, Father Nicolas Barré, a priest of the congregation known as the Minims, had been spearheading a movement in Rouen, supported by the generosity of Madame Maillefer, to establish quality schools, first for poor girls, then for boys. Nyel, as an administrator of the General Hospice in Rouen, had been recruiting young men for the same mission. Father Nicolas Roland, too, had been in contact with Barré and was so impressed by the zeal and effectiveness of the educational reforms in Rouen that he was inspired to try to do something for Reims. If the community of Sisters, founded by Roland in Reims, had done so much for the education of poor girls, modeled on the schools in Rouen, why could

Seventeenth-century Reims

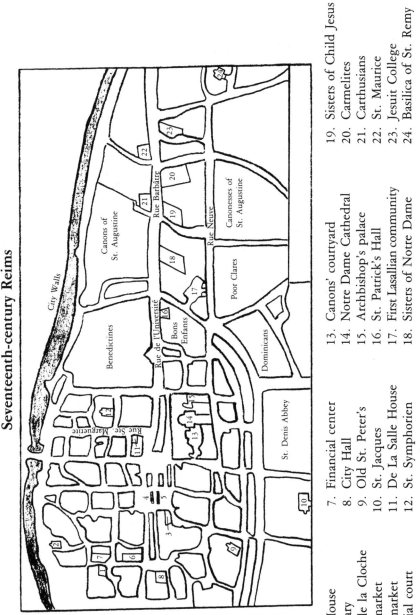

1. Moët House
2. St. Hilary
3. Hôtel de la Cloche
4. Cloth market
5. Grain market
6. Praesidial court
7. Financial center
8. City Hall
9. Old St. Peter's
10. St. Jacques
11. De La Salle House
12. St. Symphorien
13. Canons' courtyard
14. Notre Dame Cathedral
15. Archbishop's palace
16. St. Patrick's Hall
17. First Lasallian community
18. Sisters of Notre Dame
19. Sisters of Child Jesus
20. Carmelites
21. Carthusians
22. St. Maurice
23. Jesuit College
24. Basilica of St. Remy

not something be done for the poor boys of Reims? That in short was the message that Nyel brought from Madame Maillefer.

De La Salle listened to the proposal with interest. His recent experience in obtaining approval for Roland's congregation of Sisters taught him that it would not be an easy matter to win the approval of the archdiocese and the city council of Reims. There were already too many charity institutions for the resources of the city to support. If anything were to be accomplished, it would have to be done with the greatest discretion, without publicity, and without arousing the suspicions of the authorities.

After some thought, De La Salle suggested that Nyel come to stay in his house for a while. It was not unusual for his priest friends from the country to stay with him. Nyel could easily be mistaken for one of them. In that way there would be time to discuss the problems and the possibilities of the new venture.

For a whole week, in the house on the Rue Sainte Marguerite, Adrien Nyel and John Baptist de La Salle spent time together working out strategies to get the project off the ground. De La Salle called in priests he could trust and who had experience, in order to get their advice. Among them were the rector of the seminary and the prior of the Benedictine monastery attached to the Basilica of Saint Remy. Then some of the local pastors were invited to offer suggestions. They all seemed to agree that there was an urgent need to provide for the education of the poor boys who were running wild through the streets and alleys in the worst neighborhoods of Reims.

The First Schools

It was finally decided that Father Nicolas Dorigny, the pastor of the church of Saint Maurice, would provide room and board for Nyel and the 14- year-old assistant who accompanied him. Shortly thereafter (the traditional date is April 15, 1679), the first Christian School for the poor boys of Reims was opened in a small building opposite the side entrance to the parish church. It was a start. Satisfied that he had done all he could, De La Salle no doubt felt that his part in the enterprise was over. He was willing, of course, to be available again if needed, but from now on it was the responsibility of Nyel and whatever teachers he could recruit to work with him.

That is not the way things turned out. News of the success of the school in Saint Maurice soon got around. A wealthy widow named Catherine Lévesque, aware that she was mortally ill, let it be known that she was interested in endowing a similar school for her parish of Saint Jacques. Nyel did not hesitate to make contact, using the name of De La Salle to help win her confidence. Madame Lévesque, a bit suspicious of the much too eager Nyel, insisted that De La Salle be party to the contract. She agreed to endow three classes with an annual salary to support the teachers. The school opened in September 1679; six months later the foundress died, leaving in her will provision for the continuation of the school.

Now there were two schools at opposite ends of the town, while the additional teachers hired by Nyel continued to be housed at Saint Maurice. The facilities of the rectory and the resources of Father Dorigny, the pastor, were not adequate to provide for the growing numbers. De La Salle at first paid the additional expenses out of his own pocket. By December 1679 it was evident that a more permanent solution was needed. Once again De La Salle came to the rescue, moving the teachers into a house he had rented for them near his own. The lease was for eighteen months.

Nyel could not resist the opportunity to open up yet another school, in the parish of Saint Symphorien where the teachers now resided. The new school, like the others, was an instant success. But it soon became clear that, although Nyel was quite capable of establishing schools, he was not the best person to control or inspire the teachers. These rather young men were neither sufficiently trained nor adequately supervised for the work they were expected to do.

A Community in the Making

It was at this point, most probably at Easter in 1680, that De La Salle decided to invite the schoolteachers into his own home for meals. This would give him a chance to work a bit more closely with them to help overcome their deficiencies. In later years, it was this date that was selected to mark the foundation of the Institute of the Brothers of the Christian Schools by John Baptist de La Salle.

There can be no doubt that this event marked a turning point in the involvement of De La Salle with the teachers. Even at that time, however, he may well have thought of the arrangement as temporary, that the primary responsibility for the teachers and the schools lay with Nyel. There was as yet no fixed organizational structure, no plan for the future, no commitment on the part of the teachers, and they had not yet formed a community of any kind, much less one based on a religious mission.

De La Salle may well have reflected that some such steps needed to be taken if the work were to have stability. But in 1680 he little realized to what an extent he was becoming personally involved. In a memoir written much later, he expressed it thus: "I had thought that the care which I took of the schools and the teachers would only be external, something which would not involve me any further than to provide for their subsistence and to see to it that they carried out their duties in a religious and conscientious manner."

It was in the spring of that year, 1680, while all of this was going on, that De La Salle successfully passed the examinations for the doctorate in theology at the University of Reims. Both the subject matter and the significance of this degree would suggest that De La Salle had long-range plans far removed from the concerns of the barely literate teachers in the schools founded by Nyel.

It was also in that same year, 1680, that John Baptist de La Salle resumed the legal guardianship of his younger brothers and sisters. In 1676 he had relinquished this responsibility to Nicolas Lespagnol, his grandmother's cousin, in order to complete his own theological studies. Now John Baptist would have more time to devote to his family. This is yet another indication that he was concerned at the time at least as much about his family responsibilities as he was over the fate of the teachers and the schools.

During the following winter, De La Salle came close to losing his life. He was returning from a visit to the country, probably on family business as was his custom, when he was caught in a blinding snowstorm. The road became obliterated, and he fell into a deep ditch. The more he struggled to free himself, the deeper he sank into the mire. Close to exhaustion and about to lose consciousness, he made one desperate effort and was finally able to free himself. He suffered a rupture as a result; whenever it acted up in later years, he would be reminded to thank divine Providence for saving him from almost certain death in the freezing snow.

Meanwhile, the situation in the schools during the year between Easter 1680 and Easter 1681 only served to make the problems with the teachers more acute. Nyel was frequently absent; the teachers were becoming either careless or independent or both; there was no uniform policy or method to be followed in the schools; the students were becoming increasingly restless and discipline was suffering. All the good that had been hoped for seemed on the verge of falling apart.

During Holy Week of 1681, De La Salle took advantage of the absence of Nyel to call the teachers into his home for a spiritual retreat. Contrary to De La Salle's advice, Nyel had gone off to negotiate for yet another school at the invitation of the officials in the town of Guise. Although the negotiations did not succeed, this situation gave De La Salle the opportunity to spend more time with the teachers, to instill in them some sense of discipline, and to open to them a vision of the spiritual significance of the work they were doing.

On his return from his fruitless errand, Nyel was well pleased with the change he saw in the teachers. So, too, was De La Salle, even though he began to realize that if the change were to be permanent he himself would have to provide the follow-up. The lease on the house where the teachers were lodged was due to expire in another two months; a decision had to be made whether to renew it, or whether to take the next step and move the teachers into his own home.

De La Salle was torn in two. On the one hand, during the Holy Week retreat he had seen the advantages of having the teachers under his tutelage for an extended period. On the other hand, he had to consider the social status of his family, especially in the matter of a suitable upbringing for his three younger brothers, who were still living at home with him. It was bad enough to have these rough and tumble schoolteachers in for meals; to share the experience of daily living with them in such close quarters was, on the face of it, preposterous.

There was also the problem of where this was leading De La Salle personally. His original desire to help Nyel was beginning to turn into more than he had bargained for. What of his duties as a canon, for example? It was not so long ago that the cathedral chapter had to reprimand Nicolas Roland for neglecting his choir duties in favor of his work for the Sisters. Now De La Salle himself was being confronted with a similar conflict of interest. If he took one more step in favor of the teachers, there was no telling where it would lead.

True to his Sulpician training and his personal need to discern the will of God, De La Salle decided to seek spiritual direction. Accordingly he went to Paris to consult with Father Barré. In a matter of this kind it was a natural choice. Barré had known both Roland and Nyel and had long been active in the cause of education for the poor classes. Now that Barré was in Paris, De La Salle came to the monastery near the Place Royale to seek his advice.

Barré had a reputation as a gifted director who could see intuitively into the heart of a problem and the heart of a person. Sizing up both the situation and his client, Barré responded with a direct and uncompromising challenge. He advised De La Salle to take the teachers into his house and live with them.

A Critical Decision

De La Salle hesitated no longer. He was fully aware of what it would cost him by way of opposition from the family, shock in the social and ecclesiastical world in which he moved, and the need to defer or to put aside forever whatever other ambitions he may have had for himself. When the lease on their house expired on June 24, 1681, De La Salle moved the teachers into his own home on the Rue Sainte Marguerite.

The reaction of the family was not long in coming. At a family gathering, the expressions of indignation were explicit and bitter. Objections were raised concerning the impropriety of having such unworthy persons in the house at all, with special emphasis on the negative effect this would have on the training and social status of the three younger brothers still living at home. De La Salle listened patiently, but did not give an inch. As a result it was decided that Pierre, who was almost 15 years old, and Jean-Remy, who was not quite 12, would go to live with their married sister, Marie Maillefer. Only Jean-Louis, 18 years old at the time, opted to stay with his older brother and the schoolteachers.

This solution enabled De La Salle to devote more and more of his time to the teachers, and so to form them into a genuine community with a common spirit and purpose. A uniform schedule was adopted for each hour of the day, both in the house and in the schools. The customary religious exercises and ascetical practices of that era determined the routine in the house, while the best practical educational methods were consistently adopted for the schools. De La Salle was careful to move slowly. He was content to lead the teachers by the hand, so to speak, to let them see from their own experience and from his exhortations and example what was the best course to follow.

In view of these developments, Adrien Nyel was more and more content to leave the direction of the teachers in Reims to De La Salle, while he occupied himself with new foundations in the important towns outside Reims. But even there a difference became apparent. Now it was De La Salle who took charge of the negotiations for new foundations. In this way, during the year 1682, schools were opened in Rethel, Chateâu-Porcien, and Laon. At Guise, the earlier efforts of Nyel finally bore fruit when teachers from Reims, trained by De La Salle, came to take charge of the school.

All during this time, De La Salle personally supervised the situation that was developing in his family home, where the small community of pioneers had its center. Each morning and afternoon they set out for the distant schools of Saint Maurice and Saint Jacques, and the one close by near the Rue Sainte Marguerite. When they returned they shared their experiences and discussed their mistakes. De La Salle listened and gave his advice. In this situation there were present all the elements that were to characterize the organization to come: one central house servicing several schools; one person as the uncontested leader; a team of teachers, growing in professional competence and indisputably dedicated to the Christian education of the children of the poor.

The First Permanent Community

The next step was inevitable. In the spring of 1682 De La Salle received an offer for the family mansion on the Rue Sainte Marguerite. Only Jean-Louis was still living at home, and he was preparing to go to Paris to enter the seminary. There was no reason not to sell. In that year, on June 24, the feast of Saint John the Baptist and the traditional "moving day" in France, John Baptist de La Salle took his little band of teachers to live in a rented house on the Rue Neuve. In time the house would be known as the "cradle of the

Institute," the date as the birthday of the community. It is not known exactly how many teachers followed the Founder there, probably no more than five or six.

For John Baptist de La Salle, this move meant more than a change of residence. He was in fact leaving behind once and for all the comfortable world in which he had grown up to become part of the world of the poor. It is difficult for a modern reader to realize the repugnance felt by this sensitive and delicately brought-up priest when he first experienced the cramped quarters, the sounds, and the smells of a quite different social milieu. The coarse food especially brought him to the point of physical nausea, which he was able to overcome only by going without food altogether for days at a time. But once committed, there was no turning back.

In the new situation, the group of teachers that gathered around De La Salle began to assume more and more the appearances of a religious community. He was already their superior by reason of his education, his social status, and his priestly character. Now, with Nyel busy with new foundations outside Reims, De La Salle was recognized by the teachers as the superior of their community. Despite his own reluctance and the contrary custom of the time, he also agreed to their insistent demands that he serve as their confessor and spiritual director.

For a time everything seemed to be going well in the schools and in the house on the Rue Neuve. Once the novelty wore off, however, many of the young men began to chafe at the discipline imposed on them and the boredom of the routine in the school. Originally recruited by Nyel for the work of the schools, many of them were not prepared to sacrifice permanently either their salary or their independence for the sake of a venture that was chancy at best. They came to realize that the sort of commitment to a community and to a vocation that De La Salle envisioned for them was more than they were willing to bear.

De La Salle did nothing to stop those who wished to leave; in fact, he actively encouraged some of them to do so once he realized that they were unfit for either teaching or community life. Within six months all but one or two of the original group had gone to seek greener pastures elsewhere. It seemed for a time as if the entire enterprise were about to collapse. Convinced that the work was in God's hands, De La Salle remained calm, and within a short time new recruits presented themselves. These proved to be of better quality and to have higher motives than those they replaced.

Filled with new confidence, De La Salle did all he could to fortify these new candidates against the dangers of inconstancy. The new regulations he proposed were more carefully thought out and less severe. He was not in any hurry, preferring to be guided by events and by counsel before deciding what precise form the new community should take. It would be another two years or so before he would be ready to give a public and definitive sign of its existence. Meanwhile, he encouraged the teachers to be faithful to their duties in the community and the school, leaving to divine Providence any concern for the future.

A Critical Challenge

It wasn't very long before this approach began to create a certain uneasiness among the teachers. With no real guarantee for the future, they began to be concerned about what might happen to them if the fragile structure of the community should collapse. De La Salle responded by quoting the words of Jesus about the birds of the air and the lilies of the field. He renewed his appeals to them to leave everything to God and to abandon themselves to his Providence.

These pious exhortations fell on deaf ears. "It is easy for you to talk," they told him. "You have everything you need. You are a rich canon with a regular source of income and a guaranteed inheritance. You don't know what it is to have to do without. If our enterprise falls apart, you will survive and the collapse of our situation will not involve your own. But we are without property, without income, and we don't even have a marketable skill. Where will we go or what will we do if the schools fail and the people no longer want us? The only thing we will have left is our poverty and the only solution will be to go out and beg."

Their words struck home. De La Salle entered into a long period of profound meditation where he began to see the futility of giving a discourse on the Gospel that was so contrary to what he himself was living. He sought divine guidance in extended periods of prayer, sometimes lasting the whole night through. In an effort to discern God's will in his regard, to prayer he added fasting and severe forms of bodily penance. Such was to become the pattern of De La Salle's response in the many subsequent crises that he would face again and again throughout his life. After all, it was the Lord's work he was trying to accomplish.

This time, the divine imperative was clear. It was a moment of conversion, a decision even more radical than those he had already experienced leading up to this one. Remembering a suggestion that Father Barré had made once before, he knew how to meet the challenge of the teachers once and for all. Accordingly, on August 16, 1683, John Baptist de La Salle resigned his canonry in favor of a lowly priest, Jean Faubert. In this designation of a successor, he shocked the family—and the archbishop, who did all he could to dissuade him from his choice—by failing to name his own brother, Jean-Louis, then a seminarian in Paris, to the lucrative post.

De La Salle's decision had not been arrived at hastily. Not only did he ponder the move and pray over it for some time, but he afterwards put his reasons in writing, listing them under ten points. The last of these is perhaps the most interesting: "Since I no longer feel myself drawn to the vocation of a canon, it seems to me that this particular vocation has already left me long before I have abandoned it. This state in life is no longer for me. Although I entered it freely through an open door, it seems to me that today God is opening the door again so that I can leave it."

If De La Salle took his time in coming to a decision, he was not one to do things by halves. Divested of his source of regular income, he yet retained his other financial assets. These, too, he was determined to give up. It would seem quite natural, and it was the expectation of the teachers as well, that he would use his wealth to endow the schools. The memory of Father Barré's advice that "founded schools founder" seemed to suggest a different solution. De La Salle addressed himself in prayer to his Lord in these words: "If you, my God, endow the schools, they will be well endowed; if you do not, they will have no endowment. I beseech you to let me know your will."

An unexpected and tragic famine in the winter of 1683–1684 provided an answer. The high price of food and the rigor of the winter turned the city of Reims into one vast almshouse. To the three schools and to the house on the Rue Neuve the poor came in droves, children and adults alike, all close to starvation. None of them went away unprovided for. The daily distribution continued until there was nothing left. It got to the point where De La Salle himself had to beg for the bread that he could no longer afford to buy. Yet when it was all over, De La Salle reminded his community that, through it all and relying now on Providence alone, they had never lacked the basic necessities.

Going Public

With De La Salle now firmly committed to the community and the teachers themselves following his example, it was time to begin to go public with a new-found sense of identity. The best way to do so was to adopt a distinctive habit, a decision that was made most probably in the winter of 1684–1685. Up until that time the teachers had worn a waisted jacket like other laymen, with the white rabat as the only distinguishing mark to give them quasi-professional status in the schools. To protect themselves from the cold in winter, they wore a heavy mantle with pendant sleeves, but without collar or buttons in the front, the usual winter garment for ordinary folk in the Champagne region.

In order to distinguish themselves from laymen on the one hand, and from the clergy on the other, they decided to keep the mantle but to exchange the jacket for a kind of short cassock which extended half-way down the calf. The cassock was without buttons and was fastened on the inside with hooks from the top to mid-way down the front; from there down it was sewn. The purpose of this insistence on a short cassock without buttons but with hooks that did not show was to avoid the ostentation prevalent in the clerical garb of the time. The habit included a black skull cap known as the calotte, a broad-brimmed hat for outdoor wear, and heavy thick-soled shoes such as the peasants and workmen of the region were accustomed to wear.

This distinctive habit of the teachers made their existence as a community visible to their pupils, the parishioners, and the general public of Reims. It was time then to adopt a corporate title. Up until then they had been known simply as the schoolteachers of Father De La Salle. From now on they were to be known as the Brothers of the Christian Schools. And De La Salle could appropriately be called their Founder.

It is not known to what extent De La Salle wore this habit himself. He certainly did when, after the death of three young

Brothers between 1684 and 1685, he offered to take over some of the classes until replacements could be found. Twice a day he walked through the streets on his way to the school at Saint Jacques clothed in the short cassock, mantle with pendant sleeves, wide-brimmed hat, and thick-soled boots. People thought he had gone mad and accused him of an exaggerated public display of mortification and humility.

During the period from 1682 to 1685, by a sort of unwritten agreement, Adrien Nyel looked after the schools in the outlying towns of Guise, Laon, Rethel, and Chateâu-Porcien, while De La Salle assumed control over affairs in Reims. But Nyel, some 25 years older than De La Salle, was getting tired. He decided to return to the General Hospice in Rouen, whence he had started out some six years before. The entire community was now entirely in the hands of De La Salle. When news came of Nyel's death a few years later, De La Salle had a solemn requiem celebrated as a fitting tribute to the man who in one sense had been the original founder of the Christian Schools.

Training Teachers

Nyel had barely left the scene in 1685 when the Duke of Mazarin let it be known that he intended to endow a house or community of young men to be trained as teachers for the towns and villages of his dukedom. De La Salle was called to help draw up a program that would provide for 17 young candidates to be lodged in a house at Rethel. De La Salle was expected to supply the teachers from his community at Reims. This plan for a teacher-training center fell through, however, due in part to the vacillation of the duke, and partially because of the opposition of Archbishop Le Tellier of Reims.

The involvement of De La Salle in this plan is evidence that he saw from the beginning the importance of extending the work of the Society to training teachers for the schools. The concept became a reality a year or two later at the ever-expanding center in the Rue Neuve. Parish priests around Reims had been for some time sending repeated requests to De La Salle to send a Brother to take over one or another of the schools in the rural parishes. By this time the sense of community and a communal mission was so strong that De La Salle and the Brothers had adopted a policy of never sending fewer than two Brothers to a given school. The pastors, for their part, had all they could do to support even one such teacher in their country schools.

It was decided, then, that the pastors would select the schoolteachers for their parishes and send them to De La Salle to be trained. When the first group of about 25 arrived in the fall of 1687, De La Salle found room for them, apart from the Brothers, in an adjacent building which had been recently acquired for the purpose. They were put under the direction of the very capable Brother Henri L'Heureux, who taught them plainchant, written composition, arithmetic, and methods of teaching. They followed a regular schedule of religious exercises but dressed in secular clothing, and otherwise retained their independence and lay character.

This program was an outstanding success in every way. Once they returned to the parishes, the teachers were able to accomplish so much good that both the pastors and the teachers themselves remained ever grateful to De La Salle for the training he had given them. Yet, once the first class or two had completed their formation, the needs of the parishes were sufficiently provided for, and no new candidates were forthcoming.

In that same year, 1687, in addition to the Brothers and the student teachers in the training center, a third community was added to the house on the Rue Neuve. This was composed of young lads 14 or 15 years old who were interested in joining the newly formed Society of Brothers. They formed a community apart, but were introduced gradually into the religious practices and educational methods of the Brothers. At the time this group was referred to as a junior community, but in fact it was a novitiate of sorts; the program was much the same as that eventually adopted for the novitiates of the Institute.

The First General Assembly

A major factor that served to put the finishing touches on the foundation of the Institute was an assembly held prior to the opening of the teacher-training center at the Rue Neuve. By that time De La Salle realized the need to consolidate the gains that had been made up until then and to plan for the future direction of the community. For that purpose, he called 12 of the principal Brothers to come to the Rue Neuve for a period of prolonged reflection together. This first general deliberative assembly took place from the feast of the Ascension until Trinity Sunday, most probably in the year 1686.

The assembly opened with an intense spiritual retreat under the leadership of De La Salle himself, to guarantee that the negotiations would be undertaken in the presence of God and in a common search for his will. De La Salle insisted that there be a free exchange of ideas; he imposed nothing on his own authority and did not even let his own opinion be known beforehand. The topics to be discussed included the recent decisions to adopt a habit and a distinctive name for the Society, the daily regulation for the schools and the communities, and the possibility of taking vows.

Although a daily regulation of sorts was agreed upon, it was decided that it would be better to defer the drafting of a definitive Rule for the time being. More experience was needed with the regulations then in force with the possibility of adaptation to meet new situations. It was agreed that the food served should be adequate to the needs of active young men, but the quality should not exceed what was customary among the families of the poor children who attended the schools. The habit, which had been introduced probably during the previous year, 1685, was made official, as was the title, Brothers of the Christian Schools.

The subject that gave rise to the most discussion concerned the question of vows. Some argued for the three traditional vows of religion: poverty, chastity, and obedience. Although the Brothers were expected to be chaste and celibate, and although their lifestyle was characterized by poverty and sharing of goods, De La Salle ultimately advised against taking these vows. The assembled Brothers finally decided that they would take a private vow of obedience for three years, renewable annually. And so, on Trinity Sunday 1686, De La Salle and the 12 Brothers pronounced the vow of obedience for the first time. The next day they made a pilgrimage, fasting and on foot, to the shrine of Our Lady of Liesse some 30 miles distant. There they renewed the vows they had made the day before and entrusted the future of the Institute to the Most Blessed Virgin under her title of Our Lady of Liesse, derived from *laetitia,* which means joy.

As De La Salle reflected on the vow of obedience he had made, along with the others, to obey the body of the Society, he began to think that he, too, ought to be prepared to obey as well as command. When the Brothers assembled a year later to renew their vow, De La Salle insisted that it was time to elect one of their own as superior. With the greatest reluctance, the Brothers finally agreed and elected Brother Henri L'Heureux. De La Salle immediately submitted to the new superior.

Much to the embarrassment of Brother Henri, the Founder excelled all the others in demonstrations of deference and dependency. As soon as the diocesan officials heard about the matter, they were horrified that a priest and former canon should be subject to a mere lay Brother. It was only a direct order from Archbishop Le Tellier that persuaded De La Salle to resume his position at the head of the Society.

Thus, within five years, the little group that moved into the crowded house on the Rue Neuve with De La Salle in 1682 had expanded to encompass three distinct communities occupying a cluster of buildings. From out of this center there was a network of Christian Schools in Reims and in the neighboring towns providing for the children of the poor new opportunities for a Christian education according to the vision and the methods adopted by the Founder and the pioneering Brothers. The nascent Society already had an increasingly clear sense of identity and purpose. It might be said that by this time the foundation of the Institute of the Brothers of the Christian Schools was complete.

4

A Very Great Need

By the time the little community of Brothers in Reims had organized itself around John Baptist de La Salle to conduct "together and by association gratuitous schools," France was more than ready for some such educational enterprise. The need was great indeed. De La Salle himself only dimly realized it at first. Some years later, when the Institute of the Brothers was well along in its formative stages he could write in his Rule:

> The necessity of this Institute is very great, because artisans and the poor, being usually little instructed, and being occupied all day in gaining a livelihood for themselves and their family, cannot give their children the needed instruction, nor a suitable Christian education. It was to procure this advantage for the children of the artisans and of the poor, that the Christian Schools were established.

In the year 1680 the reign of Louis XIV, the Sun King, was in full flower. Having ascended the throne of France almost 30 years earlier, the fabled monarch had yet another 35 years to guide the destiny of France in the time of its greatest glory. It was an age that produced the great masterpieces of French literature, the classics of French pulpit oratory and treatises of spirituality, the palaces at Versailles and Fontainebleau, the brilliance of the royal court unmatched before or since.

It was an era, also, when the social hierarchy was beginning to change. Birth alone was no longer the criterion of worth. Some of the bourgeoisie were beginning to rise to high offices. The wealth of the merchants enabled them to build spacious mansions of their own in the towns. The rivalry for positions of influence was intense and engaged bishops, members of the town councils, and members of parliament alike.

As De La Salle himself came gradually to realize, the contrast between the nobility and the upper bourgeoisie on the one hand, and the artisans and the poor on the other, was striking. The lot of the artisans was characterized by insecurity. Unemployment was so general that craftsmen often had no steady income and no capital to help them weather an economic crisis. Even worse off were the genuinely poor, those with no other source of revenue except the work of their hands. These were the manual workers, the porters, road sweepers, water carriers, ragmen, knife grinders, and unskilled workers generally.

For nearly all of them, illiteracy was a matter of course. Marriage had to be long delayed because few under 30 could afford to raise a family. Boys had to be sent off to work at an early age. Girls were usually kept at home to care for the younger children; however, once the girls reached the age of 13 or 14, they were expected to enter service in a bourgeois household. Families suffered through periods of unemployment and semi-starvation that were inevitable and persistent.

Educational Policy

In matters of educational policy, as in all else, the power of the king was considered absolute. In view of the mutual support and interaction between the Catholic Church and the French Crown, with the king thought to be ruling by divine right, and the Church supported and often dominated by the power of the state, the religious and secular aspects of life were governed by a delicate balance between the two powers. Thus no organization, no religious community could enjoy legal status without securing letters patent from the king. Even papal documents defining doctrine, appointing a bishop, or approving a new religious congregation carried no weight in France if parliament and the king refused to recognize them.

Although educational policy was established by royal decree, the day-to-day supervision of the schools was considered to be not a civil but an ecclesiastical function. The royal policy fixed the minimum salary for the teachers and decreed that boys were to be taught by men and girls by women. On the other hand, teachers needed authorization to teach from the bishop or his delegate, unless exempted by royal letters patent. The police had no jurisdiction over school matters: this was reserved to the diocesan school supervisor, known as the *écolâtre* or *chantre* of the cathedral, a title derived from the time when the cathedral school doubled as a seminary for candidates for the priesthood who functioned meanwhile as choir boys. The local pastor might control the schools in his parish, but always as dependent upon the bishop.

Such a system, with its bureaucratic complexity, was bound to prevent any significant efforts at educational reform, as De La Salle soon found out once he became seriously involved with a new type of school. It required the greatest tact and diplomacy to win over the officials, the city council, the parish priest, the bishop, and the royal supervisor, in order to effect any change in the prevailing system. Eventually, it was only by bold and independent initiatives that De La Salle was able to bring the advantages of a good education in a new way to a new social class, the artisans and the poor.

Educational Opportunities

Nowhere was the inequality built into the social structures of seventeenth-century France more evident than in the opportunities for schooling. As we have seen in the case of De La Salle's own education, the children of the well-to-do were usually provided with private tutors in the earliest stages of their education. By the time they were nine or ten years old they were then ready to enter one of the "colleges" which provided the classical and philosophical courses required for entrance to the university.

As an alternative to the private tutors, or for children of the bourgeoisie who did not intend to enter the university, there were the "Little Schools" (*Petites écoles*). These schools were usually presided over by a single teacher who would set up shop, often in his own home. The diocesan supervisor (the *chantre* of the cathedral) was responsible for maintaining standards, protecting the rights of the teachers, and designating the precise territorial boundaries assigned to each. Although the Little Schools were required to accept the children of the certified poor free of charge, a sense of shame on the part of the poor and lack of motivation on the part of the teachers kept them away.

Instruction in the Little Schools was on an individual basis. The language used was Latin, and the emphasis was on rote memory. The pupils were expected to prepare themselves to come before the teacher to recite their lessons. There might be an assistant hired to keep the children quiet as they waited their turn. The stout leather strap known as the ferule was ever ready in the teacher's hand to make memory lapses the more memorable and less frequent.

A more specialized type of training was provided by the writing masters. These constituted a powerful guild of professional scribes under the protection of the king and parliament. Their principal function was to verify signatures and to maintain the quality of penmanship in official documents. A formal oath to preserve high standards of writing was taken by those who were admitted to the guild. Those who failed to qualify would often become public scribes, earning a modest living by writing personal letters for a fee.

The writing masters were continually feuding with the teachers in the Little Schools in an attempt to preserve their monopoly on the teaching of writing. In their view, the schoolteachers should restrict themselves to teaching reading only. Professional jealousy often resulted in complicated legal battles, and sometimes physical attacks as well.

Excluded by choice and necessity from both the university and the Little Schools, the children of the poor were relegated to the charity schools sponsored by the parish with the approval of the local bishop. Each parish was required to keep a list of the certified poor whose children alone were eligible to attend the charity schools, a policy intended to force those who could afford to pay to patronize the Little Schools.

There were no special qualifications for the teachers in the charity schools. At best, they might be retired or part-time teachers from the Little Schools, bringing with them all their inefficient methods, even less effective in an uncontrolled environment. At worst, teachers were recruited from among seminary or university dropouts who might not have progressed much beyond the elementary stages of an education. There was little by way of supervision or organization, and sessions were often interrupted for any excuse: budgetary problems, policy feuds in the parish council, lack of a teacher, needs of the harvest, or just plain lack of interest. Discipline was notoriously bad, and truancy was more the rule than the exception.

The only alternative to the parish charity school for poor children was the school usually associated with the General Hospice (the poorhouse) in the larger cities. These centers housed not only the sick and the incurably ill, but the aged and homeless, the mildly insane, migrant workers, and vagabonds. Among them would be sick or abandoned children, street waifs, or even children placed there for longer or shorter periods by their working parents. If anything, the schools in these poorhouses were even worse than the charity schools in the parishes.

It was within this framework that John Baptist de La Salle had to address the educational needs of the poor, as he began to see with ever-increasing clarity how urgent the situation was. It is worth noting that De La Salle rarely "opened" a school; he was usually invited to take over a school situation that already existed but was in desperate need of a new approach.

Movements for Reform of the Schools

In addressing the need for the reform of popular education in France, John Baptist de La Salle was not alone, nor was he operating in a vacuum. In one sense, he was not even a pioneer. All of the innovative methods he introduced into the Christian Schools had been thought of and tried elsewhere. It was his role and his genius to make them practical and effective in a network of schools animated and energized by a community of qualified and dedicated religious men.

Among the predecessors of De La Salle in this field was Father Pierre Fourier (1565–1640), the founder of the Congregation of Notre Dame at Nancy. In an age when religious women were expected to be strictly cloistered, it was his view that they could better procure the glory of God through a teaching ministry, thus integrating the religious and the apostolic life. Fourier was particularly sensitive to the need to give underprivileged young girls a solid Christian education, and for this reason he considered gratuity to be essential to the schools conducted by the Sisters.

Because Fourier wanted the education of the girls to be of high quality, he insisted that only the best qualified among the Sisters be chosen for this work, that they be well trained, that they be supervised by one of their own members, and that they work together to improve their teaching methods. Since the girls in the schools came from poor families, the accent was to be on practical subjects. The pupils were grouped in classes according to ability and rate of progress (hence an early experience with the simultaneous method, without using the word). In Fourier's view, education consisted in more than rote memory; as a result, much importance was given to developing a good rapport between teacher and pupil.

Fourier died in 1640, well before De La Salle came on the scene, but his experiment remained as an example of what might be achieved. His success was due to his clarity of purpose and creative vision, which he communicated to an able and dedicated community of religious women.

Another impetus for the movement to reform the parish schools came with the publication in 1654 of a book entitled *L'Escole Paroissiale*. The author was only later identified as Jacques de Bethencourt, for 18 years the pastor of the church of Saint Nicolas du Chardonnet in Paris. The book was a description of the policies and practices that made this parish school a model and a center of educational reform throughout the rest of the seventeenth and much of the eighteenth century.

In this highly influential little book, great stress was put on getting to know the pupils personally, especially by establishing regular contacts between the parents and the school. In order to give the students a sense of personal responsibility, certain supervisory duties were assigned to them. The simultaneous method of teaching was employed in the relatively large classes. The catechetical instruction was to go beyond mere rote memorization of formulas: the pupils were to be shown by concrete example how to live in a Christian manner. Absences were not tolerated, and truants were to be reported to the parents.

There were two interesting practices advocated in this book that were to be considerably altered in the Christian Schools of De La Salle. In the parish of Saint Nicolas du Chardonnet, the first language to be learned was Latin as more fundamental for educational purposes than French. Secondly, although the school was organized to accept both the rich and the poor, the two groups were strictly segregated. The reason given for this was practical: the dirty and unsanitary condition of the children of the poor might prove either offensive or a source of infection to their better groomed classmates.

Another center of educational innovation was the Abbey of Port Royal. The Little Schools established there lasted only from 1637 to 1660, being suppressed in the face of the anti-Jansenist stance of the king and the parliament. But they did establish a precedent for practices that would eventually become widespread. Not only did these schools pioneer in beginning the educational process in French rather than Latin, but they introduced instruction in contemporary foreign languages as well. They devised a system for taking notes while reading, a method intended to imitate the dissection process in the study of anatomy. Credited with the invention of metal pens for writing, the schools at Port Royal were famous for the fine penmanship of their students.

With the preaching of Charles Démia, the city of Lyon became identified with the movement to provide a decent and Christian education for the poor. Encouraged by what he had seen at Saint Sulpice and at Saint Nicolas du Chardonnet in Paris, in 1666 Démia addressed his famous "Remonstrances" to the "Provosts, the Merchants, the Magistrates, and the Leading Citizens Of Lyon." The subject of this impassioned plea was the urgent need for schools for the children of the poor. Démia argued that all the evils plaguing the city—moral, social, and economic—could be attributed directly to the fact that the poorer classes lacked an education. Word of this bold initiative, when it reached Paris, made a lasting impression on the young Nicolas Roland, who was studying there at the time. It played a part in his determination to bring the same message back to his native Reims.

Démia had to repeat his "Remonstrances" in 1668, and eventually he began to be heard. Appointed by the Archbishop of Lyon to take general control of the schools, he developed a program for the reform of the schools and established a school board composed of priests and laymen to supervise them. He also scheduled regular assemblies of the teachers in order to maintain quality instruction and a high level of motivation.

In an effort to recruit good teachers, both men and women, Démia founded the Seminary of Saint Charles for young men who wanted to study for the priesthood, but who were willing during the years prior to ordination to exercise an apostolate teaching children in the schools. To this group, there was later joined the community of the Sisters of Saint Charles devoted to the same purpose. The seminary did not survive the death of its Founder, but the Sisters' community developed into a religious congregation that exists to this day.

Meanwhile, in the opposite corner of France at Rouen, Father Nicolas Barré, a member of the Clerics Regular Congregation of Minims, had been busy since 1660 training women teachers for all sorts of schools, especially those devoted to the religious instruction of the children of the poor. Together with two pious ladies, Françoise Duval and Marguerite Lestocq, he had helped to found a small community known as the Teaching Women (*Maîtresses*) for the Christian and Charitable Schools. In time this group evolved into the congregation known as the Sisters of the Child Jesus of Rouen.

At the same time, Adrien Nyel, who was then the procurator general of the General Hospice at Rouen, was organizing a group of volunteer laymen to assist in attending to the many needs of the sick, elderly, and homeless poor who were housed there. Among them were many poor and abandoned children. Eventually Father Barré joined with Nyel in trying to organize a community of men to be known as the Teachers (*Maîtres*) for the Christian and Charitable Schools. Although these lay volunteers considered themselves as followers of Father Barré, it does not seem they ever formed a permanent community.

It was no doubt through his spiritual director, Nicolas Roland, that John Baptist de La Salle would have became aware of the movements in Rouen to provide religious instruction for the children of the poor. Roland had been a frequent visitor to Rouen where he was much in demand as a preacher. Father Barré and the Sisters provided both the motivation and the support for his own foundation of the Sisters of the Child Jesus in Reims. There seems to be some evidence that Roland had even tried to interest De La Salle personally in the work of the charity schools, without success.

It was his role as executor of Roland's will that first sensitized De La Salle to the urgency and complexity of the problems in popular education. His contacts with the Sisters of the Child Jesus in Reims after Roland's death led directly to that fateful meeting with Nyel in 1679. From then on John Baptist de La Salle was being drawn, one step at a time, into the mainstream of a movement in which so many others had been the pioneers.

The Christian Schools of De La Salle

The originality of John Baptist de La Salle is not so much that he was a pioneer, for example, in gratuitous schools for the poor, the simultaneous method, the use of French as a vehicle of instruction, centers for training teachers, or any of the other educational innovations with which he is sometimes credited. Rather, his contribution was to create, resolutely and against great odds, a stable community of religiously motivated laymen to construct a network of schools throughout France that would make practicable and permanent the best elements from the pioneers who had gone before him.

Father Nicolas Barré

By the time that De La Salle gathered the principal Brothers together in 1686 for their first solemn assembly, the essential elements that were to characterize the Christian Schools of De La Salle were already in place. The name itself is significant. The title "Christian" not only stressed the religious character and purpose of the school, but also served to differentiate this new type of school from the charity schools on the one hand and the Little Schools on the other.

Central to the success of the Lasallian enterprise was the community of teachers who called themselves by the name Brother. The community provided an element of stability and continuity, as well as a process of growth that came from shared experience and experimentation with new educational methods. Under the guidance of De La Salle these men adopted a lifestyle that was disciplined and even austere, prayerful and highly motivated. Great importance was attached to competence and confidence in the classroom, the religious spirit overflowing into a sense of mission and an ardent zeal to accomplish it. From the beginning the Brothers conducted their schools as a communal effort: "together and by association" was the phrase they chose to express this essential characteristic.

The method of instruction in the Christian Schools was entirely practical. Religious formation aimed at developing good Christians, that is to say, in the context of the time and place, practicing Roman Catholics. Instruction was given in French rather than Latin, a policy that De La Salle defended by advancing the most practical reasons. The emphasis was on useful subjects — reading, writing, mathematics, and other skills that would be helpful in gaining a livelihood. The simultaneous method was employed, although modified to provide for individual differences by dividing the large classes into homogeneous sections presided over by student monitors.

Discipline and good order soon became one of the outstanding characteristics of the Christian Schools. Silence reigned to the point where even the teachers spoke as little as possible. Detailed instruction was given on habits of cleanliness and the rules of politeness so that even the poorest pupils could associate with their peers without fear of offending them.

Regular attendance was insisted upon, and truancy was dealt with severely. The pupils themselves were often given the opportunity to assist in maintaining good order. Punishments were kept to a minimum, graded to meet the offense, and always administered with dignity, calm, and without any show of anger or resentment.

The original motive for the development of the Christian schools was the urgent and evident need to provide for the education of poor boys. This primary purpose was never lost sight of. However, as the schools began to prosper, more and more of the children of families who were somewhat better off began to seek admission to the Lasallian schools. The parents whose children were not destined for the university were attracted by the practical curriculum and the good order. Boys from bourgeois families learned that they could mingle easily with poor boys who were well behaved and well groomed; the children of the poor began to see new opportunities in life through the contacts they made with their better-situated classmates.

For De La Salle and the Brothers gratuity of instruction was a fundamental principle. This not only provided a quality education for the poor, but also guaranteed that no distinction would be made in the school between those who could afford to pay and those who could not. The expenses of running the school and the living expenses of the Brothers were met through contracts arranged with either the pastor or those who endowed the school. This policy left the Brothers free from any kind of external financial pressure in the running of the school. It also led to a great deal of legal trouble, as will be seen in the narrative to follow.

In retrospect, De La Salle regarded these developments as the outcome neither of his own organizational genius nor of the initiative taken by the educational pioneers who had preceded him. In his view of faith the entire enterprise was due to the working of God's Providence that enabled him to hear God's voice in the cry of the poor. He was deeply conscious that in his lifetime, and in his schools, at least one sign of the Kingdom of God was being realized: the poor had the Gospel preached to them.

5

Beginnings in Paris
(1688–1691)

In Reims in the year 1687 there was a small but highly motivated community of Brothers who had gathered around John Baptist de La Salle. They had already acquired a sense of identity and purpose, a distinctive habit, the essential elements of internal organization, and a fair amount of teaching experience, as well as a developing and corporate expertise in the conduct of schools. The schools were flourishing, not only in Reims but also in the outlying towns of Guise, Rethel, and Laon. A novitiate of sorts was functioning at the center on the Rue Neuve, as was also the teacher-training program for lay teachers in the rural schools. Some of the Brothers, including the Founder, had committed themselves by a vow of obedience which served to give a certain stability to the enterprise. The time had come to think of expanding the all-important mission of bringing the Gospel to the children of artisans and the poor.

There were already compelling reasons to think of Paris as a possible place to begin a new foundation. Father Barré had died in Paris in 1686. It was he who had guided De La Salle through the difficult choices involved in committing himself to the work of the schools. Perhaps now was the time to honor Barré's expectation that De La Salle would one day establish his Christian Schools for poor boys in the capital. The need there was even greater than in Reims. In addition, De La Salle had already promised Father De La Barmondière, one of his former teachers and now the pastor at Saint Sulpice in Paris, that he would come as soon as he could to take over the charity school in that sprawling parish.

It was while De La Salle was waiting for the right moment to make such a move that a rather different kind of proposal came from Charles-Maurice Le Tellier, the Archbishop of Reims. Delighted with the good reports that came to the chancery about the success of the schools, he offered to subsidize the work of the Brothers on condition that De La Salle would assign teachers exclusively to the charity schools in the Archdiocese of Reims. In turn, the Brothers would be given security and status as a diocesan congregation, with ultimate control in the hands of the archbishop.

De La Salle saw immediately the danger in this tempting offer. As Canon Blain remarks, he realized that Reims, which had been the cradle of the Institute, might now become its tomb. It became more urgent than ever to establish a foundation elsewhere. A foothold in the capital would provide many advantages and would serve as a more natural center from which the work could expand. Accordingly, De La Salle notified Father De La Barmondière that he was prepared to keep his promise to take over a school in Paris. The Founder's younger brother, Jean-Louis de La Salle, who happened to be a seminarian at Saint Sulpice at the time, could serve as an intermediary.

The First School in Paris: Saint Sulpice

The charity school in the parish of Saint Sulpice, with an enrollment of more than 200 pupils, had recently been placed under the direction of a diocesan priest, Father Compagnon, who had only a young layman to assist him. Aware of De La Salle's promise to the pastor and desperate for help with the large number of pupils in his care, Compagnon wrote as early as July 1685 asking for a Brother to come to teach in the school. Since by that time De La Salle, in consultation with the Brothers, had made it a rule never to send a Brother alone on a mission, his reply was evasive. Compagnon then journeyed to Reims to present his petition in person, but he found that De La Salle was out of town. When De La Salle learned of the visit, he wrote to Father De La Barmondière to say that he was interested in the project. The condition was that the pastor be willing to accept two Brothers and De La Salle along with them.

There was a series of delays over a period of almost two years before all the arrangements were complete. At first Compagnon wondered why the Brothers did not come sooner. Jean-Louis de La Salle told him that his brother was waiting in Reims for more explicit instructions. Compagnon then hesitated for a time, realizing that the presence in the school of two Brothers and the Founder himself might prove to be more than he had bargained for. De La Salle, for his part, was reluctant to come to an agreement with anyone

Lasallian Locations in Present-day Paris

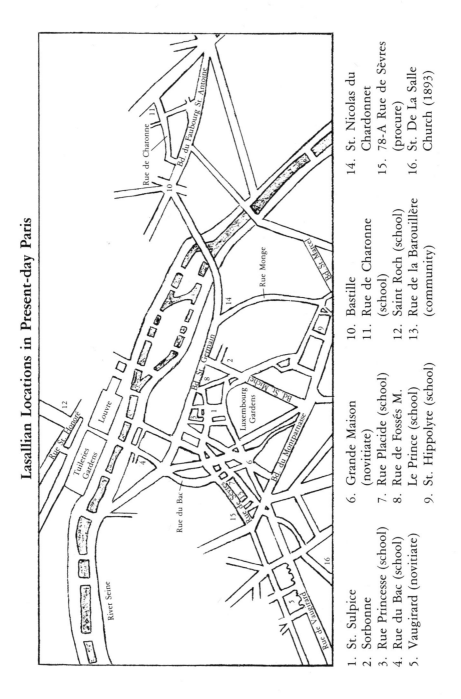

1. St. Sulpice
2. Sorbonne
3. Rue Princesse (school)
4. Rue du Bac (school)
5. Vaugirard (novitiate)

6. Grande Maison (novitiate)
7. Rue Placide (school)
8. Rue de Fossés M. Le Prince (school)
9. St. Hippolyte (school)

10. Bastille
11. Rue de Charonne (school)
12. Saint Roch (school)
13. Rue de la Barouillère (community)

14. St. Nicolas du Chardonnet
15. 78-A Rue de Sèvres (procure)
16. St. De La Salle Church (1893)

other than the pastor himself. When Father De La Barmondière finally realized the reason for the delay, he had Father Baudrand, who
was soon to succeed him as pastor, write in his name to inform De
La Salle that he and the two Brothers should come to help with the
school.

De La Salle arrived in Paris with the two Brothers on the eve
of Saint Matthias' day, February 24, 1688. They were taken to the
school building on the Rue Princesse, which also housed a hosiery
factory where the school children could be taught a useful trade.
The Brothers were to be lodged in the upper floors above the school,
but they had to share their living quarters with Compagnon's teenage
assistant and M. Rafrond, the layman in charge of the factory. Meals
were sent to the Rue Princesse from the Sulpician community where
Compagnon had his residence. The building on the Rue Princesse
still stands to this day, now a combination of apartments and small
shops, the only building in Paris associated with the Founder and
the early Brothers to have survived the ravages of time.

It did not take the new arrivals long to realize that the school
was in a state of utter chaos. The pupils came and went as they
pleased. There was no fixed schedule of classes, and school hours
varied from one day to the next. There was no provision for organized
religious instruction or for class prayers to begin and end the school
day. Card playing and gambling seemed to be the favorite pastime
during recess in the narrow courtyard behind the school. The factory was a constant distraction, but it did provide a motivation of
sorts in terms of financial profit for both the manager and the pupils.
No one seemed to care: the pastor rarely visited the school, Rafrond
was content to run the factory, Compagnon, who was nominally
responsible, was often absent and no great disciplinarian in any case.

In face of all this disorder, De La Salle urged his Brothers to
be patient, to trust Providence, and to concern themselves only with
their teaching duties. Since the role of the Brothers was limited
to classroom instruction, they used the little autonomy they had
to divide the pupils according to their age and ability. This first
small step toward organization was so effective that it soon attracted
even more new students. When one of the Brothers collapsed from
overwork, De La Salle had to take his place in the classroom until
he recovered.

As the weeks went by Compagnon began to realize that it would
be better all around if De La Salle were to take over the direction

of the school. At one point, he even made a suggestion to that effect, but De La Salle, sensing a certain reluctance and insincerity in the offer, politely declined. He was conscious, too, that such a change in administration would have to come from the pastor himself.

It was not until sometime in April, two months after the arrival of the Brothers, that Father De La Barmondière, the pastor, came on one of his rare visits to inspect the school. Quite distressed by the lack of discipline and order, he inquired as to the cause. In the face of the embarrassed and evasive replies of Compagnon, he thereupon pleaded with De La Salle to take over the direction of the school. The Founder replied that he would need more Brothers if anything effective were to be done. De La Barmondière agreed to accept as many as needed, and he offered to pay them well. This new arrangement only served to create resentment in Father Compagnon, who continued to have supervisory responsibilities for all the schools of the parish.

Reform and Resentment

Once De La Salle and the Brothers were in charge, the good order already customary in the Christian Schools in Reims was gradually introduced. The doors were not opened until the Brothers were in their place and prepared to supervise. Once classes began the doors were locked. Students who came late could not get in; those who were accustomed to run off during the day had no way to get out. Regular attendance was insisted upon, a fixed schedule of classes was instituted, and the time devoted to the manual training program in the factory was considerably curtailed. The daily catechism and the regular classroom prayers became a focal point of the school day. To fill in the long period between the end of the morning session and the return in the afternoon, the Brothers brought their pupils, lined up two by two, to the parish church for Mass. This was something new: an example of piety and decorum for the spectators on the streets of Paris, an advertisement for the school, and a feature of the schedule in the Christian Schools ever after.

These reforms only provoked jealousy and resentment on the part of Compagnon and Rafrond. Both tried to play up to the pastor. Aware that the manual training program was the pastor's pride and joy, Rafrond thought that he would force the issue by threatening to resign. When he did so, the shop closed down for a time, but the pastor did nothing to call him back. De La Salle, who had come to see some value in this type of training, engaged Rafrond, now unemployed and anxious for the money, to teach one of the Brothers the necessary skills. The Brother mastered the techniques within three weeks. Another Brother with skill in knitting was brought from Reims, and soon the factory was operating better than ever. Rafrond had only succeeded in maneuvering his way out of a job.

Compagnon was rather more insidious. He began by trying to undermine the late morning Mass favored by the Brothers by urging the pupils to attend the early parish Mass, which he knew the pastor preferred. When this ploy did not succeed, he tried to use his influence with a group of charitable ladies in the parish who were fond of him personally and generous in their support of the works of the parish. Compagnon began raising doubts in their minds about the innovations introduced by De La Salle. Included were some insinuations of mismanagement, probably on the basis of complaints from delinquent students who had been disciplined by the Brothers. In this way Compagnon was certain that the negative reactions would reach the ears of the pastor.

For some unknown reason, De La Barmondière seemed to give some credence to the complaints. De La Salle was surprised to find, on his return from a trip to Reims to secure more Brothers for the school, that the pastor's attitude had noticeably cooled. Not wanting a direct confrontation, De La Barmondière let it be known to De La Salle, through Father Baudrand, who was his confessor, that it might be better if he were to resign. As soon as the summer vacation period arrived in September 1688, De La Salle visited the pastor to bid a formal farewell. By this time, De La Barmondière was no longer quite so sure, declaring that he needed more time to think about the matter, that the Brothers meanwhile were to remain as they were. It was only after a thorough investigation of the whole matter by an outside priest that the source of the trouble became known. Within a year, Compagnon was removed from any responsibility for the schools and put in charge of the choir boys of the parish.

A New Pastor, a New School, and New Difficulties

Meanwhile, in January 1689, Father Baudrand had succeeded De La Barmondière as the pastor of the parish. The new pastor was so delighted with the conduct of the school and the progress of the pupils that he resolved to open more schools in his very extensive parish. Early in the next year, 1690, a new school was opened on the Rue du Bac. Still in the parish of Saint Sulpice, the school was near the Pont Royal connecting the Rive Gauche with the Louvre on the other side of the Seine. Two Brothers were summoned from Reims to take over the two classes in the school, and it was an immediate success.

At this point, De La Salle might well have thought that the schools in Paris were sufficiently established. They had the support of the pastor, and the lines of authority were rather clearly drawn. It seemed that he and the Brothers might now go on with their work in relative peace. But it was not to be so. This time the trouble came from the outside, from the Corporation of the Masters of the Little Schools to be exact. It was the opening of the school on the Rue du Bac that precipitated the crisis.

The basis of the complaint was that the school had been opened without authorization from the school supervisor (*chantre*) of the Notre Dame Cathedral. No protest had been raised in connection with the school on the Rue Princesse because that had always been considered a charity school and, as such, was legally under the control of the pastor. But the school on the Rue du Bac was something else. It was a new school, for one thing, and so great had the reputation of the Brothers grown that they were not only attracting the certified poor, but they were beginning to draw away from the Little Schools those who could afford to pay. The masters of the Little Schools, certainly with some reason, feared that their livelihood was being threatened by this new and highly competitive approach to elementary education.

The initial step was for the Corporation to file suit with the school supervisor for the archdiocese of Paris, Father Claude Joly. They put a seizure on all the furniture in the school on the Rue du Bac, an action they were legally entitled to take, and the school had to be closed for the time being. The first court decision went against De La Salle. Despite his thorough distaste for litigation of any kind, De La Salle was persuaded by Father Baudrand, his pastor and confessor, that he should appeal the decision as the only way to safeguard his educational mission to the poor.

De La Salle submitted his brief in writing. So cogent were his arguments, and so solid the support from the parents of the pupils, that the decision was reversed. The legal basis for the reversal was the judgment that the school was indeed a charity school under the control of the pastor, not the archdiocesan supervisor. The matter rested there for the time being, but it would erupt again in various forms as long as De La Salle remained in Paris.

Trouble in the Community

While all of this was going on, De La Salle was sorely tried by a crisis that arose within the community of Brothers. When the two additional Brothers were brought from Reims to supplement the two that had originally come to Paris, De La Salle appointed one of the new arrivals as Director of the community. This did not sit well with the two pioneers, who had endured so much in getting the school started in the first place. One of them abruptly left the community. This was a great loss to the small community and to the school as well: the man was tall and impressive looking, had many skills, was an excellent teacher, and was well liked by the boys. The second of the two pioneers continued in the community, but he was a constant source of trouble and dissension, insolent and disrespectful to De La Salle, going so far on one occasion as to raise a hand to strike him. After three years, this second of the Paris pioneers followed the first and left the Institute.

Trouble with the Pastor: The Habit and the Novitiate

Another issue that caused pain and controversy during this period concerned the habit that the Brothers had adopted earlier in Reims. The opposition this time came from Father Baudrand himself. Not only was he now the pastor of the parish, but the recent lawsuit had established the principle that the very existence of the schools depended on him. For this reason he felt justified in making representations about the Brothers' habit. He thought this strange and rather countrified sort of get-up that the Brothers wore did not reflect favorably on his parish schools. He would have much preferred that the Brothers wear a plain black cassock with the ecclesiastical mantle.

Although De La Salle had jealously guarded the autonomy of the community on internal matters, here was an issue that concerned the external relationships as well. Nevertheless he was unwilling to yield in such a matter, lest the autonomy he sought for his Society

The habit of the Brothers in the seventeenth century

in the departure from Reims might now be compromised. There was not much point in avoiding the trap of becoming a diocesan congregation, only to wind up as the adjunct of a parish. Furthermore, for De La Salle and the Brothers, their distinctive habit was the embodiment of their special identity as consecrated laymen, neither clerical nor secular. Caught on the horns of this dilemma, De La Salle had recourse as usual both to prayer and to spiritual direction. Fortunately, Father Tronson, his old spiritual director from his seminary days at Saint Sulpice, was available in Paris at the time. He advised the Founder to stand his ground.

The result was the *Memoir on the Habit,* the earliest and most precious of the autograph writings of De La Salle that has survived. In it, the Founder had an opportunity to explain publicly and in detail the special nature and mission of the young Society, all of which was symbolized by the distinctive garb they wore. Unusual as it was, people had gotten used to the Brothers' habit. It became in time a remarkable way to identify, not only the Brothers as a community, but the special type of school they conducted wherever they went.

The habit of the Brothers was not the only matter that caused tension between De La Salle and Father Baudrand, between the broader vision of the one and the narrow parochialism (in the literal sense) of the other. Once the two schools in Paris seemed to be running well, De La Salle determined to bring the young candidates from Reims to Paris so that he could personally supervise their formation. He took the precaution of obtaining beforehand the necessary permission of François de Harlay de Champvallon, the Archbishop of Paris. To those candidates who were old enough, De La Salle gave the Brothers' habit and employed them in the schools. At the request of the pastor, several of the others were assigned to spend the entire morning in the parish church to serve the many priests who came there to say Mass.

It soon became apparent that Baudrand looked upon these candidates for the Institute as somehow subject to his control. As a result, the young men were caught up in an ecclesiastical environment that was not suited to their vocation to be teaching Brothers. Many of them, in fact, began to drift away from their original fervor and dedication to the ideals of De La Salle. Once again, the Founder was in a delicate position. He was entirely dependent on the pastor for whatever authority he had over the schools; yet he wanted complete independence when it came to matters concerning the internal structure of his young Society. Eventually, he was able to withdraw the juniors from their role as acolytes. He sent home those whose fervor had faded, and admitted the others to the regular life of the community.

Baudrand, for his part, continued in his opposition to an independent novitiate outside his control. He attributed De La Salle's intransigence on these matters to stubbornness, a charge that would be repeated many times and in many different circumstances in the future. It became the customary response every time the Founder tried to preserve the originality of his creation, the independence of his young Society, and its internal cohesion and identity.

Another Brush with Death

Toward the end of 1690 De La Salle fell ill and almost died. Although he was only 39 years old, it is not surprising that his physical frame, which had always been somewhat delicate, should become exhausted from the excessive burden of the work, the stress and anxiety in facing almost constant opposition, the long hours devoted to prayer, and the austerity of a lifestyle that included rather severe penitential practices.

The first attack came after De La Salle had undertaken to go by foot on the long journey from Paris to Reims in order to attend to some urgent business. Although he wished to return quickly to Paris, he was unable to ignore or to conceal his weakened condition, and was forced to take to his bed. The Brothers at Reims, who had not seen him in two years, were horrified at first when they saw how emaciated he had become. But they lavished on him all the care that the love of devoted sons could devise and all the remedies that their meager resources could provide. In a short time the needed rest and nourishment began to have their effect in restoring him to health.

It was during this illness that his maternal grandmother, Perrette Lespagnol, now the widow of Jean Moët, came to visit him at the Rue Neuve. She asked to be shown to his sick room. De La Salle sent word that she was not to be admitted to the upper floors of the house. She, who of all the family had always sided with John

Baptist, insisted that it was her right to visit a sick man who was her very own grandchild and godchild. Instead, De La Salle made the effort to get dressed and to receive her in the parlor. He calmed her remonstrances by pointing out that it was a strict rule — as it was in most religious communities of men — that women not be allowed in the living quarters of the house. He did not want to make an exception in his own case, but he assured her that he loved her all the same and that he was recovering nicely.

As soon as he was able, De La Salle set off again for Paris, much against the doctor's advice. When he arrived back at the Rue Princesse he was so exhausted and so ill that he again had to be put to bed. This time, despite the attentive care of the Brothers, he did not rally and his condition grew worse. Within six weeks he was suffering intensely from a retention of urine and it seemed that death was imminent.

Filled with consternation the Brothers began to storm heaven, praying that their Father not be taken from them so prematurely. They contacted the famous Doctor Adrien Helvétius, well known to the Sulpician community for his effectiveness in treating Father Tronson three years earlier. The doctor proposed a remedy, warning De La Salle that it would either cure him or kill him. In an attitude of submission to the will of God, John Baptist agreed to go through with the remedy. The doctor recommended that Holy Communion in the form of Viaticum be administered beforehand to support the patient.

The procession with the Blessed Sacrament to the bed of the sick man was a solemn affair. Father Baudrand himself headed the group of several priests from the Sulpician community and the seminary, all dressed in surplices and carrying lighted candles. In the sick room, the Brothers were all in tears, begging their Father's blessing. Baudrand assured them that if the worst were to happen, he himself would be a father to them. De La Salle, dressed in surplice and stole to receive his Lord, could barely speak, but Blain tells us that he finally whispered, "I recommend that you remain closely united and in complete obedience." Someone had to hold his hand to give his blessing. He then received the sacrament with his customary fervor and faith.

After the priests had left, Helvétius administered his remedy. He stayed with the patient for a considerable time until he was sure that the remedy was producing the desired effect. De La Salle soon began to show signs of recovery. Within a few days he was able to take some nourishment, and his strength began to return.

During his long convalescence, the holy priest protested all the special care that was being taken of him, saying that he ought to be sent to the General Hospice with the rest of the sick poor. Through it all, he remained utterly calm and resigned to the will of God. Once his recovery was sufficiently advanced, he resumed his work and his austere life, confident that the success of the Christian Schools depended not on his health or even his life but on the will of God. As long as possible he would continue to exert himself to the utmost to procure God's glory as far as he was able and as God would require of him.

6

Crises and Consolidation
(1691–1698)

The years 1690 and 1691 that almost witnessed the death of the 40-year-old Founder were years that came close to witnessing the death of his Institute as well. The personal antagonisms that made the early years in Paris so difficult were now succeeded by organizational problems that threatened to overwhelm the entire enterprise. It looked for a while as if the newly born Society might not survive its infancy.

Brother Henri L'Heureux

De La Salle had realized for a long time that sooner or later he himself would have to be replaced as superior of the community. As early as the General Assembly of 1686, he had persuaded the Brothers that they should choose a successor from among themselves. The election of Brother Henri L'Heureux on that occasion had been quickly annulled by Archbishop Le Tellier, shocked to learn that a mere lay Brother had become the religious superior of a priest, much less of a doctor of theology who had been a canon of the cathedral. In order to forestall any such objection for the future, De La Salle undertook to teach Latin to Brother Henri, and then enrolled him in the theology program at the Abbey of Saint Denis in Reims with the intention of preparing him for the priesthood.

In making the choice of Brother Henri, De La Salle was not only following the expressed preference of the Brothers, but he discerned a person of high quality as well. Brother Henri had been one of the first to join De La Salle and so had shared with him all the deprivations and humiliations of the early years. A model of religious fervor and humility, L'Heureux also had an agile mind and he could speak well. At the Abbey of Saint Denis he had a reputation for being hesitant in replying to questions, but profound and eloquent in his responses once he penetrated to the heart of the matter. In a relatively short time he completed his studies, whereupon De La Salle brought him to Paris prior to presenting him for ordination.

It was at this time that De La Salle fell ill. Once his recovery was assured, he returned to Reims to complete some unfinished business. As was his custom, he left Brother Henri in charge of the Brothers in Paris at the Rue Princesse. No sooner had De La Salle reached Reims than a letter arrived informing him that Brother Henri had suddenly been taken ill. A second letter soon followed saying that the case was serious, and a third that the doctors had given up hope. At first De La Salle was inclined to consider these reports exaggerated since he had left the Brother in apparently good health. Once convinced that the case was indeed serious and the concern of the Brothers genuine, the Founder set out hastily for Paris. He arrived about midnight a day or two later, only to find that Brother Henri had been dead and buried for two days.

In one of his few admissions that De La Salle ever showed any human emotion, the biographer Blain tells us: "The news broke his heart. Never in his whole life did it receive a deeper wound. The first onslaught of sorrow caused him to break down and cry." More typically, Blain continues: "He appeared ashamed of this weakness and reproached himself for it. The first movement of human grief was followed by a deeply religious response of resignation to God's will."

The shock of this tragedy did in fact compel De La Salle to ponder its providential meaning, what it was that God might be saying to him through this event. The Founder soon discerned that perhaps the Institute should not have priests among its members. He came to see with increasing clarity that the priesthood would be incompatible with the vocation and mission of a teaching Brother, that the introduction of the priesthood might well weaken the very foundation of the Institute. The presence of priests in the Society might also open the door to the ever-present possibility of external ecclesiastical control. In time, the Rule of the Brothers would become explicit on the exclusively lay character of the Institute.

Trouble in Reims

With his plans to groom a successor in abeyance for the time being, De La Salle had even more pressing organizational problems to deal with. Principal among them was the deteriorating situation back in Reims. When De La Salle left from there for Paris in 1688, there were three flourishing schools in Reims, three more in the outlying towns, a functioning juniorate for young candidates at the Rue Neuve, and a teacher-training program for rural teachers. Now, after two years of successful operation, the teacher-training program had been terminated, mostly because there was no longer any need for it. As for the juniorate, that too came to an end when De La Salle brought the candidates to Paris to continue their formation there under his direction.

Only the community of teaching Brothers was left in the house on the Rue Neuve. In 1688 there had been 16 of them, not counting the two that De La Salle took with him to Paris. Three years later only eight remained. What was worse, only one new recruit had been attracted to the community. The problem centered on the personality of the superior De La Salle had left in charge, a young man in his early twenties who was also known as Brother Henri. As a Director this Brother Henri was a man of piety and exact in observing the regulations, but he was harsh and indiscreet in dealing with the Brothers. His total lack of human understanding was more than many of them could endure, and so they left.

Facing an Uncertain Future

Things were not much better in Paris. De La Salle himself was still recovering from the double shock of his own illness and the death of Brother Henri L'Heureux. He felt himself to be totally alone, with no clear plans for a successor in case his health should soon again fail. Most of the Brothers, too, were exhausted from overwork, and many of them were ill. Religious fervor and discipline were not at all as intense as had been the case in the beginning. The presence of the candidates in the crowded quarters on the Rue Princesse created more problems than it solved. And then there was Father Baudrand, the pastor of Saint Sulpice to deal with. Realizing that the Society was in a precarious position, he seemed to be all too anxious to take it over himself at the first opportunity.

As was his custom, De La Salle took his time in weighing the alternatives before deciding on a course of action. He spent long hours in prayer for divine guidance, convinced that his work would survive and prosper if that were indeed God's will. The plan that emerged was twofold. First of all, he would seek a property suitably located, somewhere near Paris, that could serve as a center for the physical and spiritual renewal of the older Brothers and as a novitiate for the training of new candidates. Secondly, he would associate with himself one or two Brothers capable of maintaining the Institute in case anything should happen to him.

Vaugirard

After a careful search, De La Salle found the property he was looking for. It was in Vaugirard, at that time a small village just outside Paris, about a mile or so from the school on the Rue Princesse. On the grounds there was an unpretentious but sufficiently large house with a garden surrounded by ample open space and plenty of fresh air. It seemed ideal for the purposes De La Salle had in mind.

The first Brothers to be moved into the new center were those who were sick or ailing. Then, when the school year was over in the late summer of 1691, De La Salle summoned to Vaugirard all of the Brothers from Reims, Laon, and Paris who had joined the Society during the previous three or four years. Many of them had experienced little by way of a novitiate, in some cases not more than a few weeks before they were sent into the classroom. The Founder wanted to make up for this lack and renew them in their first fervor with an intense spiritual retreat under his direction. The retreat had barely begun when De La Salle learned that his beloved grandmother and advocate, Perrette Lespagnol, had died on October 7. Whatever grief he felt, he kept to himself in the conviction that nothing was more important than the work he had in hand.

De La Salle soon realized that the time available for the renewal program was too short to accomplish all that he had hoped for. Rather than lose the momentum of what he had begun, he arranged to replace these Brothers in the classroom with student teachers and so prolonged the retreat until well into December. Thus Vaugirard served as a sort of "second novitiate" even before the novitiate proper could be opened. The project was so successful that over the years the Founder continued to call the Brothers by turns to Vaugirard for an annual period of spiritual renewal. Out of this experience there was established a practice that has endured in the Institute in one form or another to the present day.

When De La Salle sent the retreatants back to their schools and communities, he instructed them to write to him regularly to give an account of their behavior and of their interior dispositions as well. The Founder was faithful in replying, often at some length, to these "redditional letters," as they came to be called. Fortunately, some of his replies have been preserved. In due time, the practice of writing for spiritual direction to the Superior or his Assistant, in addition to the regular personal interview with the local Director, became part of the Rule of the Institute.

The Heroic Vow

Once the morale of the Brothers had improved and religious discipline had been reestablished, the next step was to try to provide for the future of the Society in the face of the crises, opposition, and uncertainty that had been its experience thus far and that seemed likely to continue. For this purpose, De La Salle chose two zealous and courageous men who seemed to be the most committed to their vocation and on whom he thought he could depend. They were Brothers Nicolas Vuyart and Gabriel Drolin. He proposed that the three of them bind themselves by vow to establish the Society, no matter what it might cost them, and even if all the others should abandon it—a not unlikely possibility at the time.

At Vaugirard, on November 21, 1691, the feast of the Presentation of Mary in the Temple, the three men made their "heroic vow," as it has been called, in these terms:

> Most Holy Trinity, Father, Son, and Holy Spirit, prostrate with the most profound respect before your infinite and adorable majesty, we consecrate ourselves entirely to you to procure with all our ability and efforts the establishment of the Society of the Christian Schools, in the manner which will seem most agreeable to you and most advantageous to the said Society.
>
> And, for that purpose, I, John Baptist de La Salle, priest, I, Nicolas Vuyart, and I, Gabriel Drolin, from now on and forever until the last surviving one of us, or until the complete establishment of the said Society, make the vow of association and union to bring about and maintain the said establishment, without being able to withdraw from this obligation, even if only we three remained in the said Society, and if we were obliged to beg for alms and to live on bread alone.

In view of which we promise to do, all together and by common accord, everything we shall think in conscience, and regardless of any human consideration, to be for the greater good of the said Society.

Done on this 21st of November, feast of the Presentation of Our Lady, 1691. In testimony of which we have signed. . . .

The Novitiate at Vaugirard

The difficulties surrounding the opening of a formal novitiate were of a somewhat different order. When De La Salle informed Father Baudrand what he was planning to do, the response was emphatic and negative. The pastor told him not even to think about it. Once again this put De La Salle in a bind. Not only was Baudrand his pastor and confessor, but in one sense his superior besides. Yet from his recent experience De La Salle knew the unfortunate consequences that follow on an inadequate program of training and formation. Now that he had a suitable center for a novitiate, he was determined to take advantage of it. But Baudrand remained adamant.

In his customary way, De La Salle remained calm and had recourse instead to intensified prayer. In addition, he began to multiply his already much too austere penitential practices with a view to winning this favor from heaven. When Baudrand heard about it, he sent word that De La Salle might as well cease torturing himself since he had no intention of changing his mind. But De La Salle had an alternative. He enlisted the support of a former classmate from seminary days, Paul Godet des Marais, who was now Bishop of Chartres and who had great influence in Paris. After almost a year of waiting, in August 1692, permission finally came from the Archbishop of Paris himself, François de Harlay de Champvallon, for De La Salle to establish his community at Vaugirard.

The advantages of the house and grounds at Vaugirard during the summer months soon turned into a test of virtue during the long Parisian winter. The old house was falling apart with the loose doors and windows no proof against wind, snow, or rain. There was only one small stove and, of course, no indoor plumbing. The furniture consisted of a few benches to sit on and, for beds, straw pallets laid on wooden planks stretched over saw horses. There were no facilities for cooking in the house; the coarse and scanty food was brought each day in a hamper from the kitchen on the Rue Princesse. Laundry was done once a week. The clean undergarments provided on Saturday morning were often frozen stiff. The only way to dry them out was to wear them.

In sum, the privations at Vaugirard were such that the name has become associated in the Brothers' tradition with unbearable living conditions whenever and wherever they had to be endured, which happened again and again in the Institute's long history.

As if the privations imposed by circumstances at Vaugirard were not enough, the Brothers there, novices and veterans alike, vied with one another in the practice of voluntary penance, especially in the use of the scourge or "discipline," as it was called. Since no fixed policy had yet been set on the matter, permission had to be obtained to engage in such practices of corporal penance. The permission was eagerly sought and willingly granted. The customary time for taking the discipline was just before supper after the daily accusation of faults. The Brothers would inflict this punishment on themselves, each in some remote corner, often to the point of drawing blood. Some would get so carried away that they would miss part or all of the meal, which always began and ended at a specific time.

These penitential practices were but an adjunct and support of a regimen of intensive prayer over and above the regular religious exercises observed in all the Brothers' communities. The Office of the Blessed Virgin was recited each day, meditatively and standing. There were supplementary periods of meditation preceded by an hour of spiritual reading both morning and afternoon. The novices were joined in these pious and penitential exercises by the school Brothers whenever they could get away, the Brothers from Paris over the weekends, and those from Reims and Laon during vacation periods.

The religious fervor and the austere rigor of the lifestyle at Vaugirard renewed the Brothers in the spirit of their vocation. In addition, it attracted a number of worthy candidates, some of them from rather well-to-do families. On the other hand, the rigorous regimen served as a screening process to separate out the fainthearted and the unworthy. On November 1, 1692, only a year after the house was opened, De La Salle gave the Brothers' habit to six novices, one of whom was to be a serving Brother.

During the following two years there was a widespread famine in France that served to increase dramatically the number of candidates who applied. Relying on statistics supplied by the Founder himself, Blain tells us that only one or two out of every dozen who presented themselves remained, yet in the period between 1692 and 1694 a total of 35 novices persevered at Vaugirard.

It was at this time, incidentally, that the category of serving Brothers was introduced. This made it possible to admit those who had a strong sense of vocation and some manual skills but no aptitude for teaching; more important, it freed the school Brothers from the burden of shopping, cooking, and cleaning that too often interfered with their school duties and regular religious observance. The serving Brothers wore a brown habit to distinguish them as they went about their functions in the streets and the markets, but in every other respect they were the equal of the other Brothers in the community.

Rheumatism and Its Remedy

Inevitably, De La Salle's austerities caught up with him. This time it was a severe attack of rheumatism brought on by sleeping on the stone floors in the drafty old house, to say nothing of the lack of adequate nourishment combined with the other penances he inflicted on his poor body. He tried to ignore the intense pain as long as he could, but it finally got to the point where the man could no longer move about, so rheumatic had his whole body become. Forced to seek some relief in order to continue his work, De La Salle agreed to allow the Brothers to call once again for Doctor Helvétius.

The remedy proposed was painful in the extreme. The patient was laid on a grill of hardwood with iron pots of burning coals underneath. On the coals were placed leaves of juniper and other herbs so that the smoke might penetrate the pores of the body and draw out the inflammation. While one side of the naked body was exposed to the burning heat, the other was covered with blankets so as to concentrate the heat. The room was stifling and filled with smoke. When the Brother in attendance tried to adjust the wooden slats he found them so hot he could not keep his hands on them. De La Salle suffered heroically through all this torture without complaint. Although the procedure proved effective, it would have to be endured again in later years.

The Winter of 1693-1694

Due in part to a scanty harvest, and in part to the drain on the food supply by the armies of King Louis XIV, engaged at the time in military adventures against the Hapsburgs in Spain, Austria, and Flanders, the winter of 1693-1694 brought another devastating famine throughout all of France. Vaugirard was no longer a safe place for the Brothers. Even in the best of times, it was not uncommon for thieves to rob the Brother who carried the food each day from the Rue Princesse. Now it became an almost daily occurrence. Even the house itself was sometimes invaded by vagabonds in the mistaken notion that food, however scanty, was kept stored there. De La Salle, reluctant to leave his beloved retreat, nonetheless decided that it would be better to take his novices back to the Rue Princesse until the worst of the famine should be over.

Although the building on the Rue Princesse was more secure, there was no way to escape the impact of the famine that was especially severe in the city. The price of bread doubled and tripled, and it was not always available. Sometimes the Brothers had to make do with a thin soup made from cabbage leaves. Through it all, De La Salle was patient and urged the Brothers to take literally the gospel maxim that they should not be anxious about what they should eat, that their heavenly Father would provide for them. Although they were all hungry most of the time, none of them starved. Relief in one form or another always came just as things were most desperate.

Throughout that terrible winter, the pastor, Father Baudrand, seems to have remained insensitive to the plight of the Brothers. It may be that he never quite forgave De La Salle for opening the novitiate that he had so firmly opposed. He may even have wanted to remind De La Salle of how dependent the young community was on his good will. At the beginning of 1694, when the famine was at its worst, he withheld the salary of the Brothers teaching on the Rue du Bac. On one occasion, a pious and influential lady of the parish spotted the Brother cook in a line of beggars seeking a handout. It was only at her insistence that the pastor sent some money to the Brothers to tide them over. When that ran out, De La Salle was forced to go to the pastor personally to beg as an alms for what his community needed and was entitled to. Baudrand had just received some emergency funds from the government, and these he shared with the Brothers. But later, he charged the sum against the money due to them for their salary.

The biographers are not agreed on how to interpret the apparent indifference of the pastor to the needs of the Brothers. There is no doubt that his own resources were strained throughout that difficult winter. At the same time, however, it does seem that he used every opportunity to try to keep the community of the Brothers, and De La Salle in particular, dependent on him in every way possible. Thus it was not long afterwards that Baudrand decided to move the school and the community from the Rue Princesse to the Rue Guisarde. De La Salle did not consider the new location at all suitable. To force the move, the pastor refused to renew the lease on the Rue Princesse. Thereupon De La Salle signed the lease himself and kept the Brothers where they were. Baudrand is said to have remarked that De La Salle "was a stubborn man who always wanted to have his own way in spite of myself or the pastor who was here before me."

The Rule and Perpetual Vows

Once the spring of 1694 arrived and there was some relief from the famine, De La Salle took the novices back to Vaugirard. There he had enough time to begin composing a Rule for the Brothers, a process that involved as many hours of prayer and penance as in the actual writing of the text. There was an opportunity now to reflect on and incorporate into a Rule the experience of the Society since the assembly of 1686. In submitting a draft text to the Brothers, the Founder made it clear that it was up to them to eliminate or to add whatever they considered necessary, and ultimately to approve the Rule he was proposing.

Another question that had been put on hold since 1686 was the matter of perpetual vows, whether some Brothers might be ready for this step and, if so, what vows they should take. Ever since the introduction of the temporary vow of obedience, some of the Brothers had been asking to commit themselves for life to the service of the Lord in the educational ministry proper to the Society. Unwilling to make such a decision on his own, De La Salle wrote to those he judged most dependable, asking them to consider the question prayerfully during the early months of 1694. Then he invited each of them in turn to come to Vaugirard to make a private retreat and to ponder with him the problem of when and how to introduce perpetual vows.

Finally, at Pentecost in 1694, he brought all 12 of these senior Brothers together at Vaugirard to decide the question in a solemn assembly—later to be known as the first General Chapter. There was much give and take in the discussion, and each was left free to express his own opinion on the matter. The most controverted question concerned whether or not to include the vow of chastity. The Founder urged caution in this matter, and his view was eventually accepted. Poverty seems not to have been seriously considered, perhaps because it was superfluous: extreme poverty had been their experience from the beginning. It was finally decided that they would take perpetual vows of obedience, stability in the Society, and association to conduct the gratuitous schools.

Accordingly, on Trinity Sunday, June 6, 1694, De La Salle and the 12 principal Brothers made the first perpetual vows in the Institute. Since it was considered wise to keep the event secret for the time being in order to test its impact, the ceremony was held in a remote room in the house at Vaugirard. The formula of vows was similar in structure to that of the heroic vow of 1691. The text follows:

> Most Holy Trinity, Father, Son, and Holy Spirit, prostrate with the most profound respect before your infinite and adorable majesty, I consecrate myself entirely to you to procure your glory as far as I am able and as you will require of me.
>
> And for this purpose I, John Baptist de La Salle, priest, promise and vow to unite myself and to remain in Society with Brothers Nicolas Vuyart, Gabriel Drolin, and [the other ten names follow] to keep together and by association gratuitous schools wherever they may be, even if I were obliged to live on bread alone, or to do anything in the said Society at which I shall be employed, whether by the body of the Society, or by the superiors who will have the government thereof.
>
> Wherefore I promise and vow obedience to the body of the Society as well as to the superiors: which vows of association, as well as stability in the said Society, and of obedience, I promise to keep inviolably all my life.

Each of the other 12 pronounced his vows in exactly the same way. All 13 of the signed formulas are preserved in the archives of the Brothers' generalate in Rome.

This text has served as the pattern of the vow formula in use in the Institute ever since. The formula is so structured that the basic element in the commitment, consecration to the Triune God, is

De La Salle's formula of perpetual vows, 1694

expressed prior to any mention of specific vows. Although the designation and the content of the individual vows have changed over the years, this fundamental expression of commitment to procure the glory of God has remained invariable from the beginning.

In the later paragraphs of the formula, this consecration becomes both personal and interpersonal: the Brother mentions his own name and then refers to his associates; it is total, without any thought of turning back; it is apostolic in its thrust and its specific commitment to the gratuitous schools. Taken as a whole, the vow formula integrates all the elements of the Brother's life: religious consecration is joined to association in community for an apostolic purpose.

The Election of a Superior

On the day following Trinity Sunday in 1694, De La Salle reassembled the Brothers who had made perpetual vows the day before to consider quite a different matter. He proposed that they elect one of their own as Superior. The reasons he advanced were serious and sensible: his own health was precarious, and death might claim him at any time; it would be better to be prepared for such a possibility in advance; the enterprise should not rely on one person alone, much less himself; the election of one of themselves would strengthen the bond of union just forged by the vows they had made; it would protect them against having a priest superior imposed on them at some later time.

But the Brothers would have none of it. When De La Salle insisted more strongly, they agreed to an election, but the ballots turned into a unanimous affirmation of the Founder as Superior. Upset by this deception and even a bit angry, he called for a long period of prayer, after which he proposed that they have another ballot. The result was the same. This time they pointed out to him that his resistance seemed to be contradicting the will of God. He finally had to give in, but not before having them all sign the following declaration:

> We, the undersigned [the names follow], after associating ourselves with John Baptist de La Salle, priest, to keep together gratuitous schools, by the vows which we pronounced yesterday, declare that as a consequence of these vows and of the association which we have formed by them, we have chosen as our Superior John Baptist de La Salle, to whom we promise obedience and entire submission, as well as to those whom he will assign to us as our superiors.
>
> We also declare that it is our understanding that the present election will not have the force of a precedent for the future. Our intention is that after the said John Baptist de La Salle, and forever in the future, no one shall be received among us or chosen as Superior who is a priest, or who has received Holy

Orders; and that we will not have or accept any Superior who has not associated himself with us, and has not made vows like us and like all those who will be associated with us in the future. Done at Vaugirard on June 7, 1694.

Relative Peace

Having survived so many crises, and with its internal structure more fully consolidated, the Institute was able to enjoy a few years of relative peace. The Brothers had a Rule, a core group committed by perpetual vows, an elected Superior in the person of the Founder himself, and a formal decision to remain forever exclusively lay. Meanwhile the communities and the schools continued to prosper.

Life at Vaugirard went on as before with prayer, penance, and deprivation the characteristic lifestyle. During the years from 1691–1698, De La Salle was able to concentrate on his writings, especially a series of Catechisms, the *Conduct of the Schools,* and the *Rules of Christian Politeness.* He was also able to obtain ecclesiastical approval for the *Exercises of Piety for Use in the Schools.*

In August 1695, Louis-Antoine de Noailles was named Archbishop of Paris to succeed François de Harlay de Champvallon, who had just died. In the beginning, the new archbishop seemed favorably disposed to De La Salle. Up until that time, there had been no chapel in the house at Vaugirard, with one of the rooms serving as a simple oratory for community prayers. The Brothers had to go to the nearby church of Saint Lambert, where De La Salle celebrated Mass for them privately, except on feasts when they attended the parish Mass. In 1697, once again through the influence of his friend Paul Godet, Bishop of Chartres, contrary to archdiocesan policy at the time and over the objections of the pastor of Saint Lambert, De La Salle obtained from Archbishop Noailles permission to celebrate Mass and reserve the Blessed Sacrament in the novitiate house. Bishop Godet himself presided at the formal blessing of the chapel in June of that year.

As De La Salle's reputation for sanctity spread far and wide, and the community became known as a rival to the Trappists for its austerity of life, Vaugirard attracted more and more priests and laymen who came there to make a retreat under De La Salle's direction. The holy priest and former canon seems to have had a special gift for dealing with hardened sinners and fallen-away priests; many miracles of grace were attributed to his ministry to such persons in distress. Devout persons, too, profited from his guidance and example. On one occasion, the Count of Charmel, a nobleman who lived nearby, was greatly impressed by his visit to Vaugirard. On his return home, he sent to De La Salle a richly decorated antependium for the altar and a chasuble to match.

Back at the Rue Princesse, there was a new pastor of Saint Sulpice. In 1696 Father De La Chétardie was appointed to succeed Father Baudrand, who had to resign as pastor because of ill health. At first, the attitude of the new pastor was very favorable to the Brothers. Soon after he assumed office, he visited the school to see the situation first hand. Surprised by the lack of even basic necessities, he made it one of his first concerns to see that the needs of the Brothers were provided for.

As the seventeenth century was coming to an end, it seemed that a new era for the Institute of the Brothers was on the horizon. The years ahead were indeed destined to bring new growth and expansion. But there would also be new crises and struggles to be overcome in the face of continued misunderstanding, opposition, and outright persecution.

7

Experimentation and Expansion
(1698–1703)

The presence of a new pastor in the parish of Saint Sulpice seemed to augur well for the future of the Brothers in Paris. In the fall of 1697, less than a year after taking office, Father De La Chétardie agreed, on De La Salle's suggestion, to open yet a third school in the parish, this one on the Rue Placide. Many students flocked to it, and it was not long before the number of Brothers assigned there had to be increased from four to six.

As had happened before, this success served only to reignite the fury of the Masters of the Little Schools when they saw so many of their pupils transferring over to the school of the Brothers. The first challenge came in the form of a physical attack on the school and its furnishings. De La Salle arrived on the scene as the schoolmasters and their henchmen were making off with whatever they could lay their hands on. Utterly defenseless, the holy priest retained his usual calm. "Here I am, take me along too," he is reported to have said to them.

The Brothers were summoned into court, and all their schools in the parish had to be shut down for three months. The issue centered on whether or not the Brothers were accepting fees from those who could afford to pay. The schoolmasters presumed that they did. Reluctant as De La Salle was to fight the case, he did so at the pastor's insistence. In an eloquent defense, he won the case by challenging the schoolmasters to show that the Brothers received a single penny from the pupils, or that they profited financially in any way. This victory only served to enrage the schoolmasters all the more. They would be heard from again before long.

The Grande Maison

By 1699 the number of young men wanting to join the Brothers had increased to such an extent that De La Salle began to search for a new and more suitable site for a novitiate. After seven years, Vaugirard had more than outlived its usefulness. There was within the limits of the parish of Saint Sulpice a sizable property that had once belonged to a small congregation of nuns. Known as the *Grande Maison,* the house was surrounded by open spaces and extensive gardens that were protected by solid gates and thick walls.

The asking price was rather more than De La Salle could afford, but Father De La Chétardie came to the rescue by raising the salaries of the Brothers, so happy was he to have the novitiate back within the confines of the parish. He also put the Founder in touch with a wealthy widow, Madame Voisin, known for her support of charitable causes. She agreed to supply the furnishings for the house at the cost of 7,000 livres, a large sum indeed, since 200 livres was the customary annual stipend for each Brother. The large chapel that had previously been used by the nuns was blessed anew by the vicar-general of the archdiocese and placed under the patronage of Saint Cassian, who from that time on has been considered a patron of the Institute. It is easy to understand why, since Saint Cassian was an early Christian teacher who was ordered to be bound and put to a slow and painful death by his students.

The Brothers had barely settled in the Grande Maison when De La Salle was asked to provide instruction and lodging for a group of 50 or so Irish boys who had followed King James II of England into exile. This was the first time that boarders had ever been accepted in a Brothers' school. Yet De La Salle felt compelled to yield to the request of the archbishop and the pastor, who were finding it difficult to provide for the education of these young refugees. Furthermore, these boys were somewhat beyond the elementary level in their education and in need of more advanced instruction, quite possibly including Latin, which had been forbidden to the Brothers. For these reasons, De La Salle took charge of them himself. This incident is a good example of the Founder's willingness to adopt innovative procedures as Providence provided new opportunities and challenges in the ministry of education.

In due time King James, accompanied by Archbishop, now Cardinal, Noailles and Father De La Chétardie, came to visit the school. The king expressed complete satisfaction with the care being taken of his young subjects and the progress they were making in their studies. On this occasion, some of the Brothers wanted to ask the king to use his influence in Rome to obtain papal approval for the Institute. The Founder dissuaded them, however, preferring to wait until Providence should provide a more favorable opportunity to have the Institute formally approved on its own merits.

The Grande Maison provided other opportunities for the Brothers to expand their educational horizons by innovative programs of a practical nature that would enable the sons of poor and working class families to earn a decent living. Thus in 1699 a manual training program was introduced at the Grande Maison, motivated by and modeled on the success of the similar program at the Rue Princesse.

The Christian Sunday School

It was most likely in 1699, also, that a Sunday School, the "Christian Academy," as it was called, was opened at the Grande Maison for young men under 20 years of age who were occupied during the rest of the week in earning a living. The school was soon filled to capacity, with some 200 students divided into several classes. Some learned how to read and write for the first time. The more advanced followed courses in practical drawing, geometry, or other branches of mathematics. Classes began at noon on Sunday, lasted for two hours, and were followed by a Catechism lesson that concluded with a spiritual exhortation given by one of the Brothers.

De La Salle had assigned two of his most talented Brothers to this work, and even provided them with advanced training in their special fields. One of them was particularly gifted in art, the other in mathematics. Unfortunately, after a few years, these Brothers began to realize that their talents could be used to their personal profit elsewhere. Finding the temptation too great, they left the Institute. As a result, the Christian Academy had to close temporarily. It was some time before De La Salle was able to find a qualified Brother to continue the program on a modified basis.

A New Teacher-training Program

A work that had always been dear to the heart of De La Salle was the training of lay teachers for the rural schools. He preferred to restrict the Brothers to city parishes where three or more of them could conduct schools "together and by association." Most country schoolteachers, by contrast, had to maintain a school singlehandedly and in isolation. A program to train teachers for the rural schools had been one of De La Salle's first ventures in the early days in Reims, but it did not long survive his departure. Ever since, he had been looking for an opportunity to revive it.

In 1699, at the request of Father Lebreton, the pastor of Saint Hippolyte, De La Salle sent two Brothers to take over a school in the remote Parisian suburb of Saint Marcel. The pastor was so pleased with the results that he consulted with the Founder on the possibility of opening in his parish a center for training lay teachers. De La Salle was more than willing to cooperate. The pastor was able to enlist the help of generous donors: a devout layman provided a house on the Rue de l'Ourcine; another, a priest, volunteered an annual sum to support the project. De La Salle agreed to screen the applicants. In addition, he sent one of his best teachers and longtime associate, Brother Nicolas Vuyart, to take charge of the program.

The student teachers followed much the same program that had been in use at Reims. They continued to wear secular dress, but otherwise they followed much the same schedule as the Brothers: early rising, extended periods of prayer and spiritual reading, together with courses in subject areas and in educational methods. Since the house was adjacent to the parish school, there was an opportunity also for supervised practice teaching.

The teacher-training program prospered for five or six years, and then the pastor died. He had wanted it to continue after his death and so tried to insure its survival. Realizing that the Institute of the Brothers had no legal status, the pastor had decided to name Brother Nicolas Vuyart as heir to the invested funds that supported the program. This seemed like a sensible arrangement. Brother Nicolas, after all, had vowed "heroically" with De La Salle and Gabriel Drolin in 1691 to stay together, no matter what might happen, in order to establish the Institute. Not only was he an effective teacher himself, but he had a talent, besides, for passing on his skills to others. Under his direction the teacher-training program had made great progress.

Unfortunately, as we shall see in a later chapter, it was just at this time that the definitive judgments against De La Salle were handed down by the tribunals in Paris. Perhaps Vuyart thought that he might salvage the enterprise by dissociating himself from De La Salle and taking charge of the program himself. In any case, he decided to put aside the Brothers' habit and send away the Brother who had been working with him in the parish. When the priest who had provided the annual income to support the teachers in training heard of it, he revoked his donation. The center had to close as a consequence, much to the regret of De La Salle, who was helpless to prevent it.

Vuyart continued to maintain the parish school at Saint Hippolyte on his own for the next 20 years. At one point he even applied for readmission to the Institute. Although De La Salle was willing to forgive and forget, the Brothers advised against it. Blain's judgmental and vindictive description of the fate of Vuyart is worth quoting, as much for its dubious theology as for its rhetoric:

> The perfidious disciple of whom we have spoken survived his master, but not for long. After continuing the school in the parish of Saint Hippolyte for over 20 years, he fell ill of a mortal ailment the day after De La Salle died. The Servant of God died on Good Friday, April 7, 1719; and it seemed that on the very next day he interested heaven in avenging a crime which during his life he had pardoned so wholeheartedly. The former Brother fell ill on Holy Saturday, the day the Servant of God was buried; and after five months of suffering, he went to give an account to his Judge for the tremendous injustice he had been guilty of toward the Church, for the affront he had offered his Superior, for his scandalous desertion which had shocked his Community, and for the complete ruin of the training college for the country schoolmasters which he had brought about.

This second attempt to establish a permanent teacher-training center proved to be relatively short-lived, as were the innovative programs at the Grande Maison, the secondary instruction for the Irish boys in a resident setting, and part-time courses on Sundays for working teenagers. But these ventures illustrate a certain openness on the part of the Founder and the Brothers to explore new possibilities in the field of education as the seventeenth century turned into the eighteenth. At that same moment, the Institute was beginning to move into new geographical areas as well, beyond the confines of the parish of Saint Sulpice and the Archdiocese of Paris.

Chartres, 1699

As the reputation of the Brothers began to spread, the first prelate to call them to his diocese was Paul Godet des Marais, the Bishop of Chartres. This was not surprising. He had been a companion of

De La Salle in his seminary days, and later served as the effective intermediary between De La Salle and the authorities in securing permission to open the novitiate and later the chapel at Vaugirard. His appeal to the Founder for Brothers for his diocese came at a particularly good time since the schools in Paris were closed over the trouble with the schoolmasters. Furthermore, the bishop's request was supported by a petition signed by the pastors of Chartres, urging quality schools for the poor. Before making a move, however, De La Salle called the Brothers together to get their consent.

Just prior to the arrival of the Brothers, the bishop issued a pastoral letter to the clergy and the people of Chartres explaining how important it was to have good schools, for boys as well as girls, especially for the children of working parents who had neither the time nor the talent to educate them at home. On October 12, 1699, two Christian schools were opened in Chartres, one in the parish of Saint Hilary, the other in Saint Michel parish. There were seven Brothers in all, three for each of the schools and a serving Brother to take care of the temporal needs of the community.

Bishop Paul Godet was a remarkable man in many ways. An ardent defender of orthodox doctrine, especially against Quietism and other exaggerated approaches to spirituality that were current at the time, he yet had the common touch and moved easily among his people. He took particular care of the Brothers, saw to their every need, and was most solicitous when some of them fell sick. He did what he could to mitigate the austerity of their lifestyle and to moderate their penchant for bodily mortification. He would say to them: "If you are unwilling to fatten up the victim before immolating it, you should at least give it enough to eat."

On one occasion, when De La Salle came to the bishop's residence to pay his respects, Godet tricked him into staying for dinner by having all the doors locked behind him. Present also for the meal was the vicar-general, Father D'Aubigné, who would one day become the Archbishop of Rouen. Already at Chartres, he did not conceal his disdain for the shabby appearance of De La Salle and his Brothers.

Over dinner, Bishop Godet made three recommendations to the Founder concerning the Brothers. He thought that the Rule ought to be modified to mitigate the much too austere lifestyle of the Brothers, especially in the matter of penitential practices. Secondly, he asked the Brothers to attend Mass on Sundays and feasts in each of the city parishes in turn so that people might profit by their good example. Finally, he argued that in the schools, the Brothers should adopt the traditional practice of having the students learn to read Latin before studying French.

Once again, the Founder felt compelled to hold his ground. To the first point, he replied that the Rule had been adopted after consultation with all the Brothers and could not be changed without their consent; that, in any case, there was no corporal penance required by the Rule. To the second point, De La Salle replied that such a procedure would put an intolerable burden on the Brothers; in addition, the Rule required that they be in church with their pupils on Sunday morning and then teach them catechism for an hour and a half. Sunday afternoons before Vespers were to be free for the recreation and spiritual renewal of the Brothers in the community house.

Concerning the teaching of Latin, De La Salle promised to reply more at length, which he did in an extended memoir addressed to the Bishop of Chartres in 1702. His arguments against the use of Latin as a vehicle for elementary education were of a practical order: French is easier to learn than Latin, it takes less time, it is more useful, it is a vehicle for learning Latin, it is a necessary tool for learning Christian doctrine both in school and in later life; Latin, by contrast, is more difficult, there is no time to master it before the students have to leave school to go to work, it is of no use to working class people in later life, those with only a smattering of Latin make fools of themselves when they try to use it.

The bishop seems to have accepted these responses, such was the great respect he had for De La Salle, his character, and his vision. He continued to support the Brothers as long as he lived, doing whatever he could to make their life more bearable and their work more productive and appreciated.

Calais, 1700

While Chartres is not far from Paris, only a few miles beyond Versailles to the southwest, Calais is a port town on the English Channel far to the north. In 1700 the pastor of the principal church and dean of the clergy in Calais was a certain Father Ponton. His nephew, also a priest and a student of theology at Saint Sulpice, had been attracted by the Brothers and their work with the children of the parish. He wrote such glowing reports back to his uncle that the pastor urged him to do all he could to interest the Brothers in coming to Calais, noting that the local schoolmaster had just died. To help move the negotiations along, the pastor persuaded the city magistrates to enlist the support of the Duke of Bethune, the Governor of Calais, who was living in Paris at the time.

The duke invited De La Salle to come to his palace in Paris to discuss the matter. Arriving somewhat too early for his appointment, De La Salle stopped in the nearby church, only to find the duke himself attending Mass and receiving Communion with the greatest fervor. This helped the negotiations on both sides: De La Salle disposed to accommodate such a devout Christian gentleman, the duke willing to grant all the support and approval that the Brothers would require. By July 1700 the arrangements were complete and two Brothers arrived in Calais to take over the parish school. One of them was Brother Gabriel Drolin, who had made the heroic vow in 1691.

At De La Salle's insistence and before beginning their mission, the two Brothers went to Boulogne to receive the blessing of Bishop Pierre de Langle in whose diocese Calais was located. Not only did the bishop bless the Brothers, but he issued a proclamation to the people of Calais urging all the parents to send their children to the Christian School. The civil magistrates, the clergy, and the people of the city joined in making the Brothers feel welcome.

Although ample housing had been provided for the Brothers, it seems that there was no dependable source of revenue to guarantee that the school could continue. Feeling that death was near and wanting the work to continue, the pastor wrote to the Marquis de La Vrillière, who promised to bring the matter up at the next meeting of the king's council. King Louis XIV responded favorably and in the next two years saw to it that the Brothers were given a considerable sum derived from the sale of the confiscated property of the Calvinist Huguenots.

At the same time, Father Le Prince, chaplain of the port district, began a campaign to have a Christian School for the children of the sailors. Through the good offices of the Minister Pontchartrain, Chancellor of France and the official responsible for the port, the school was opened in 1705 in an old guardhouse adapted for the purpose. A regular income was provided for the Brothers by royal decree and augmented by the city officials from import duties on goods entering the city.

Troyes, 1702

In 1702 De La Salle received a request for Brothers from the pastor of Saint Nizier at Troyes in the province of Champagne. A pious lady had left an annuity of 200 livres to the pastor, Father Le Bé, to be used for a gratuitous school for the parish. Although the sum was less than what was customary and necessary for the support of the Brothers, De La Salle agreed on condition that housing should be provided for them. This was no problem since the pastor preferred to live in the seminary, and so the rectory was available for the Brothers.

When Le Bé died and the new pastor took over the rectory, the Brothers had a difficult time for a while. But then the townspeople came to the rescue with an annual sum to rent a house for them. Soon after, an Oratorian priest named Chantreau came back to Troyes, his native city, and began a campaign of preaching in favor of gratuitous schools for the poor. So successful was he that the citizens this time raised enough money to support two more Christian Schools, one in the parish of Saint Mary Magdalen, the other in that of Saint John.

Rome, 1702

As the network of Christian Schools began to spread throughout France, De La Salle began to think seriously about establishing a foothold in the Eternal City. From his seminary days, he had always had a high regard for papal authority, contrary to the Gallican tendencies of some of his professors and most of the higher clergy of France. A foundation in Rome would be a symbol of the attachment of the Institute to the Apostolic See founded on the rock of Peter and his successors. At the same time, it might eventually pave the way for the papal approval that alone could guarantee the Institute its autonomy and freedom from the perennial threat of control by local bishops and pastors.

In the summer of 1702, De La Salle decided it was time to act, despite the difficulties that such a project entailed, not the least of them financial. Brother Gabriel Drolin was summoned from Calais, and on one September morning he and Brother Gérard Drolin, his blood brother, set out from the Grande Maison with the blessing of the Founder and only 100 livres between them for expenses. It was not nearly enough but it was all that the hard-pressed Superior could afford. He urged them to rely on Providence, which did not fail them, but neither did it spare them the perils and the fatigue of the long journey, most of it on foot.

When they finally arrived in Rome, total strangers, unexpected, and unprovided for, unable to speak the language, and dressed in a garb that even the blasé Romans found strange, the Brothers might well have thought that getting there was the least of their problems. To make matters worse, César d'Estrées, the Cardinal Bishop of Albano, who was also French Ambassador to the Vatican, and to whom they had a letter of introduction, was away on an extended mission. His vicar managed to get them settled for the time being, but it was clear that any possibility of establishing a permanent foundation would be a long way off, if not impossible.

The school system in the Papal States at the time was complicated and tightly controlled. The traditional regional schools in

Painting by Mariani (1906) of the departure of the Drolin brothers for Rome in 1702.

the 14 sectors of the city were under the control of the rector of the University of Rome, La Sapienza. The recently established papal schools were open only to girls. In addition, there were the Pious Schools for the poor conducted by the priests of the congregation founded by Joseph Calasanctius. In short, the Brothers found that there was little need for their services and little interest in breaking from the tradition in Rome that teachers in schools for boys should be clerics.

The situation was so unpromising that, after a few months, Gérard Drolin, discouraged and unable to adapt, headed back for France, where he soon left the Institute. Gérard had once been with the Trappists. De La Salle remarked that he should have left him there, that Gérard was not suited to live as a secular, but neither could he make up his mind what he wanted.

Gabriel Drolin remained at his post. Shortly after his brother left Rome, Gabriel found a fellow countryman, Claude de La Bussière, who offered him a permanent place to stay. But it took a long time before he could break through the highly organized and clerically dominated school system of ecclesiastical Rome. In 1705, he was accepted temporarily as a teacher in the regional schools; it was not until 1709 that he obtained his license to teach in one of the papal schools, which by that time had begun to accept boys as well as girls.

Drolin remained alone in Rome, faithful to the Institute, to his mission and his vows, for 26 years until he was recalled by Brother Timothée in 1728. Of the many letters written by De La Salle to his isolated disciple, 20 have survived. The Founder kept promising to send another Brother, and even to come to Rome himself, but he was never quite able to do either. And although he sent news and words of encouragement, De La Salle seems never to have completely understood the problems Drolin had to face, often showing impatience at Drolin's lack of progress in establishing a school in Rome that the Brothers could call their own.

Avignon, 1703

The establishment of a Christian School in Avignon was significant in many ways. It marked the expansion of the Institute for the first time into the southern part of France known as Provence. Since

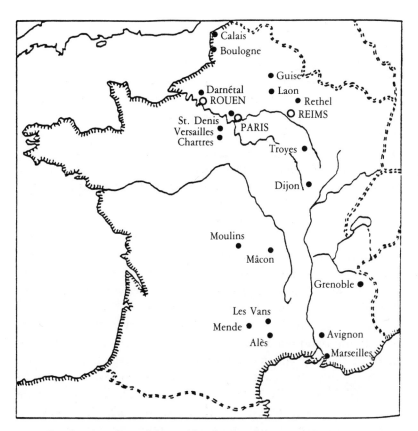

Brothers' communities at the death of De La Salle in 1719

Avignon had long been a papal city and part of the Papal States, it afforded a direct connection between France and Rome. Whatever the Brothers were able to accomplish in Avignon was bound to be known and recognized in Rome; in one sense, the schools in Avignon carried more weight in the Vatican than anything Gabriel Drolin was able to do in Rome itself.

The idea of founding charity schools for the poor of Avignon originated with the wife of the papal treasurer, Jean-Pierre de Château-Blanc. When she died she left a legacy so that her husband could carry out her dying wish. By then the reputation of the Brothers had already penetrated that far south, but the Founder was slow in responding to the initial appeal for Brothers. But when Gérard Drolin was on his way back to Paris from Rome, he stopped at Avignon and lodged with Château-Blanc. He agreed to act as intermediary with De La Salle and was eventually successful in this, his last act of service for the Institute before abandoning it.

All the arrangements were complete by 1703. The Archbishop of Avignon at the time was Laurent Fieschi, who had a residence in Paris where he also served as papal nuncio to France. Speaking of the Brothers he had chosen for this mission, De La Salle wrote enthusiastically to Gabriel Drolin in Rome: "I presented them to His Excellency, the Archbishop of Avignon, Extraordinary Nuncio to France. He received them cordially and gave them his blessing before they left [for Avignon], and he did so with great pleasure." De La Salle also told Drolin to keep the matter secret.

This blessing was important to De La Salle since Fieschi could not have been ignorant of the difficulties De La Salle was having at the time with the church authorities in Paris. The blessing implied more than approval of the three Brothers: it could be interpreted as some kind of approval for the distinctive lifestyle and the legitimate autonomy that the Founder wanted for his Institute.

When the Brothers arrived in Avignon they were well received by Antoine Banquieri, the vice-legate in charge of the papal territory in the city and its surroundings. As happened almost everywhere, the school was an instant success and soon had to be expanded. In 1705, De La Salle could write to Drolin: "The schools in Avignon are going well. We have four Brothers there now and we will soon have a house that can accommodate as many as 20."

Eventually Fieschi was summoned to Rome and made a cardinal, while Banquieri was named Governor of Rome. Both became powerful advocates for the Institute at the papal court. The favorable testimony of Archbishop François de Gontery, who succeeded Fieschi in Avignon, had great weight in obtaining the Bull of Approbation for the Institute after the Founder's death.

But that is to get ahead of the story. There were many more trials to be endured before the Institute would be so firmly established. Meanwhile, during all the time De La Salle was negotiating for these new foundations to the north, south, and east, his personal reputation, as well as the distinctive character and autonomy of his Institute, were all in serious jeopardy back in the capital.

8

Paris: The Ecclesiastical Establishment (1702–1705)

One of the characteristic traits of John Baptist de La Salle, attested to in all the sources and highlighted by all the biographers, was his disciplined equanimity, his absolute calm in the face of either success or disaster. His typical response in either case was: "God be blessed!" This expression, deeply rooted in his own implicit trust in divine Providence, concretizes the spirit of faith that he wanted to communicate to his disciples. In the Rule he wrote:

> The spirit of this Institute is first, a spirit of faith, which should induce those who compose it not to look upon anything but with the eyes of faith, not to do anything but in view of God, and to attribute all to God, always entering into these sentiments of Job: "The Lord gave and the Lord has taken away; as it has pleased the Lord, so it is done."

Never was this spirit more tested than in the face of the persecution he had to endure in Paris that began during the years that his Institute was meeting with such marked success in so many other cities outside the capital.

The "Secret Enemy"

Unlike many of the obstacles that the Founder had to surmount during the earlier period, those that had their origin in the early 1700's were neither fortuitous nor easy to identify. It seems beyond doubt that De La Salle was the victim of a calculated plot to take the Institute out of his hands. The means used were devious: manipulation, misrepresentation, and subterfuge were all employed in an attempt to discredit the Founder and alter the nature and purpose of the foundation.

In relating the story, the biographer Blain attributes the plot to the machinations of a "secret enemy." The consensus of most scholars is that Blain is referring to none other than the pastor of Saint Sulpice, Father De La Chétardie. Although Blain does not name the "enemy," and indeed speaks glowingly of the pastor as a living saint and disparagingly of "the enemy" as an agent of Satan, he leaves enough clues to enable the reader to judge that the "enemy" and the pastor are one and the same person. There is also an independent source, a letter written by Father Charles de La Grange to a priest friend in Laon in response to a request from the Brothers there for detailed information about the problems De La Salle was having with the cardinal in Paris. The letter is quoted by the biographers without mentioning the name of the Founder's adversary; in a copy of the original that has been preserved, he is identified as the pastor of Saint Sulpice.

This is somewhat surprising in view of what is known of the character of De La Chétardie. He was evidently quite saintly and a wise shepherd that cared for his flock, enterprising and tireless, generous and sensitive to the needs of the poor. He does not seem to have been ambitious: when he was offered the post of Bishop of Poitiers in 1702, he cited 66 reasons (that was his age) for remaining as he was. He was deeply concerned to foster the work of the Brothers, supervising and supporting not only the schools in his parish, but also the novitiate and the innovative projects at the Grande Maison, of which he was especially proud. For all of that, he seems to have developed a growing resentment against De La Salle for his intransigence in matters of policy and his consistent refusal to allow any interference in the affairs of the community or the schools of the Brothers.

In treating of this period, the biographer Maillefer, always quite discreet in such matters, may be closer to the mark when he speaks in the plural of "his enemies" and "those who started the trouble." In view of the attitude of Father Baudrand earlier and Father De Brou in a later period, there seems to have formed within the Sulpician community a conviction that the idea of a community of Brothers to teach gratuitous schools was a good one, but that it could be better controlled and its future assured if it were under the direction of the Sulpician pastors, rather than left to the unreasonable demands and obstinate attitude of the troublemaker from Reims.

Complaints

The occasion for the move to oust De La Salle had its origin when, shortly before the move from Vaugirard in the winter of 1693–1694, the Founder thought it best, in view of the multiple and complicated negotiations that were then underway for schools in distant places, to give over the direction of the novices to Brother Jean-Henri. When Brother Jean died soon after, he was succeeded by Brother Michel, an uncompromising sort of person with little understanding of human nature and more zeal than discretion. He treated the novices with such severity that two of them went to De La Salle to complain. He, deeming it wise not to interfere, encouraged the aggrieved young men to find peace in patience, obedience, and mortification.

This approach was satisfactory only as long as the Founder was available to give encouragement and solace. As soon as De La Salle was called away on business, the Director intensified the penances he imposed on the novices, including physical beatings which left their scars. Having no other ready recourse, the two novices went to De La Chétardie who listened sympathetically to their tale of woe. He then asked them to put their complaints in writing, which they were happy to do. This gave the pastor a good excuse to take action, but he decided to wait for more evidence.

It was not long in coming. The Director of Novices had his counterpart in Brother Ponce, the Director of the community on the Rue Princesse. One day, dissatisfied with the performance of a novice who had been assigned to his school for practice teaching, he subjected the terrified young man to a cruel scourging. Unable to bear such treatment, the Brother fled and went straight to the pastor to display the welts left by the blows. Without waiting for the return of De La Salle, Father De La Chétardie drew up a memorandum which he sent to Cardinal Noailles, describing these incidents. He added some observations of his own, alleging that there was dissension among the Brothers and that many were disillusioned with their vocation. He concluded by stating that De La Salle was no longer fit to be Superior and that he should be deposed.

Investigation and Condemnation

Cardinal Noailles, who all along had held De La Salle in high esteem for his ability, his honesty, and his saintliness, found the accusations hard to believe. At the same time, he respected De La Chétardie as a zealous and effective pastor, and one not easily given to intrigue or self-seeking. Not wishing to act without a better knowledge of the facts, the cardinal assigned his 70-year-old vicar-general, Edme Pirot, to conduct an on-the-spot investigation.

The investigation lasted throughout most of the month of November 1702. Pirot came to the community once each week to observe what was going on. Each Brother was brought in and interrogated privately under oath. Secrecy was insisted upon with strict instructions not to discuss with the others what had transpired during the interview. De La Salle, who had returned by this time, could not help but notice that something was going on. Yet he remained detached from the proceedings and made no attempt to find out

Cardinal Noailles

what the investigation was all about. No one had the heart to tell him or the temerity to violate the secrecy that had been imposed.

Pirot's report, which was never made known to De La Salle or anyone else except the cardinal, must have been negative, in view of subsequent events. It is difficult, all the same, to imagine what evidence he could have gathered against De La Salle. Granted that the complaints of the abused novices were justified, it was the Directors who inflicted the punishment and not De La Salle, who was away at the time it happened. The biographers suggest that Pirot probably based his report, not on what he heard and saw in the Brothers' community, but rather on the repeated insistence by the pastor that De La Salle be replaced.

Some idea of the contents of the report can be gathered from the letter of Father La Grange, referred to earlier, in which he reports the results of a visit he himself made to the cardinal to discover the facts. Speaking of De La Salle, he wrote to his correspondent in Laon:

> He is accused only of being too severe toward his Brothers, of practicing and encouraging penances that are too severe. He has been described to the cardinal as being a person not suited to direct others, and above all as a person extraordinarily committed to his own sense of purpose, directing himself and his Brothers solely according to his own manner of thinking.
>
> His great crime, as far as I can find out, is that he does not act according to the views of the pastor of Saint Sulpice. He would like to meddle with the administration and even the personal affairs of the Brothers, but up to this moment De La Salle has refused. I do not know how these things will turn out, for you know as well as I the mentality of the pastor. He is the key to the difficulty; if De La Salle could agree with him, there would be no trouble with the archbishop.

After the investigation was over, De La Salle went to see the cardinal to thank him for the official display of interest in his community. The cardinal received him graciously, as always, with the usual signs of friendship. Then came the blow. Gently but emphatically, the cardinal told him that he could no longer be the Superior, that another was being appointed in his place. Difficult as it must have been, De La Salle accepted this judgment in silence and with equanimity. He did not ask the reasons why, and none were offered. When he got back to the community, he said nothing about what had happened. He went about his business as usual, confided in no one, and sought no other comfort than the peace that he always found in bowing to the inscrutable designs of God in his regard.

Confrontation and Resistance

A day or two after the interview with the cardinal, Pirot sent word to De La Salle that a date had been set to install the new Superior and to have him acknowledged by the Brothers. Once more, secrecy was imposed. Without giving any hint as to the reason, De La Salle sent word to all the Brothers in Paris that they were to assemble at the Grande Maison after Vespers on the first Sunday of Advent.

Not expecting anything unusual, the Brothers gathered in the community room at the appointed hour. Soon a carriage drove up to the door, and Pirot emerged accompanied by a priest they had never seen before. Once they all were settled in their places, the vicar-general launched upon a lengthy discourse praising De La Salle for having instituted a work so useful to the Church and for having guided it so well up until then. Finally, he had to come to the point. He told them that the cardinal had decided to name a new Superior, and introduced Father Bricot as a man worthy of esteem and confidence, one they should be prepared to obey in all things.

At the mention of the word "Superior," one of the Brothers respectfully whispered to Pirot that they already had a Superior, and it would be better not to mention another. Pushing aside the Brother who had interrupted him, Pirot was forced to be more explicit: the Brothers had no choice but to obey the cardinal's orders. The Brother then repeated out loud what he had whispered the first time. Pirot tried to continue, but by now it dawned on all the Brothers what was happening. They drowned out his final words, shouting that De La Salle was the only Superior they needed, that he and the cardinal were the only superiors they would recognize, that the cardinal must be somehow mistaken, that they would appeal.

De La Salle, appalled at the response of the Brothers, called for silence. He did all he could to try to persuade them to be reasonable, imploring them on his knees and with tears in his eyes to be quiet and submit. He was no more successful than Pirot had been. The Brothers replied that they would gladly obey him in all other things, but in this they could not and would not. At this point, Brother Michel, the Director of Novices, intervened to speak on behalf of the Founder. In exasperation, Pirot shouted at him: "What? You? You dare to speak? You, who are responsible for all this trouble in the first place!"

Father Bricot, tall, young, and dignified, was more embarrassed than anyone at the situation in which he had been placed. All he wanted to do was to get out of there. To put an end to a scene that had already lasted too long, he suggested quietly to Pirot that they withdraw and leave well enough alone. De La Salle accompanied them to the door, apologizing profusely for the stubbornness of the Brothers and their refusal to obey.

Compromise

The sequel is best described in the letter of Father La Grange to his priest friend in Laon, and through him to the Brothers:

> On his return, the vicar-general was emphatic in his praise of the zeal and affection of the Brothers for De La Salle, and he told the archbishop that "if all the members of communities of men and women were as united with and as fond of their Superior as were the Brothers to De La Salle, there would not be so many disorders in Paris." He then described all that had taken place, making it clear that the Brothers would not listen to any reasons given for accepting a new Superior.
>
> The cardinal was so annoyed that he there and then sent to the royal palace to find out how the situation might be remedied and how the Brothers might be punished for their failure to submit to his orders. Some time later, the vicar-general returned to inform De La Salle that, unless he made his Brothers obey the orders of the cardinal, he would be exiled from the country. De La Salle replied that the vicar-general well knew the efforts he had already made, but to no purpose. As for being exiled, he was prepared to go wherever His Eminence might care to send him, and that this would afford him much consolation since he could find God everywhere. As for food and clothing, he could hardly be worse off than he already was.
>
> The vicar returned without carrying out his threat, full of admiration for De La Salle's lack of concern for his own fate. When the Brothers heard the news, they decided to spend the whole day and night in prayer, without food or drink, imploring the help of heaven in their anxiety and affliction. The following day, they decided to leave their schools in Paris and

abandon the house. As they started to make arrangements to depart, the news was brought to the pastor of Saint Sulpice. He immediately went to De La Salle and begged him to stop them. At the same time, the cardinal sent word to parliament to suspend the decree of banishment and to leave things as they were.

It was a sort of armistice. Truth to tell, the Brothers won out. But it was still necessary to find a peaceful settlement that would save face and leave the last word to the archdiocese.

For quite a while, De La Salle and the Brothers were left in peace. In the meantime, however, there were several meetings. De La Salle and some of the principal Brothers visited the vicar-general, and several priests were sent either by the vicar-general or the pastor of Saint Sulpice to the Brothers' house to speak and confer with each Brother in private.

Some eight or ten days later, the ninth of this month [probably January 1703], the vicar-general and Father Bricot returned to the Brothers' house and asked that the Brothers be assembled. They made a thousand promises, among them that nothing would be changed, that the would still keep the same Rule, that De La Salle would not be taken from them. Although it was necessary for them to accept and obey Father Bricot as their Superior, they would have the consolation of having De La Salle still with them, and the new Superior would visit them only once a month.

They agreed to these conditions, or at least they did not resist as they did the first time; if the proverb is true that silence means consent, they did consent to the choice of this priest, since not one of the Brothers said a word in objection.

This compromise seems to have satisfied the archdiocesan authorities. From then on they refused to get involved in the affairs of the Brothers, especially in anything that concerned the pastor of Saint Sulpice.

The Persistent Pastor

Father De La Chétardie did not give up so easily. Once he understood that he could not dislodge De La Salle by invoking church authority, he had recourse to more indirect means. Father Bricot was soon replaced as ecclesiastical superior of the Brothers by a priest more in sympathy with the pastor's attitude. Whenever this new superior came to visit the Brothers, which was rather more often than Bricot had been used to doing, he subtly suggested alternatives to the austerity of their lifestyle, their extreme poverty, the harsh conditions under which they lived, if only they would accept himself as their superior infact as well as in name. He even suggested that they might well be opposing the will of God in preferring De La Salle to an appointee of the cardinal.

Although most of the Brothers treated the man as an intruder and avoided him as much as possible, some of them fell victim to his blandishments. Religious fervor suffered to some degree, and as many as eight or nine Brothers left the community. De La Salle himself reluctantly agreed to mitigate some of the rigor and penitential practices, especially the public use of the discipline, which he eliminated altogether.

One Brother who favored more rather than less in the way of penitential rigor was Brother Michel, the Director of Novices, a typically rigid sort of person, harsh on others and as harsh on himself. One night he and a companion climbed over the wall at the Grande Maison and headed for the Trappist monastery, where they presented themselves for admission. The trappist superior, an admirer of De La Salle, refused to accept them, and sent them back to their community. A year or so later, Brother Michel was transferred to Chartres. He died there in the plague of 1705 that carried off four of the Brothers, including the infirmarian who had been sent from Paris to take care of the plague victims.

It was at this time, also, that the two Brothers teaching in the Sunday Academy became dissatisfied with their location and decided to leave the Institute. This project was particularly dear to De La Chétardie, and he did all he could to persuade De La Salle to continue it. The Founder was willing, but he was having difficulty finding Brothers willing to be trained in drawing, mathematics, and the other advanced studies offered in the Academy. The Brothers felt that to acquire such skills might put their own vocation in the same danger. One of them even drew up a lengthy memorandum explaining this point of view.

When De La Chétardie saw the text of the memorandum, he was furious. He accused De La Salle of writing it, or at least inspiring its tone and content. The Founder protested that he had nothing to do with it, whereupon De La Chétardie called him a liar. Taken back by such an insult, De La Salle replied quietly: "If that is true,

Reverend Father, then it is with that lie on my lips that I am going now to celebrate Mass."

The departure of the two Brothers forced the Sunday Academy to close for the time being. To show his annoyance, the pastor immediately reduced the salaries of the Brothers teaching in the parish. Then one of the Brothers, concerned for the survival of all the rest, volunteered to study drawing. He was ready in a fairly short time to reopen the Academy on a modified basis. As soon as he did so, the pastor restored the salary cuts.

Loss of the Grande Maison

This continued interference in the affairs of the community led some of the Brothers to urge the Founder to move the novitiate and his headquarters to some other location outside the parish of Saint Sulpice. But De La Salle loved the Grande Maison for its convenient location, its extensive rooms, and its spacious grounds well protected from the noisy city outside its thick walls. Soon he had no choice. In the early summer of 1703, the property was put up for sale and, modest as was the price, De La Salle had no means to purchase it. Things looked bright for a moment when one of the wealthy parishioners left a legacy of 5,000 livres precisely to endow the novitiate. Since, however, the Brothers had no legal identity, the pastor was able to deprive them of the entire sum and turn it to other purposes.

The house was soon sold to an outsider. The new proprietor was good enough to allow the Brothers to remain for a while, rent free, while they sought another site for the novitiate. The only condition was that they should not gather fruit from the orchard and that they should allow the gardener and his family to continue to live on the property. The gardener, ostensibly to guard the owner's fruit, decided to move to a room overlooking the orchard. Much to the annoyance of the Brothers, he would now have an unobstructed view of all their activities, depriving them of the privacy they had hitherto enjoyed. The gardener did not keep his lookout for long.

For years, the house had an unenviable reputation for being haunted, based no doubt on the fact that the deceased nuns who had built the place were buried in the crypt beneath the chapel.

Two of the Brothers claimed that one of the dead nuns, Sister Saint Fiacre, appeared to them regularly. She revealed to them her name and the fact that she was spending her Purgatory there. To humor the impressionable Brothers, De La Salle celebrated a Requiem Mass for her soul and had the Brothers receive Communion. But she still did not rest in peace.

During the first night the gardener moved into his new quarters, Sister Fiacre became active again. Her ghost waited until the gardener and his family were asleep and then woke them up by turning everything in the room upside down. Dishes, chairs, and furnishings were flying all over the place. Even the little baby was taken from its crib and placed in the center of the room. After two successive nights of such visitations, the gardener had enough. He packed up and moved his family to some rooms above the stables, far away from the Brothers. The ghost seemed satisfied and bothered them no more.

The dear dead nun was apparently unhappy to have the Brothers leave. She let her displeasure be known once again in a last attempt to keep them from going. Just as the last wagon carrying their furniture was about to depart, she shook it so violently for several minutes that it almost toppled over. At least that was the interpretation given by some Brothers who saw it happen while the wagon was standing at the door with no one around it.

Even Blain relates these incidents with a skeptical tone. The Brothers may have been less naive and more resourceful in having their way than we are inclined to think. Or perhaps one of them was a poltergeist. Or, despite the skeptics, it may have been a true ghost after all. In any case, ghost or no ghost, the Brothers left the Grande Maison for good in August 1703. They had been only five years in a house that might otherwise have become the center of a prosperous educational enterprise. But Providence had other plans.

The Rue de Charonne

The new house was located on the Rue de Charonne in the distant faubourg Saint Antoine not far from the infamous Bastille. Since the house was within the confines of Saint Paul's parish, the pastor's permission was necessary to relocate the novitiate there. The pastor had a long-standing policy of not admitting any new communities and had, in fact, already turned down several similar requests from other congregations. Yet he was aware of the reputation of De La Salle and the good that a school might procure for the children of the parish, and for that reason he made an exception in this case, assuring the Brothers of his protection and patronage.

Wary of further involvements with the archdiocesan authorities, De La Salle did not renew his request to celebrate Mass in the novitiate chapel. There was no real need. Just across the street there was a chapel in the convent of the Dominican Sisters of the Cross. They were more than willing to allow the Brothers to use it, especially when they saw the fervor with which the Founder celebrated Mass. Very early on they asked that he serve as their confessor, a favor which he granted but with considerable reluctance.

For the next several years, this community of Sisters was the principal source of support for the Brothers whenever they needed help, even after the school on the Rue de Charonne had to be closed. The Sisters could afford to be generous because the convent was well endowed and well known — it features in *Cyrano de Bergerac* — and many of the Sisters were from noble families with influential connections. Often in later years, when De La Salle would be at the end of his resources, he would say to the Brothers, "Let us go to the Cross." The Sisters of the Cross never let him down.

Once the novices were settled in their new home, it was already September 1703, and time for the school year to begin. There was first of all a new Christian School for the children of the parish. Then the Sunday Academy for working teenagers was reopened in this new location on the Rue de Charonne. Both met with the usual success and were soon filled to capacity. The faubourg Saint Antoine to the northeast of the central city was a long walk away from the faubourg Saint Germain on the left, or south, bank of the Seine, where the house on the Rue Princesse was located. Nevertheless, the school Brothers continued to come to the novitiate on Sundays and feasts for growth and renewal as a community under the personal guidance of their Father and Founder.

As a sign — in more ways than one — of the new beginning in a new center, a huge placard was hung over the door with the legend *Frères des Ecoles chrétiennes*. This was a way of proclaiming to the world that the Society had found its identity, that it had achieved a modicum of independence, at least from the pastor of Saint

Sulpice, and that it was prepared to move ahead with the business of providing Christian teachers and a quality Christian education for the poor and anyone else who cared to profit by it. But the sign, to use the gospel expression, would soon be contradicted.

9

Paris: The Educational Establishment (1703–1706)

The new center on the Rue de Charonne provided a retreat and a respite from whatever designs the pastor of Saint Sulpice may have had on the burgeoning Society of the Brothers. At the same time, it left them more vulnerable to the attacks of other enemies who could only profit from their demise as a community.

In order to understand the complex legal entanglements that followed upon the move to the faubourg Saint Antoine, it is necessary to realize what a challenge the Lasallian enterprise was to the educational establishment in Paris at the time. By long-standing tradition, the schooling was in the hands of three groups: the Guild of Writing Masters, under the jurisdiction of the parliament, a judicial and not a legislative body with its court at the Châtelet; the Corporation of the Masters of the Little Schools, under the jurisdiction of the archdiocese, specifically the diocesan supervisor (*écolâtre*); and the charity schools in the parishes, under the jurisdiction of the local pastor. The policies that De La Salle introduced into the Christian Schools were in direct conflict with all three.

Admission to the Guild of Writing Masters came only after a long and difficult apprenticeship. Its members were sworn to safeguard the quality of penmanship and the authenticity of signatures. Its monopoly in these areas, which had been extended to include mathematics, was under the protection of the king. In the view of the writing masters, it was bad enough that writing and arithmetic were being taught in the Christian Schools, although that was already a matter of contention with the Little Schools as well. The real threat to their monopoly was that teachers of these restricted subjects were being trained in the Brothers' novitiate and in the Sunday Academy, both recently transferred from the Grande Maison to the faubourg Saint Antoine, as well as in the teacher training program at Saint Hippolyte.

The challenge that the Brothers represented to the schoolmasters in the Little Schools was competition of a different sort. The simultaneous method employed in the Brothers' schools was more efficient, the curriculum was more practical, and there was better discipline. In short, it was a better educational situation. The real bone of contention, however, was that the Brothers provided gratuitous instruction for all, including those who could afford to pay. The schoolmasters complained, not without cause, that they were being put out of business in those areas where the Brothers had opened competing schools in territory officially and exclusively assigned to them.

Technically and legally, the Brothers' schools belonged to the category of charity schools under the control of the pastor. De La Salle and his Brothers did not "open" schools; they took over the direction either of charity schools already functioning or of new schools that the pastor opened for them. Yet the Christian Schools of De La Salle did not easily fit into the traditional pattern. They differed from the ordinary charity schools as much as they did from the Little Schools conducted by a single schoolmaster. And, as can be seen from the conflicts in the parish of Saint Sulpice, there were many policies concerning the teachers and the schools where the Brothers would not allow the pastor to interfere, even though they operated under his authority.

Furthermore, the Brothers formed a nascent community with a network of schools, innovative educational methods, and a distinctive garb to signify their corporate identity. Although the Society of the Brothers as yet had no legal existence in either civil or canon law, it did exist in reality. As such it was a threat to the established order: to the diocesan and parish authorities who wanted to control it and to direct its future course; to the writing masters and schoolteachers who wanted to destroy this new corporate structure intruding on the educational scene.

The Writing Masters Go to the Police

The opening of the novitiate on the Rue de Charonne, with the placard boldly proclaiming for all to see that the Brothers of the Christian Schools were in business, led the writing masters to decide that it was time to act. The new school seemed to be the most vulnerable as a target for the initial attack. If successful, it would then be easier to force the Brothers out of Paris altogether, or at least restrict them to charity schools for the certified poor.

In January 1704 the Guild of Writing Masters lodged their complaint with the Lieutenant General of the police, the Marquis d'Argenson, who was the official competent to deal with a civil case. De La Salle was accused of assuming the title of Superior of the Brothers of the Christian Schools without legal authorization, of conducting without authorization or competence several schools on the pretext that they were charity schools, and of accepting into the schools all those who applied, whether rich or poor. A list was appended giving the names of sons of artisans enrolled in the school who could afford to pay. More than likely, these were the names of pupils who had left the writing masters to transfer to the Brothers' schools. Among the parents there were two surgeons, a locksmith who owned two houses, a wine merchant, a butcher, and several innkeepers.

The complaint also accused De La Salle of training teachers and teaching subjects reserved by law to the writing masters. The sign over the door was adduced as evidence that a rival corporation was being formed illegally. The complaint demanded that the furnishings and school supplies from the building on the Rue de Charonne be confiscated and handed over to the guild.

When De La Salle failed to reply to the complaint, D'Argenson gave the order for the confiscation. Two officers of the court, accompanied by a sergeant-at-arms, appeared at the school on February 7, 1704. They took an inventory of all the school furnishings — desks and chairs, pens, inkwells, and writing samples — and put them under seal for safekeeping pending the judgment of the court. Two days later De La Salle was summoned to appear at the Châtelet to face the accusation of conducting several classes and schools throughout the city and for demonstrating the art of penmanship. He was informed that the confiscation was to be confirmed officially and the materials were to be put at the disposal of the Guild of Writing Masters.

De La Salle made no move to defend himself. Apart from an innate reluctance to engage in litigation of any kind, he knew it would be useless. As a priest, he might have pleaded that the Châtelet, a civil court, had no jurisdiction over him. But this would not exempt his Brothers since they had no ecclesiastical status. Besides, a judgment by default could always be appealed if the opportunity presented itself. De La Salle probably realized that a condemnation might actually win sympathy and support for the

Brothers, especially among the parents or the young adults who were profiting from the innovative methods and the quality education offered in the Christian Schools and the Sunday Academy.

Inevitably, on February 22, 1704, De La Salle was condemned in the Châtelet by default. The writing masters were given title to all the furnishings of the school that had been used to teach writing. De La Salle was forbidden henceforth to accept in his school any but the children of the certified poor. In addition, a fine of 50 livres was levied against him personally for violating the city ordinances by "conducting classes and schools that taught the art of writing."

It was true, of course: in modern terms, an act of civil disobedience. Not only was writing taught in the Brothers' schools, but the novitiate and the training program at Saint Hippolyte were turning out fine calligraphers independently of the guild. But there was no way that De La Salle was willing to back away from the course he had set for himself. It was time to challenge the traditional system that made it impossible for the children of the poor either to share an educational experience on an equal basis with those who were better off, or to learn those skills—writing and arithmetic as well as reading—that would enable them to break out of the social bind in which their poverty had placed them.

The Masters of the Little Schools Go to the Chancery

Meanwhile, sensing the rift between De La Salle and De La Chétardie, the Masters of the Little Schools decided that they could safely proceed against De La Salle without objection from the pastor of Saint Sulpice. There was a new archdiocesan supervisor responsible for the Little Schools, a priest less favorable to the Brothers than his predecessor had been, and one sensitive to the mood of the cardinal, who had become annoyed with De La Salle ever since the trouble over the Bricot appointment. In any case, from the point of view of the archdiocese, De La Salle was no longer the ecclesiastical superior of the Brothers.

On February 14, 1704, just one week after the confiscation order by the civil court, an edict was issued from the diocesan chancery forbidding De La Salle to teach, to engage or assign other teachers, or to conduct schools in Paris or any of its environs without being assigned a specific territory by the diocesan supervisor of schools. In addition he was fined 50 livres, and all the furnishings in his

A master of the Little Schools

schools were to be confiscated. In effect, De La Salle was being condemned for intruding on the rights of the Little Schools.

De La Salle Decides to Appeal

This judgment by ecclesiastical authority was a devastating blow. With the cardinal in his present mood, De La Salle realized that an appeal in that direction would be useless. By the same token, he could not accept the interdiction which forbade him to assign teachers or conduct schools. That would, in effect, destroy the Society that he had vowed in 1691 to establish. This time, he knew that he had to act. He engaged a lawyer, M. Guillaume Quellier, to represent him. Accordingly, on March 19, 1704, the feast of Saint Joseph, patron of the Institute, De La Salle lodged an appeal through his lawyer to the court of parliament against the decision of the diocesan supervisor given on February 14. It would be another year before the appeal would be heard.

Meanwhile, on May 4, De La Salle filed a petition with the Lieutenant General of the police to recover the furnishings that had been confiscated at the Rue de Charonne. The basis of the petition was that the sentence of the Châtelet of February 22 was invalid since it conceded to the writing masters school furnishings that the diocesan supervisor had already assigned on February 14 of the previous week to the schoolmasters of the Little Schools. By these legal maneuvers, De La Salle and his lawyer were putting the police at the Châtelet in opposition to the diocesan supervisor of schools, and the writing masters against the schoolmasters of the Little Schools.

In a hearing held on May 30, the judge at the Châtelet refused to accept the petition of De La Salle and sentenced him to pay the court costs. The sentence of February 22 would stand, pending any appeal. There did not have to be an appeal, since the decision left unresolved the question of the furnishings, which the Châtelet had awarded to the writing masters and the diocesan supervisor had assigned to the schoolmasters. For his part, De La Salle could only await the eventual outcome. In the meantime he had taken the precaution of putting into storage in a rented building the novitiate furnishings which had been donated by Madame Voisin.

The Writing Masters Press Their Advantage

Encouraged by their victories in court, the writing masters decided to widen the attack. On June 7, 1704, they petitioned D'Argenson at the Châtelet to issue a restraining order on De La Salle, Ponce, Nicolas, and the 16 other Brothers, mentioned by name, who were teaching in Paris without authorization of the diocesan supervisor. They demanded that the Brothers cease their corporate activities at once and that a fine be imposed of 500 livres per Brother (almost three years' salary!) and an additional fine of 2,000 livres on De La Salle.

On July 11 a restraining order was issued to that effect, except that the fines were reduced: 50 livres per Brother and 100 from De La Salle, a moot point since they had no money to pay anything. In addition, the decree stated that any parents who could afford to pay would be liable to prosecution if they sent their children to the "Christian gratuitous schools," which were no longer to be considered open to the general public, but only to the certified poor.

Frustrated at not obtaining any money from De La Salle or the Brothers, the writing masters thereupon undertook to sell the furnishings that were still at the Rue de Charonne. They arrived at the school accompanied by wreckers and their tools. The sign over the door was torn down; benches, desks, books, and all the teaching materials used in the Sunday Academy were carted off in wagons. De La Salle and the Brothers witnessed the devastation without complaint. There was nothing they could do to stop it. In this fashion, the Sunday Academy, that had done so much good for so many young men since its foundation, came to an end.

The End of the Teacher-training Program at Saint Hippolyte

The repercussions of these events reached all the way across town to the faubourg Saint Marcel, where Brother Nicolas Vuyart and Brother Gervais were directing the teacher-training program. The decree of the Châtelet of July 11 applied to this enterprise more than to any other; Nicolas Vuyart was one of the first named after the Founder in the condemnation. The pastors of the parishes of Saint Martin and Saint Hippolyte, who stood the most to lose, consulted with the two Brothers to see what could be done to save the program. They decided to apply independently for authorization for each of the Brothers to teach, using their secular names without reference to De La Salle or the Christian Schools. The pastors would submit the petition in their own name.

The writing masters were not deceived. They easily gathered enough evidence to show that Nicolas and Gervais were in fact associated with De La Salle and guilty of conducting a school "under his orders." On August 29, 1704, the inevitable sentence fell. The Lieutenant General of the police, rejecting the petition of the two pastors, confirmed the previous decrees of February 22 and July 11 against the Brothers; in addition, under penalty of the law, the "Brothers of the Charity Schools" were forbidden to live in community or constitute themselves as a Society until such time as they received letters patent from the king. The decree left the pastors free, however, to engage anyone they wished to teach writing in their schools to the children of the poor, provided that they submitted the names of the poor students to the approval of the writing masters.

This created a dilemma for the two Brothers. In order to continue the program, they would have to put aside the habit and sever any organizational link they had with De La Salle and the Brothers. Vuyart had already inherited in his own name the funds that had been left by the previous pastor, Father Lebreton, to insure that the program would continue. In deciding to break definitively with the Brothers, Vuyart's motives may not have been as traitorous or self-serving as the biographers attribute to him. The pastor of Saint Hippolyte, after all, allowed him to teach in the parish school for the next 24 years.

Vuyart may have thought—incorrectly as it turned out—that by leaving the Brothers he could save the training program and so protect the legacy and fulfill the last wishes of Father Lebreton. But Vuyart did not get along well with Brother Gervais, who was forced to leave Saint Hippolyte since he wanted to remain faithful to the Brothers. The end result was that the program had to be closed, probably during the vacation period in September 1704.

The Writing Masters and the Schoolmasters Join Forces

During the vacation period in September 1704 the writing masters decided to suggest to their ancient rivals, the schoolmasters, that they work together in their common cause against De La Salle and the Brothers. Their aim was to gather evidence that De La Salle was ignoring the ban pronounced on August 29 by the Lieutenant General of the police. In this way they hoped to bolster their case when the appeal of De La Salle against the decision of the diocesan supervisor would come before parliament.

A meeting was held between representatives of the two groups on September 30. A statement had been prepared by the president of the Guild of Writing Masters for the schoolmasters to sign, which they eagerly did. The statement accused "Master John Baptist de La Salle, so-called superior of the Brothers of the Christian Schools, and the self-styled [*prétendus*] Brothers of the aforesaid Schools" of continuing "since the first of the present month of September to assemble children of bourgeois parents into their various locations in the different sections of this city where they openly teach these children contrary to the instructions from the police."

The statement goes on to maintain that what the Brothers are doing is prejudicial to the plaintiffs, stripping them of their best scholars who were children from good families, and making it difficult for them to earn a living. Accordingly, the statement demands that the sentence of the police be carried out and that action be taken against "the aforesaid De La Salle and the self-styled Brothers and the others mentioned in the judgments already referred to."

The "judgments referred to" were those from the Châtelet of February 22, July 11, and August 29, which referred explicitly and respectively only to the teacher-training establishments in Saint Antoine and Saint Marcel, the principal targets of the writing masters. By signing the statement which made no mention of these specifics, the schoolmasters were trying to apply the decrees to the schools in the parish of Saint Sulpice, which was their concern, but outside the jurisdiction of the Châtelet.

The only one who could clarify this issue and defend the right of the Brothers to teach in his parish schools was Father De La Chétardie. But he did nothing. Meanwhile, once the four schools pertaining to Saint Sulpice reopened in October, the Brothers continued on with their daily tasks in the classroom. They were continually harassed by the writing masters, who kept threatening to produce the signed agreement if the Brothers continued to accept others than the certified poor. Hired spies would follow the children on their way to school to see if any of those listed in the petitions were still attending the Brothers' classes. The Brothers themselves were threatened with more legal action and the parents with prosecution and fines unless they could prove their inability to pay.

De La Chétardie soon found his sources of support for the schools drying up. A whispering campaign spread the word among wealthy donors that the Christian Schools in his parish had no legal status and would soon be shut down. The alms that had been allotted to the parish from the royal treasury for the relief of the poor were considerably reduced, so much so that De La Chétardie had to protest to the royal treasurer. On the advice of the charity board of the parish, in the fall of 1704, De La Chétardie closed the recently opened school on the Rue des Fossés-Monsieur-le-Prince. It was hoped in this way to cut down on the number of Brothers teaching in the parish, reduce expenses, and make a token gesture to show good will to the writing masters.

Parliamentary Decisions

The schoolmasters of the Little Schools, however, would not be satisfied with half measures. In December they, too, decided to bring their case before the parliamentary court in a petition to have the sentence of the diocesan supervisor against De La Salle (which was still under appeal) applied to Brothers Ponce, Nicolas, Jean, Joseph, and others teaching in the Christian Schools. The only way the Brothers could defend themselves legally, without risking a royal judgment from parliament against the entire community, was to respond as distinct individuals. In a response dated January 7, 1705, each of them insisted that his school was dependent on the pastor of Saint Sulpice and therefore not implicated in the condemnation of De La Salle. From a legal point of view, the cases were distinct.

The ploy might have worked if De La Salle's appeal to the Châtelet against the judgment of the diocesan supervisor, lodged a year earlier, had not come up for judgment at the same time. The court decided to deal with the cases together. On March 26, 1705, the schoolmasters petitioned the court to challenge the Brothers named in the suit to furnish proof that they had no connection with De La Salle or his Christian Schools. It was one thing to hide behind a legal fiction, but to turn it into a reality was quite another matter. To do so, the Brothers would have had to make a formal renouncement of their association and put aside their distinctive religious habit. This they could not bring themselves to do, and so their case was doomed.

Realizing that the situation in Paris was hopeless, De La Salle was already involved in negotiations to establish the Brothers in Normandy. By July 1705 he had opened a school in Darnétal. Soon thereafter he signed a lease for the property at Saint Yon just outside Rouen. Quickly and quietly he had the novitiate furnishings that had been donated by Madame Voisin for the Grande Maison taken out of storage and transported to Saint Yon. The Archbishop of Rouen and the president of the Rouen parliament paid the expenses.

The appeal before the Paris parliament moved slowly during the winter of 1705–1706. The schoolmasters did not cease to lobby with prominent persons in a position to influence the outcome. D'Argenson at the Châtelet, for example, was won over to the idea that all teachers in the schools should be subject to one diocesan authority. On a higher level, the Procurator General of the King, Henri D'Aguesseau, held long conversations with Cardinal Noailles about the legal status of the Brothers. The king himself let his judgment be known through his secretary, the Count of Pontchartrain: no such community should be allowed to operate until it had received letters patent.

The final decision was handed down by the court of the parliament on February 5, 1706. Sentence was pronounced against "John Baptist de La Salle, so-called superior of the Brothers of the Christian Schools, as also against those named Jean, Ponce, Joseph, and the others, who were conducting schools under the auspices of the aforesaid De La Salle without authorization or competence." De La Salle was forbidden "to establish any community under the name of a training school for teachers in the primary schools, or anything similar, or to post on the door any special inscription similar to the one that had been confiscated."

On March 19, 1706, the feast of Saint Joseph, the decree of parliament was communicated to De La Salle at the Rue Saint Honoré, where he had been staying, and separately to the other Brothers at the Rue du Bac. The Brothers who had been teaching in the three schools in the parish of Saint Sulpice throughout the long months of opposition and uncertainty were thoroughly disheartened at the final outcome. They asked De La Salle for permission to close the schools, and after some hesitation he agreed.

One day in July of that year, without giving any advance warning, the Brothers simply took off from Paris for parts unknown, leaving only one Brother at the Rue Princesse to watch over the house. The next day the children were surprised to find the doors of the schools locked against them. When the Brothers failed to return after a few days, the parents became alarmed and went to the pastor to seek an explanation. He had to admit that he was as surprised as they and equally at a loss as to what to do.

De La Chétardie and the Final Compromise

Some months before the final decision of parliament and the subsequent withdrawal of the Brothers, the pastor of Saint Sulpice had already decided that he had to do something to save the schools in his parish. He was aroused to action for the first time in the fall of 1705 when the writing masters appeared at the Rue Princesse in an attempt to have the furnishings confiscated. They were stymied by the owner of the building who had registered a prior claim to seize the furnishings as security for the payment of the rent. This did not keep the writing masters from continually harassing the Brothers, disrupting the classes, demanding proof that such and such a student was truly a charity case, and threatening further police and legal action.

As soon as De La Salle and the novices had left for Rouen, De La Chétardie decided to take legal action to assert his rights. The judgment of the Châtelet was a civil act and had no application to him as a pastor or to his parish schools. Although De La Chétardie had no great attachment to De La Salle personally, and probably thought of himself as better qualified to direct the Brothers, he did regard the Brothers themselves very highly. He approved thoroughly of their educational policies and methods as well as the importance they gave to association and community life.

Accordingly, on November 19, 1705, he lodged a petition with the Lieutenant General of the police in favor of Brothers Ponce, Jean, Joseph, and the others, carefully avoiding any mention of De La Salle, from whom he dissociated himself. In the petition, De La Chétardie insisted that the school furnishings on the Rue Princesse belonged to him by right and that the seizure should be lifted, that the Brothers were in his employ, that all disturbances against them should cease, and that they be given the respect due to them according to the rights of the charity schools. No immediate action was taken at the time, since the appeal was still pending before parliament.

Once the final decree had been issued, De La Chétardie was summoned to meet with representatives from the writing masters for a hearing before the lieutenant of the police. The writing masters objected that the pastor could in no way prove that the Brothers were teaching in charity schools, since so many of the pupils could afford to pay. They added that the pastor was free to engage anyone he wished to teach writing to the really poor of the parish, provided that the names be certified by the police and communicated to the guild for their approval.

While the legal status of his parish schools was very much up in the air, and especially after the Brothers withdrew, the suggestion was made to De La Chétardie that the Brothers be replaced. The pastor refused even to consider it. Every bit as much as the parents, he genuinely appreciated the Brothers and wanted to keep them for his schools.

With that in mind, De La Chétardie contacted De La Salle and begged him to allow the Brothers to return to Paris. The Founder replied that he would rather yield to his enemies than to have the Brothers exposed to continual disturbances with no appreciation for what they were trying to do. He went on to say that the way the Brothers had been treated over the last few years had discouraged many of them and that he could not easily replace them. He was adamant on this point. He said that he would not send any Brothers back to Saint Sulpice unless he could be assured that they would be allowed to work undisturbed. He insisted that De La Chétardie assume personal responsibility for protecting them. The pastor readily agreed, and the Brothers returned in time to open the schools in the fall of 1706. De La Chétardie even offered to pay for their transportation back to Paris, so happy was he to see them return.

It remained only to come to terms with the Guild of the Writing Masters. The pastor met with some of their leaders and had a document drawn up before two notaries. In it De La Chétardie stated that it was he who commissioned the Brothers to teach in the charity schools of the parish; that De La Salle had used his disciples in this work only on the orders of the pastor; that he, the pastor, had provided lodging, paid the salaries and the rent; that he wanted the Brothers to continue their work in full liberty without further interference.

For their part, the writing masters insisted that the Brothers accept in their schools only those whose poverty could be attested to by one of the priests of the parish. Parents soon came flocking from all over the parish to obtain the required certificates attesting to their poverty. It seems that few of them were refused by the priest in charge. This face-saving device changed very little: by and large the same students as before were enrolled in the parish schools conducted by the Brothers.

De La Salle in the Face of Crisis

Throughout all of these difficulties De La Salle retained his characteristic calm, remained in the background as much as possible, and went about his business as usual. With his equally characteristic tenacity, he never surrendered any of the principles that he considered essential to the Brothers and the Christian Schools: that they should conduct schools together and by association as a Society, with or without legal status; that in order to educate the poor the schools be gratuitous for all without discrimination; that the teachers be trained religiously and professionally, within the Society, for their educational mission. On all three counts, as can be seen from the intensity of the legal debates, De La Salle had set himself in direct conflict with the educational theory and practice of the time.

The secret of De La Salle's imperturbable confidence and calm in the face of opposition and defeat lay in his deep religious faith, the "spirit of faith," as he called it, that he left as a legacy to his Institute. The biographer Blain, probably citing a written memoir he had in hand, quotes the Founder in these words:

> In the words of Gamaliel, "If this undertaking is from God, who can destroy it?" If my work does not come from God, I would consent to its ruin. I would join our enemies in destroying it if I thought that it did not have God for its author, or that he did not will its progress. But if he declares himself its defender, let us fear nothing. . . . If contradiction is a proof

that an enterprise comes from God, let us be happy; our Institute is indeed his creation. The cross which follows it everywhere gives us assurance that this is so.

This same sentiment found an echo in one of a series of retreat resolutions that he made for himself:

I shall always consider the establishment and the direction of our community as the work of God. That is why I have entrusted it to his care, in such a way that as far as I am concerned, I shall do nothing that concerns the Institute except by his orders. For that reason I shall always consult extensively concerning what I ought to do. I will often speak to God in the words of the prophet Habacuc: *Domine opus tuum.* [Lord, the work is yours.]

This attitude of resignation to the divine will and radical trust in divine Providence did not prevent De La Salle from using every available human resource and strategy to assure the continuation of the work he had begun. The events in Paris only served to strengthen his conviction that his Institute could never survive so long as it was dependent on an individual pastor or bishop. That was why he moved the novitiate from Reims to Paris in the first place. That was also one motive for opening the school in Avignon and a factor in the decision to send two Brothers to Rome. Now he was establishing a new center in Rouen for the same reason.

During all the difficult years in Paris, despite the opposition, the uncertainty, the reversals, and the compromises, there was notable vitality and progress elsewhere in France. During this period there were more than 50 Brothers teaching in the Christian Schools in Reims, Rethel, Guise, Laon, Chartres, Calais, Troyes, and Avignon. The reputation of the Brothers and their schools was spreading rapidly throughout France, with requests for new foundations coming all the time. There were signs that the cross might yet lead to a glorious resurrection.

10

Beginnings in Rouen and Elsewhere (1704–1708)

During all the time that the legal proceedings in Paris were moving toward their inexorable conclusion, De La Salle was trying to find an alternate location for the Brothers and for the novitiate that had been forced to close down on the Rue de Charonne. When an invitation came to open a school on the Rue Saint Honoré in the parish of Saint Roch on the right bank of the Seine, he sent two Brothers there and went himself to live with them. In a residence that they shared with two or three priests, the Brothers were far enough away from the faubourg Saint Germain and the parish of Saint Sulpice to be able to keep a somewhat independent foothold in the capital. The Saint Roch school did not last long, but it served its purpose for the time being. The five or six novices from the Rue de Charonne were sent to the Rue Princesse until a suitable permanent location could be found for the novitiate.

Darnétal

In the circumstances, it is no wonder that De La Salle responded eagerly to an invitation to open a school in Darnétal, just outside Rouen. It was in Darnétal that Madame Maillefer had earlier founded a gratuitous school for girls. A similar school for boys had been supported for some time by a group of former students of the Jesuit College. The schoolmaster had just died in the summer of 1704, and they were looking for a replacement. Father Deshayes, who had known De La Salle in his seminary days at Saint Sulpice, had heard about the work of the Brothers in Paris and recommended that they be invited to take over the school. De La Salle expressed interest, but insisted that he could not send fewer than two Brothers. The best stipend that the sponsors could afford was 150 livres for the two Brothers plus the use of lodgings that had been occupied by the deceased schoolmaster.

De La Salle made a quick trip to Rouen to visit the parish. Once he was sure that the population was sufficient to support a school, and the living conditions suitable for a Brothers' community, he agreed to the less-than-generous terms. He was evidently anxious to establish a foothold in or near Rouen, the capital of Normandy and a city hallowed by memories of Barré, Roland, and Nyel. It was more than 25 years since Nyel had left Rouen to open a school in Reims; it was time for De La Salle to bring the maturing project back to the site of its origins. The school in Darnétal opened after the September vacation period in 1704 with Brother Ponce, the "strong man" from the Rue Princesse, as the Director, and another Brother to assist him.

As happened everywhere, the school was an immediate success and was soon filled to capacity. But the living conditions of the two Brothers were far from ideal. The house was badly in need of repairs that the pastor was unwilling or unable to provide. The promised stipend was often delayed and sometimes not paid at all. The parish managed to support the Brothers in this hand-to-mouth existence by taking up special collections whenever the Brothers seemed to be getting ready to give up the school. Canon Blain, writing from Rouen, devotes long pages in his biography of the Founder to the stinginess of his fellow townspeople.

Archbishop Colbert

The Archbishop of Rouen at the time was Jacques-Nicolas Colbert, 80 years old, the son of the famous Minister of Finance in the early years of the reign of Louis XIV, a doctor of the Sorbonne, and a member of the French Academy. Toward the end of Lent in 1704 he was in Rouen to preside at the ordinations for the archdiocese. When the Brothers from Darnétal came to pay their respects, the archbishop inquired about the possibility of obtaining Brothers for the charity schools in Rouen. The Brothers assured him that De La Salle would probably be willing to send as many as he could spare.

Archbishop Colbert instructed his vicar-general, Father Couët, to write to De La Salle asking him to come to Rouen, before Easter if possible, since the archbishop had to leave town shortly after that. In his letter, the vicar-general assured De La Salle of a warm welcome, and even hinted at the possibility of allowing him to establish a novitiate. It seems that De La Salle's difficulties in Paris were already becoming widely known. The Brothers wrote to the Founder urging him to accept the invitation. This he did, making the journey from Paris to Rouen by stagecoach. The interview was fruitful, and it was agreed on both sides to move the plan forward.

The supervision of the charity schools in Rouen was rather different from the system in Paris. There was a charity school in each of the four quarters of the city: Saint Maclou, Saint Goddard, Saint Eloi, and Saint Vivien. These were administered, not by the pastors of the parishes, but by the administrative board of the General Hospice, otherwise known as the Bureau of the Ablebodied Paupers. Adrien Nyel had at one time been Director General of the institution. The teachers lived in the hospice and set out each day for their respective schools. The greater number of them were seminarians working to finance their studies for the priesthood; in addition, there were a few unmarried laymen, the successors of the group that had worked with Adrien Nyel.

Under this system, the charity schools were not functioning very well. The problems were similar to those that plagued the charity schools everywhere: poor discipline, ragged attendance, unsanitary conditions, and segregation of the poor. The teachers had little or no training and little motivation or interest in their work. To earn their food and lodging at the hospice, they were required after school hours to serve the meals and otherwise care for the needs of all the "ablebodied paupers" who lived there. For most of them, seminarians and laymen alike, teaching in the schools was a temporary way of earning one's keep until something better came along.

Impressed by the success of the school in Darnétal, the archbishop conceived a plan to have the Brothers replace the teachers and take over the direction of the four schools. But any such new contractual agreement needed to be approved beforehand by the municipal charity board. To help win the necessary approval, Archbishop Colbert enlisted the support of an interested and influential layman, the President of the Parliament of Normandy, Monsieur Nicolas-Pierre Camus, the Seigneur de Pontcarré. Already well disposed to the Brothers, that gentleman promised to do all he could to have the proposal succeed.

The board showed little enthusiasm for the archbishop's plan, with one or two of the more influential members totally opposed. For one thing, they were fearful that the introduction of the Brothers might require more money than they could afford; for another, they

Seventeenth-century Rouen

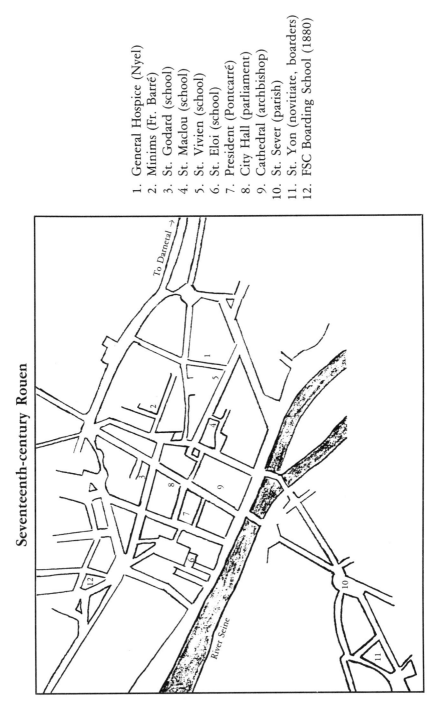

1. General Hospice (Nyel)
2. Minims (Fr. Barré)
3. St. Godard (school)
4. St. Maclou (school)
5. St. Vivien (school)
6. St. Eloi (school)
7. President (Pontcarré)
8. City Hall (parliament)
9. Cathedral (archbishop)
10. St. Sever (parish)
11. St. Yon (noviitate, boarders)
12. FSC Boarding School (1880)

To Darnetal →

River Seine

were reluctant to give up control over the charity schools. It took all the powers of persuasion of Archbishop Colbert and President De Pontcarré to get the board to agree at least to try the plan on an experimental basis. As soon as he was able to squeeze this concession from the reluctant board members, the archbishop suggested to De La Salle that he send some Brothers at once before the board had a chance to change its mind—which it did, several times, before the Brothers finally were in control of all four schools.

Although Archbishop Colbert was unable to control the policies of the charity board, he did what he could to make De La Salle feel welcome in the archdiocese. He gave him extensive faculties to exercise his priestly ministry, even expressing the hope that the holy priest might use them rather widely in spiritual direction, as he had often done in Paris. But De La Salle was content to function in this ministry only rarely, restricting himself for the most part to the direction of his novices.

The General Hospice

In mid-May of 1705 De La Salle set out for Rouen from Paris with two Brothers to begin the new enterprise. They travelled by foot, making all the community exercises en route, staying overnight at wayside inns where their pious demeanor and unusual habit, unknown in the countryside, attracted a good bit of attention. On May 19, a few days after they arrived in Rouen, they were formally admitted to the General Hospice, where they were to live and take their meals. They were, in effect, assimilated into the prevailing program designed for seminarians, with the same duties and the same stipend (36 livres a year in addition to room and board).

The Brothers were able to take charge of the schools only gradually. One Brother went to the school at Saint Maclou, which was the first to open, then the other was sent to Saint Goddard. By the end of the year two more Brothers had arrived, one for Saint Eloi and the other to teach the children resident in the hospice. Meanwhile, De La Salle transferred Brother Ponce from Darnétal to serve as Director of the community and to teach at Saint Maclou. It was not until some years later, after the Brothers had left the hospice, that a Brother was assigned to Saint Vivien.

The reluctance of the charity board to have the Brothers at all, much less to allow them to effect any change in the conduct of the charity schools, was soon made evident. Heavy demands were put upon them in an obvious effort to have the experiment fail. The Brothers were required to get the residents of the hospice out of bed in the morning, get them dressed, and preside over their prayers before going off to school. They were expected to provide instruction for the children living in the hospice as well as in the outside schools. There were over 100 students in each of the classes; the Brother who remained to teach at the hospice had even more. The Brothers had to come back from even the distant schools to serve the noon meal to the residents before they themselves could eat, and then return in a hurry to be on time for the afternoon classes. At the end of the day they had again to preside at religious instruction and night prayers of the residents and put them to bed.

The situation was made the more intolerable when the board refused to allow De La Salle to increase the number of Brothers beyond the five that had been originally bargained for. The health of the Brothers suffered from all the overwork. It became impossible, besides, to maintain any kind of community life or regular religious exercises. When one of the Brothers succumbed to illness or exhaustion, De La Salle would send another more vigorous Brother to replace him, but that could not go on indefinitely. The board was determined to get rid of the Brothers, but De La Salle was equally determined to keep his foothold in Rouen.

After two years, and with the help of President Pontcarré, an alternate plan was worked out. The Brothers would leave the hospice, move into a rented house of their own, and continue to direct the charity schools on their own terms. De La Salle, for his part, agreed to supply ten Brothers for the four schools, plus two to take care of the temporal affairs, and to accept the wholly inadequate stipend of 600 livres a year for the 12 of them (200 livres per Brother was the usual sum). Poor as they were, they at least had the freedom to live their own community life, free from the burden and distraction of caring for the residents in the hospice. Pontcarré and Archbishop Colbert provided what assistance they could, and often visited the schools. One such occasion has been immortalized in a well-known nineteenth-century painting by the artist Gagliardi.

The Novitiate at Saint Yon

Without any doubt, one of the principal reasons that motivated De La Salle to encourage the Brothers to endure the privations at Darnétal and at the General Hospice in Rouen was the prospect of establishing a permanent novitiate in the archdiocese. The archbishop and his vicar-general were well disposed to the idea; it remained only to find a suitable location. In the summer of 1705 an ideal property in the faubourg Saint Sever on the west bank of the Seine was put up for lease. Known as Saint Yon, the property had originally belonged to an aristocrat of that name who built a chapel there dedicated to his patron, Saint Yon, a disciple of Saint Denis. More recently, the property had housed a community of Sisters. The owner in 1705 was Madame De Louvois, the sister-in-law of Archbishop Le Tellier of Reims. Knowing the high esteem in which that prelate held De La Salle, she agreed to let him have the property for a modest sum and signed a lease for six years.

It was in August 1705 that De La Salle had the novitiate furnishings and then the novices themselves brought from Paris to Rouen. The Sisters who had recently vacated the premises donated to the Brothers the tapestries and paintings that still adorned the chapel, and all of the furniture that they had left behind. Monsieur De Pontcarré contributed handsomely to the expenses of the installation. He continued to show support for the Brothers whenever possible. They, in turn, reserved an area of the property for him to come, as he often did, to walk and otherwise enjoy the serenity of the grounds in undisturbed isolation.

De La Salle, too, loved the place. The house was large and comfortable, the gardens spacious, the fresh air invigorating, and the peace and quiet a welcome relief from the bustle of the city. Yet the faubourg Saint Sever was close enough to Rouen to maintain regular contact with the Brothers in the schools. De La Salle spent as much time at Saint Yon as he could. As he had done earlier at Vaugirard and the Grande Maison, he brought the community Brothers to the novitiate as often as they could get free, at least once a year, for recreation, retreat, and renewal.

The novitiate itself was soon thriving under the Director of Novices, Brother Barthélemy. Only six novices had come with him from Paris in August 1705; ten more joined before the end of the year, and another ten in the following year. These developments at Saint Yon were of critical importance at this moment in the history of the Society still struggling for its existence. On the one hand there were the disturbances and disruptions to contend with in Paris; on the other, the many new foundations being established in cities all over France. Saint Yon served as a secure and salutary center to hold the entire enterprise together.

Diversification at Saint Yon

The spacious manorhouse and the extensive property at Saint Yon made it possible for De La Salle to respond to a request to open a school for boarding students. This venture proved to be quite successful. The parents were pleased at the transformation the boarding experience accomplished in the children they sent there, a good number of them somewhat older and from well-to-do bourgeois families. In addition to the elementary curriculum of reading, writing, and arithmetic, more advanced courses were offered in drawing, geometry, and architecture. The fame of the school soon spread, and applications for admission began to come from as far away as Paris.

The significance of this introduction of advanced practical courses should not be missed. Brother Clair Battersby, in his biography of De La Salle, cites an impressive list of authorities who have considered this an important step in the history of education. It was one of the few educational ventures of the time that aimed to bridge the gap between the charity schools established for the poor and the colleges that prepared the children of the upper classes for university studies. The curriculum at Saint Yon was advanced well beyond the elementary level, but it was also practical. Instead of the Latin and Greek classics in literature and philosophy that constituted the curriculum in the colleges, the courses at Saint Yon were professional and even scientific, designed to advance the education of the sons of the bourgeoisie who were destined for careers in commerce and industry.

The success of the boarding school led inevitably to another educational adventure. There was soon pressure to extend the facilities of Saint Yon by offering a center for delinquent children whose presence in the boarding school would only be disruptive. And so a special program was developed just for them. Outside of class time, the boys in the house of correction, as it was called, were kept separate from those in the boarding school, and the supervision was much more strict. When facilities had to be shared, as at meals and chapel services, the delinquents were kept with the Brothers. It was a relief to the troubled parents and the concerned magistrates of Rouen to discover that the Brothers of Saint Yon could achieve remarkable results in a short time with young lads in need of correction and reform.

Some years later, yet a third group of paying residents was accepted at Saint Yon, this time turning part of the facilities into a house of detention that was effectively a prison. It was probably at the suggestion of De Pontcarré that De La Salle agreed to accept a certain number of young men condemned in the courts by *lettres de cachet*. That was the legal term for sealed orders signed by the king ordering such persons to be kept under confinement for a specified time. This device was used for renegades among the upper classes, including some clergy, to remove them from society where they could be an embarrassment to their families.

Upon their arrival at Saint Yon, these men had to be confined to cells that were locked and barred. Many of them were violent, yelling and screaming, cursing and swearing at the Brothers, who now became their jailers. But as they calmed down, the inmates were given more freedom and privileges until they were considered ready for release. Some of them responded well to the unselfish treatment and kindly services provided by the Brothers. Blain tells us that religious conversions were not rare at Saint Yon. But some inmates proved to be incorrigible. The records over the years show that episodes of resistance and violence were rather common. It was an occasional source of merriment for the neighbors to see the Brothers chasing after an escaped prisoner in the dead of night; needless to say, the popular tendency on those occasions was to cheer for the escapee.

With all of these programs functioning in addition to the novitiate, the population of Saint Yon at any one time might reach as many as a hundred persons. Yet the order and the discipline were such, especially the insistence on silence, that visitors could hardly believe all that was going on in the place. The varied programs provided the Brothers with new opportunities to exercise their spirit of faith and zeal as they acquired more and more expertise in these creative educational activities. The resident programs also provided a much needed source of revenue to support the novitiate and to supplement the inadequate stipends provided for the Brothers teaching in the gratuitous schools in the city. This pattern would constitute a valuable precedent for the future.

Away on Business in Paris

Much as De La Salle loved the peace and solitude of Saint Yon, he found that he could not always spend as much time there as he would have liked. Affairs in the capital often demanded his presence there; at the same time, the expansion at Saint Yon and the problems with the charity board sometimes required him to be in Rouen. During the years from 1705 to 1708 he frequently had to commute between the two centers.

The novitiate was barely settled at Saint Yon when De La Salle decided to close the schools at Saint Sulpice and reassign the Brothers. Then he had to deal with De La Chétardie, who was begging to have the 18 Brothers return to Paris. Once a satisfactory agreement was worked out, he found that he could spare only 12 Brothers for Saint Sulpice, one as Director, ten for the schools, and one, named Brother Thomas, to take charge of the temporal affairs of the community. The schools in Paris were soon working normally again, although with reduced numbers because of the restrictions imposed by the agreement with the writing masters.

Once things were somewhat back to normal De La Salle came to Paris to pay his respects to Father De La Chétardie. Although the pastor was happy to have the Brothers back, he continued to nurse his old resentment against De La Salle. He received him ungraciously and continued to create difficulties over money matters. Sensing that the pastor had a much better rapport with Brother Thomas, De La Salle stayed in the background.

On one occasion, when a discussion over finances was at a critical stage, De La Salle disappeared from the scene altogether. Always a devotee of Saint Teresa of Avila, he went to make a prolonged retreat at the nearby monastery of the discalced Carmelites. No one knew where he was, least of all De La Chétardie. Blain suggests that the pastor may have taken advantage of the Founder's absence to try to persuade Brother Thomas to take over as Superior under his protection. Fortunately, that good Brother had an unswerving loyalty to De La Salle. None was more relieved than he when the Founder reappeared to free him from the embarrassing situation in which he had been placed.

One day during the winter of 1706–1707 De La Salle was returning from the schools in Saint Sulpice to Saint Roch on the other side of the Seine, where he usually stayed when he was in Paris. He had just left the Brothers on the Rue du Bac, crossed the Pont Royal, and was about to enter the path through the Tuileries gardens when he stumbled and fell. His knee, which had already been cut open to drain an inflamed swelling, was pierced through by a concealed spike in the gateway. He fainted on the spot. The bystanders at first thought he was drunk, but when they realized his condition they half carried him across to the Rue Saint Honoré. Barely able to knock on the door, he fainted again in the arms of the Brother who opened it.

It was during his convalescence at Saint Honoré that De La Salle was visited for the first time by a young layman named Jean-Charles Clément. As we shall see in a later chapter, this encounter would eventually have far-reaching and dire consequences for De La Salle and the Brothers.

Another problem that engaged the attention of De La Salle every time he came to Paris concerned the living conditions on the Rue Princesse. For some 20 years the Brothers had been living there in a facility that was never intended as a residence in the first place. There was no privacy: the front of the building opened directly on the street, there was no surrounding lawn or garden, the courtyard in the rear was exposed to the view of all the neighbors. Also, the living accommodations within were not adequate for the number of Brothers. For a long time it had been evident that they needed a suitable residence; it was equally obvious that it might be difficult to obtain the permission of the pastor for them to live elsewhere while teaching in his parish schools.

De La Salle wisely commissioned Brother Thomas to take full charge of the matter. It did not take him long to find a suitable property on the Rue de la Barouillère near the Sèvres gate. The house was large enough, the property isolated, and there was a garden. De La Salle went personally to look it over and was much pleased with it. Brother Thomas then approached the pastor for permission to lease it. After a favorable report from his assistant pastor, Father Languet de Gergy, whom he sent to investigate, De La Chétardie gave his consent. The Brothers now had a house of their own, apart from the building in which they taught class.

The Wise Administrator

These problems in Paris were not the only ones that occupied the Founder during the years from 1705 to 1708. Much as he loved the solitude and opportunities for extended periods of prayer that he found at Saint Yon, he had to deal with a multitude of administrative affairs connected with the rapid expansion of his Institute. It was during this time that the crucial negotiations with the charity board in Rouen were taking place. There were legal problems back in Reims as well, involving legacies of funds and properties in various places and the extension of the holdings adjacent to the house on the Rue Neuve. Then there were requests coming all the time to open up new foundations to the South and to the North. It is only recently that letters and documents have come to light that give us a glimpse of John Baptist de La Salle as a conscientious and efficient administrator.

Another time-consuming burden was the correspondence the Founder kept with all of the Brothers, widely scattered as they now were. All of them were required to write to him once a month giving an account of their conduct in the school and the community, their life of prayer, and their interior dispositions. Out of the thousands of letters he must have written over the years, a precious handful have survived. These are sufficient to give an insight into the personality of the Founder, especially his compassion and patience in dealing with the Brothers in their personal and professional difficulties.

Among the most interesting letters are those addressed to Gabriel Drolin living in Rome. In them De La Salle shares with his isolated disciple the major developments affecting the Institute — usually the "good news" first and very little of the "bad news," except perhaps the lack of money. He is sometimes encouraging to Drolin, sometimes impatient with his lack of progress in getting established in Rome, always promising to send help, and now and then enclosing whatever money he could spare.

New Foundations in the South: Dijon

Two Brothers were sent to Dijon in May 1705 at the request of Monsieur Claude Rigolet, a renowned magistrate of the city, a member of the city council, and royal secretary. He had a reputation for great piety as well, and was the brother-in-law of Father Languet de Gergy, the assistant pastor of Saint Sulpice in Paris. Through the generosity of the Rigolet family, and with the approval of the mayor and the city council, the Brothers were soon entrusted with schools in three sectors of the city.

Marseille

One of the results of the success of the Brothers' schools in Avignon was the first foundation in Marseille, a completely different and much more tumultuous city. The parishes surrounding the old port were filled with wandering ragamuffins with nothing to do but watch the coming and going of the ships. The sailors themselves could neither read nor write. Most of them had no religious training, some were Moslems, and a good number found it profitable to sign up with whatever band of pirates made the best offer. Faced with this situation, the municipal authorities had opened a school in the port district of Saint Laurent, but neither the young deacon who had been hired as schoolmaster nor the results with the pupils had been very satisfactory.

It so happened that two rich merchants from Marseille named Morelet and Jourdan were visiting Avignon in 1705. There they saw the Brothers' work first hand. On their return to Marseille they persuaded the authorities to extend an invitation to De La Salle to supply some Brothers to take over the school at Saint Laurent. Two were sent from Avignon for this purpose, and classes began on March 6, 1706. The success was instantaneous: more than 200 pupils presented themselves on the second day the school was opened. This encouraged the officials in Marseille to think of entrusting all four parish schools in the city to the Brothers, but specific action was delayed for some years. By that time the Founder himself was on the scene.

Mende

Avignon and Marseille are on a direct route along the Rhône River, south from Paris and Lyon. But there were other southern towns to the west that were also seeking the Brothers for their schools. Farthest west and most important of these was Mende, the capital of the Gévaudan, more than 140 miles from the Rhone valley. The countryside between is most beautiful but difficult of passage, even today, with roads ascending and descending through canyons and gorges, twisting and turning up steep mountains and across rough plateaus.

This whole area had been thoroughly infiltrated with Calvinist Huguenots during the seventeenth century and served as a hideout and center of resistance against the religious policies of the Catholic Louis XIV. To support the king in his attempt to eliminate the Protestant religion from Catholic France, bishops in this region were particularly anxious to obtain competent and orthodox teachers to counteract the Protestant influence and to give a thorough and effective indoctrination into the Roman Catholic faith.

In 1707 François-Placide de Piencourt had been Bishop of Mende for almost 30 years during the worst of the war and the bloodshed between the forces of the king and the Protestant resistance. After an agreement with the municipal authorities, by which he would provide the necessary funds from his personal fortune, he appealed to De La Salle for Brothers to train the new generation in the Catholic faith. De La Salle sent Brother Ponce, the tough disciplinarian of the Rue Princesse, and more recently the pioneer in Darnétal and Director-General in Rouen, to go personally to Mende to investigate.

Brother Ponce took over the first class in the school all by himself. On April 8, 1707, the bishop wrote to De La Salle to say how pleased he was with Brother Ponce and asked for "another Brother able to teach both writing and arithmetic." When Ponce fell sick after two weeks, De La Salle sent two Brothers to fill out the community. One of them was Brother Matthias, a good teacher but a rather unstable young man at the time. The ten letters of De La Salle to Brother Matthias that have survived give a marvelous insight into the personal relationship between De La Salle and his Brothers: the Brother impatient with the harsh superior, always asking for a change of assignment; the Founder counselling patience, asking that the Brother be reasonable, and chiding him for his sloppy penmanship.

Toward the end of the year 1707, Bishop Piencourt died, but not before leaving a legacy that would provide for the maintenance of three teachers in perpetuity, with specific instructions that preference be given to the Brothers of the Christian Schools. He was the only bishop in De La Salle's lifetime to provide in this way for the Brothers. But the small size of the Mende community, its distance from the principal centers of the Institute, and the constant changes in its personnel made this remote outpost a source of great concern to De La Salle.

Alès

A few months after the foundation in Mende, De La Salle received a request to take over a school in Alès, not quite half-way on the road from Avignon to Mende. In the heart of the mountainous Cévennes, Alès was one of the last strongholds of the Huguenots, staunch adherents of the French Calvinism that Blain describes as "the cruel hydra that Calvin had nurtured for the misfortune of his own country." It was hardly an ecumenical age.

The request came to De La Salle from Father Guillaume-Ignace de Mérez, the vicar-general of Alès, writing at the request of François-Maurice de Saulx, the first Bishop of Alès, recently created a diocese precisely to combat the residual Calvinism in the town. After recalling their time together at Saint Sulpice, in his letter of June 2, 1707, Father Mérez explained the reasons why the Bishop wanted the Brothers in Alès:

> We need them here, where it is difficult for us to find Catholic teachers to whom we can entrust the education of the young. We need two right now at Alès. The problem is to root out heresy in this area and to establish the Catholic religion. It is an important task, calling for excellent workers. We shall have their expenses paid by the town; thus, your Brothers will not need to ask anything from the children's parents. The salaries of the teachers have already been fixed by His Majesty; hence it will be nothing new. But we need to make these Huguenots understand where their true interest lies by showing them that these new teachers will train their children in good penmanship.

As at Mende, De La Salle seems to have been attracted by the opportunity to have the Brothers enlisted in the struggle against heresy. In 1708, a year after the school was opened, the bishop was so pleased with the Brothers that he wrote De La Salle asking for more. In his concern for orthodoxy the bishop would allow no other teachers in his diocese, and parents who refused to send their children to the schools were fined. In this situation, neither the parents nor the Brothers were quite so happy. The parents, most of them still convinced Calvinists, would get the children at home and refute all that the Brothers had taught in the religion classes. This made it difficult for the Brothers, who were used to a more strictly Catholic clientele.

Grenoble

Grenoble is situated in the heart of the French Alps, southeast of Lyon and not far from the Swiss border in the region known as the Dauphiné. Although the Huguenots had been strong there at one time, by 1707 the region was thoroughly Catholic. The negotiations for a Christian School in Grenoble had begun in Paris as early as 1705, under the initiative of two alumni of the Seminary of Saint Sulpice, subsequently canons of the collegiate church of Saint André in Grenoble, Fathers Yse de Saléon and Claude Canel. They were leaders of a movement to provide all kinds of social benefits for the poor of the city, including a suitable education for the children.

Arrangements were completed in 1707 for the Brothers to come to Grenoble, with the sponsors paying their travelling expenses. That had never happened before. But the death of the bishop apparently caused a delay. Finally in 1708 the Brothers arrived and were entrusted with the school in the parish of Saint Laurent. A house was provided for them where the Founder himself would one day come to live. It still stands today. Also in the future was another school that would be opened in the parish of Saint Hugh, but that would not be until 1715.

Saint Denis

It was during this period when De La Salle was directing the expansion of the Institute in the South from the center at Rouen, that negotiations were underway to open a school in Saint Denis. An extensive suburban town just to the north of Paris, Saint Denis is famous for its abbey church, one of the oldest examples of French gothic architecture, and it is there that the tombs of the French monarchs are to be found. The initiative for a Christian school at Saint Denis came from a Mlle Poignant. As early as 1705, she had declared her intention to provide the necessary funds to establish and endow the school.

De La Salle was reluctant at first to send only two Brothers to such an isolated outpost. Yet there were certain advantages. Saint Denis was far from the center of the troubles and outside the jurisdiction of the authorities in Paris. Besides, the generous disposition of Mlle Poignant gave promise that the enterprise might eventually involve a greater number of Brothers. Finally, persuaded by the prior of the monastery of Saint Denis, De La Salle agreed to send two Brothers, and the school opened in 1708.

Unfortunately, Mlle Poignant died shortly thereafter. As a result, the school was never able to expand. Other developments at Saint Denis, however, would soon be the occasion of a major crisis in the life of De La Salle and his Institute.

New Problems in Rouen

With the death of Archbishop Colbert of Rouen in December 1707, De La Salle and the Brothers lost a good friend and a source of support. The new archbishop was Claude-Maur d'Aubigné. He had been vicar-general to Bishop Godet des Marais in Chartres and so was well acquainted with the Brothers. But he had little interest in them and was even less kindly disposed to De La Salle personally. The appointment did not augur well for the future.

De La Salle was finding it increasingly difficult to administer his rapidly expanding Society from his remote northern outpost in Rouen. In 1708 he began to delegate some of his powers as Superior to help preserve the essential spirit of the Society as one community conducting schools "together and by association." Brother Ponce, a strong personality with wide experience, was put in charge of all the schools in the South, with the center at Avignon. On July 15, 1708, De La Salle commissioned Brother Joseph to visit the schools in Reims and the neighboring towns. Thus, in the Founder's lifetime, the structure of regions and districts headed by a Brother Visitor was already beginning to emerge.

Before the year 1708 came to an end, a combination of an early and severe winter, coupled with a series of military defeats suffered by the French army, brought about a devastating famine through all of France. This created the necessity for the Founder to shift the base of his operations back to Paris.

11

Famine, Fame, and Defamation (1709–1711)

Nothing could have made John Baptist de La Salle happier as he approached his 60th year than to settle down in the peace and solitude of Saint Yon, contributing to the formation of the novices, corresponding by mail with his widely scattered Brothers, and making arrangements for an orderly transition of the superiorship to a worthy successor. But it was not to be. In 1709, De La Salle had ten more years to live; serenity and security were to elude him to the bitter end. A whole new series of problems drew him increasingly from his rural retreat outside Rouen to the center of the action in Paris.

The Famine of 1709

The winter of 1708–1709 was the most severe anyone could remember. One cold wave after another effectively ruined the winter crops; what provisions had been stored were soon exhausted by the armies of Louis XIV engaged in the War of the Spanish Succession. Famine was everywhere: there were food riots in the streets, plundering and pillage were commonplace, the hospitals were filled to overflowing with the sick and undernourished, bread was expensive and of poor quality, meat and vegetables were not available anywhere.

The Brothers suffered terribly, as did everyone else. Used as the disciples of De La Salle were to meager rations, periodic fasts, and doing without comforts of any kind, they weathered the crisis better than most. But De La Salle had to make some emergency adjustments. To ease the plight of the teaching Brothers in Rouen, he moved the novices to the house on the Rue de Barouillère in Paris, where they were to remain for the next six years. Young men in desperate need of even a skimpy meal applied to enter the already overcrowded novitiate. No one who seemed in any way sincere was turned away, but not many could endure the austere regimen of the novitiate for very long. To those who complained that he was too lenient in accepting such candidates, De La Salle remonstrated that at least they had the benefit of a good spiritual retreat.

As always, De La Salle urged the Brothers to rely totally on divine Providence. And as always, Providence did not let them down. On more than one occasion, when the Brothers were reduced to their last few pennies, some unexpected benefactor would come to their aid. There were even some "miracle" stories. Brothers related how there were times when only a few crusts of bread would be served up at the main meal, not at all enough to go around. Thereupon the Founder would say the grace, pray over the meager rations, and somehow there would be enough for each to have his fill.

When it was all over, the Brothers had managed to survive. Some of the wealthier congregations went bankrupt, and most of them lost a large percentage of their membership to sickness and to death. Such was not the case with the Brothers. Blain quotes one of the priest friends of the Brothers:

> If you suffered hunger, at least it did not destroy you. Your community is the poorest in the realm, yet it survived the cruel years which, it would seem, should have put an end to it. You have neither property, capital, nor endowments, yet you survived a time when famine made itself felt, or at least was feared, in the wealthiest families. Many rich, well-endowed communities were ruined during those times or emerged from them laden with debts. But you, you are just as you were before. If you have nothing, at least you owe no one anything, and your numbers even increased during those doleful days.

The fact is that some half-dozen Brothers did develop serious cases of scurvy. The always dependable Doctor Helvétius came to the rescue. He put the sick Brothers in the charge of a skilled colleague, and paid out of his own pocket for all the medicines and treatments until they recovered.

The most serious case was that of the Director of Novices, Brother Barthélemy, whose scrofulous tumors seemed to resist all medication. The Brothers were all for dismissing him from the Institute and sending him home, on the pretext that the pastor at Douai was anxious to have him back as a lay teacher to replace his recently deceased father. The Founder was on the verge of agreeing, but after a whole night spent in prayer, he decided to allow the sick Brother to remain. In time, the tumors healed. It was this Brother Barthélemy who would one day succeed De La Salle as the Superior of the Institute.

Problems in Chartres

Famine or no famine, the year 1709 provided little respite from the problems De La Salle had to face in administering his relatively far-flung Institute. The Bishop of Chartres, Paul Godet des Marais, as we have seen, had a high personal regard for De La Salle, whom he knew from seminary days, and was more solicitous than most ecclesiastics of the time for the temporal needs of the Brothers. At the same time, Bishop Godet was the sort of man who wanted to get his money's worth in terms of control. He had already made an attempt to mitigate the austerity of the Brothers' Rule and to have them begin the elementary lessons with Latin rather than French. De La Salle had been successful in dissuading him on both counts.

Now, in the spring of 1709, the Brothers in Chartres were told that they would have to move from the house where they had been living for ten years and which had proven adaptable in every way to their needs and lifestyle. Bishop Godet planned to install them in a vacant priory he had recently acquired that was adjacent to the junior seminary. When De La Salle heard of it, he was totally opposed. As he wrote to Brother Hubert, the Director, on July 20, 1709, "It has neither courtyard nor garden," and there, he said, the Brothers would be "very uncomfortable." The need for a courtyard and a garden was a recurrent concern of the Founder in choosing a house for the Brothers. Much as he encouraged mortification and bodily austerity of all kinds, De La Salle always insisted on the therapeutic value of fresh air, especially since the Brothers were confined all day long in the fetid atmosphere of overcrowded classrooms.

Faced with this new intervention on the part of his friend, the bishop, De La Salle instructed Brother Hubert to begin a campaign of prayer involving the students and the Brothers. Special attention was to be given to devotions at the Lady Chapel in the great Chartres Cathedral. The rest was to be left to Providence. For his part, De La Salle planned to speak once more to Godet when next the bishop would come to Paris, sometime before the opening of the school year in October. As it happened, Godet des Marais died in September that year, 1709, and the proposed move never took place.

The new bishop was Charles-François de Mérinville, the nephew and auxiliary bishop to his predecessor, Paul Godet. Although the new bishop shared his uncle's appreciation for the Brothers, he saw no reason to continue to support them out of his personal funds. This new situation put the Brothers in desperate financial straits for a time, and at one point the numbers had to be reduced from seven to four. It was only because of the concern of a canon of the cathedral, Father Charles de Truchis, that they were able to survive at all.

There were other problems as well. Once the personal support of Bishop Godet was gone, the writing masters in Chartres raised the usual difficulties, claiming unfair competition because the Brothers were teaching writing gratuitously to those who could afford to pay. Eventually the guild won at least the passive compliance of the new bishop for a policy that would limit the schools of the Brothers only to the certified poor.

On one occasion, the financial problems of the community in Chartres came close to solution when the Brothers were left a legacy intended to support the Christian Schools. The will was contested and the Brothers lost the case. Without corporate legal status they had no right to inherit anything. It was suggested that it might be possible for the Brothers to apply for letters patent that would give them legal incorporation. But De La Salle was opposed. "I prefer that you yourselves be guided by Providence," he wrote. "You can get letters patent after my death if that is what you want." Eventually, that is what the Brothers did, but out of Saint Yon rather than Chartres.

Versailles and the Vincentians

The year following the great famine of 1709 saw a new wave of expansion as the fame of the Institute spread. One such venture was the school at Versailles in a town dominated by the newly built palace and the legendary court of Louis XIV. A Vincentian priest, Father Claude Huchon, had earlier opened two charity schools, one in the king's Deer Park, and the other in the local parish. Well aware of the Brothers' reputation, Father Huchon persuaded De La Salle to send two Brothers to take over the Deer Park school.

The older of the two served as the Director and was, in the words of Blain, "an excellent Brother and a first-rate teacher." Father Huchon had a high regard for him. Unfortunately, this Brother soon acquired a taste for the heady life of the town, made extensive contacts with the notables of the court, and gradually lost the spirit of his vocation.

On his first visit to the community, De La Salle saw what was happening. Recognizing the early stages of disenchantment with community life, the Founder decided that an immediate transfer was in order. The pastor, however, had become so taken in by the Brother's talent, and so dependent on him, that he would not hear of any change. De La Salle had to yield, and the Brother remained at his post.

Before long, De La Salle's intuition proved to be correct. Unable any longer to endure the constraints of the school and the community, the Brother one day put aside his religious habit and took off without saying a word to anyone. When the Brother failed to show up in the school, the pastor sent a holy old Vincentian after him. The priest caught up with the fugitive at the gates of the town, but all his spiritual insights and powers of persuasion were in vain. The pastor learned his lesson. From then on he never interfered again in the affairs of the Brothers.

Huchon's successor as pastor in Versailles was equally supportive of the Brothers. Soon two more Brothers were invited to take over the school in the town, and another was added to provide for the temporal needs of the community. From then on the schools at Versailles prospered, animated by the prototypical Lasallian community of at least five Brothers, one of whom was charged with temporal affairs and available as a replacement in the schools in case of emergency.

De La Salle always had a high regard for Saint Vincent De Paul and the Congregation of the Mission, commonly known as the Vincentians or the Lazarists. He often proposed them to his Brothers as models of religious observance and of devotion to the poor. In addition, it was through Father Divers, the Procurator of the Vincentians with the Holy See, that De La Salle often addressed his letters to Brother Gabriel Drolin in Rome.

It was just about the time of the Versailles incident, however, that the Vincentians in Rome were beginning to persuade Gabriel Drolin to replace the Brothers' habit with the clerical soutane and to accept the tonsure. In his letters to Drolin from 1709 to 1711, the Founder is adamant on both points, insisting that these priests no longer interfere with the internal affairs of the Brothers. He wrote to Drolin on August 24, 1711: "Do not heed what the Lazarist [Vincentian] Fathers may say. Those in Paris are acting in a way that could well result in the destruction of our Institute."

Les Vans

Les Vans is a small town in the diocese of Uzès, nestled in the cavernous Cévennes and deep in the heart of the Huguenot country. In the year 1708, Father Vincent du Roure, a priest zealous for orthodoxy, whose family had once owned property in Les Vans, was passing through Avignon. Impressed by what he saw of the Brothers' work there, he determined to disinherit his relatives and leave his modest fortune of 7,000 livres to endow a Brothers' school at Les Vans. He thought this would be the best way to help to counteract the Protestant influence. When Du Roure died in 1710, De La Salle accepted the inheritance and delegated Brother Ponce to make the final arrangements from the center at Avignon.

The school opened in the following October with Brother René as Director assisted by Brother Maximin. Since the annual revenue of 350 livres from the legacy was not enough to support the two Brothers, the municipal authorities agreed to provide an additional 130 livres to make up the difference. In addition they ordered new furniture for the school and lodged the Brothers in a house facing the square in front of the church. The house, which still stands, proved to be comfortable for the Brothers, but there was little privacy in the heart of a small town accustomed to neighborly relationships where whatever went on was the subject of continual gossip.

As in Alès, there was in Les Vans considerable resistance to the repressive policies of Louis XIV against the Huguenot Protestants. Inevitably, the Brothers became one of the targets of the resistance. On at least one occasion, the townspeople blockaded the house and hurled rocks at the windows in an attempt to drive the Brothers away. The police intervened and dispersed the mob.

Some of the biographers estimate the size of the crowd in the thousands. Since, however, there is no mention of the incident in the minutes of the town council, it seems that a legend of sorts may have grown up around it. It is true that the Bishop of Uzès threatened strong penalties against the leaders, but De La Salle, when he heard of it, urged the Brothers to trust only in Providence to vindicate their rights.

Moulins

In 1710 De La Salle sent two Brothers to take over the school at Moulins in the Bourbon country. The request came from Father Louis Aubrey, who for years had been devoting his considerable energy to the education of the poor. The older of the two Brothers, and the Director, was a man named Brother Philippe. He made such an impression that the vicar-general of the diocese, Father Languet de Gergy, brother of the assistant pastor of Saint Sulpice, asked him to give model lessons in the parish church for the benefit of the younger clergy and the catechists of the town. Although this was a departure from Institute policy, it did serve to enhance the reputation of the Brothers, which endured through the years as the school prospered and expanded. More than a century later, Brother Benilde Romançon, the first Brother after the Founder to be canonized, would teach in this school.

Boulogne-sur-Mer

The foundation in Boulogne, a seaport on the English Channel, was the last in which De La Salle would be personally involved. The Bishop of Boulogne, Pierre de Langle, was already familiar with the work of the Brothers in Calais, which was in his diocese. The suggestion to open a Christian School in Boulogne came once again from a Vincentian priest, the rector of the diocesan seminary, Father Bernard. He proposed the idea to a devout and celibate layman, Jacques Abot de La Cocherie, who had already devoted a considerable amount of his time and money to charitable works for the Church. De La Cocherie was able to obtain contributions from his influential friends and from the bishop himself. As soon as the necessary funds were raised, De La Salle was contacted. In 1710 he sent four Brothers to open the school.

The Brothers were well received by the bishop, who lodged them in the seminary until a house could be provided for them.

At first the school was located in what was known as the lower town, the commercial center near the port. After a few years, the bishop was so pleased with the results that he decided to open a second school in the upper town near the cathedral. For this purpose he obtained two more Brothers from De La Salle.

The house that had been rented for the Brothers proved to be too small for such a number and the distance between the two schools too great. Such was the enthusiasm of the townspeople for the Brothers and their work that the original founders decided to build for them a new residence between the two schools on a plot of land obtained by a grant from the king. The governor of the town himself drew up the plans.

Construction was started, but soon the money began to run out and the work slowed down. To move things along, the governor, the Marquis de Colembert, with connections in high places, managed to obtain the needed building materials and to have them transported to the site. He recruited volunteers to lend a hand with the work and soon the building was completed. De La Salle himself would one day be received with great honor and enthusiasm when he would have the occasion, some years later, to visit Boulogne en route to Calais.

The Teacher-training School at Saint Denis

The origins of this enterprise, which was to turn out so tragically for De La Salle, go back to December 1707 when the Founder was recuperating at Saint Honoré from the wound sustained when he fell near the Tuileries and his knee was pierced by a spike. The details of the history of the foundation at Saint Denis are narrated by the biographer Blain, who had before him an account, which has since been lost, written by De La Salle himself in order to clear his good name.

It all began innocently. De La Salle was visited in the house on the Rue Saint Honoré by a young layman named Jean-Charles Clément. Impressed by what he saw of the work of the Brothers at the Rue Princesse, Clément asked for some Brothers to help inaugurate a program that he had in mind to give training in useful trades to teenage boys. Money, he said, would be no problem: he had, in fact, already begun to gather some of the necessary materials.

Besides, his father was a well-known surgeon, and negotiations were then underway whereby he himself would receive as a benefice the revenues of the well-endowed Abbey of Saint Calais.

De La Salle replied that he could do nothing unless the project being proposed conformed to the nature and purpose of the Institute. He thereupon drafted a written statement for the young man's benefit, outlining the specific apostolic works to which the Institute was committed, and suggesting that he study it carefully.

Clément returned three days later, admitting that he was not really interested in the work of the Christian Schools as such. But he was much taken with the Founder's long-range plan to open once more a center to train schoolmasters for the country parishes. Such a project might even be expanded eventually to include his own plan for training teenage boys in manual skills. Clément was eager to start at once, expressing his willingness to use for the purpose a good part of the allowance he had from his father until such time as he would have an independent income of his own.

Although De La Salle was himself eager to reopen the training school for teachers, he decided that it would be wiser to proceed cautiously with this enthusiastic young man. The more Clément urged immediate action, the more De La Salle insisted on reflection and delay. In addition, there was the problem of a suitable site, since De La Salle was formally forbidden by the court order of February 5, 1706, from opening anything like a training school for teachers within the jurisdiction of the Châtelet of Paris.

As time went by, Clément became impatient with the delay. He decided to use his considerable influence to involve the archdiocesan authorities in the project and, in this way, to put pressure on De La Salle. In contacts initiated by Father Vivant, the archdiocesan *officialis,* De La Salle was assured that Cardinal Noailles would approve of the project provided that the training school would be located outside the city limits of Paris.

The first offer of a site came from the pastor at Villiers, a small village about ten miles from Paris, but Clément was not at all pleased with such a remote location. Then another and seemingly providential opportunity presented itself in Saint Denis where the Brothers had just opened a school. The sister of Mlle Poignant, who had founded the school, had a house in Saint Denis that she was ready to sell for 13,000 livres. The contract was signed on October 23, 1708.

Since Clément was not yet 25 years old, and still legally a minor, the house was purchased for him by the lawyer, Monsieur Louis Rogier. The down payment of 5,200 livres was supplied by De La Salle from a fund that he had set aside precisely for this purpose. Clément signed a receipt, which he entrusted to Rogier. In it he affirmed his intention to reimburse De La Salle and to pay the balance due so as to become the sole proprietor of the house.

The training school opened in 1709 with three candidates. Except for a brief period when it had to close because of the famine, it soon began to prosper. Cardinal Noailles took a positive interest in the program. Through the good offices of Madame de Maintenon, the Cardinal was able to obtain a royal decree of exemption from the obligation to quarter soldiers. The program itself followed that of the earlier centers in Reims and Saint Hippolyte. There is reference in the sources to instruction in plainchant and to the presence of the student teachers at church services dressed in cassock and surplice, as would be expected of them when they assumed their duties in the country parishes.

In 1710 Jean-Charles Clément came into possession of the revenues of the rich abbey of Saint Calais, probably when the previous holder of the benefice, Charles-François de Mérinville, succeeded his uncle, Paul Godet, as Bishop of Chartres. The sudden access to independent wealth and the title of Abbé, even though he was not in Holy Orders, seem to have turned the head of the ambitious young man. He made no attempt either to reimburse De La Salle for the money he had advanced, or to pay the balance due to Mlle Poignant. She, in turn, was trying to get the house back from Rogier, the titular owner, who had plans of his own to resell it to a prospective new buyer. Although he made no further effort to assume any of the debt, Clément insisted that he wanted the house for himself.

In the midst of these negotiations, Doctor Julien Clément, the young man's father, learned of the business. Accusing his son of being a light-headed simpleton, he declared that the entire arrangement should be judged invalid by reason of his son's legal incompetence as a minor.

De La Salle Visits the South

Such was the state of affairs in 1711 when De La Salle decided to undertake a project he had long envisioned of visiting the schools and communities that had been established over the previous eight years in the South of France. Little is known of the precise itinerary. Blain gives no details about the journey, except to say that De La Salle was received with joy by the Brothers wherever he went, and with great respect by the bishops in whose dioceses the Brothers were conducting schools.

It seems likely that De La Salle would have set out from Paris in February 1711, probably stopping at Dijon and Macon en route to the South. There is documentary evidence that he was at Avignon in July; in Grenoble, the account books for that year make reference to his visit to the community there, but no precise date is given. Blain's generalizations would suggest that De La Salle also visited the remote communities at Mende and Alès, either before or after the Avignon visit.

It is certain that he traveled as far south as Marseille. A letter, dated August 24, 1711, that De La Salle sent from Marseille to Gabriel Drolin in Rome, has survived. In it the Founder says that he is about to "return to France," that is to Paris, as if he had been in a foreign land. No doubt, the deepening crisis of the Clément affair demanded a hasty return to the capital.

The Clément Vendetta

In 1711 the Clément family was granted noble status by King Louis XIV. This, together with the recent accession of the young abbé to the benefice of Saint Calais, may have prompted the family to want to sever any connection with a priest as socially and legally out of favor as was De La Salle. Their ploy was to depict their young son as the dupe and victim of the wily innovator from Reims. This time, as Blain points out, it was not De La Salle's possessions or even his schools, but his very honor that was at stake.

On his return from the South De La Salle found the cards stacked against him. All attempts to make a reasonable settlement with the Clément family were in vain. De La Salle offered to withdraw from the entire enterprise without compensation for his investment in it. He was willing to swear on his honor that he had not acted in any malicious way in his dealings with the young zealot. But the elder Clément would have none of it. He would be satisfied with nothing less than the vindication of his son through a public and juridical condemnation of De La Salle.

On January 23, 1712, De La Salle was cited to appear in court to answer to charges of suborning a minor for the purpose of extorting money from him. To defend his honor, De La Salle prepared a dossier containing 13 letters that Clément had written to him, the signed receipt for the 5,200 livres, and a long memoir detailing the history of the foundation at Saint Denis. When Rogier came to tell him that the case was lost, the house was to be confiscated, and that a warrant was out for his arrest, De La Salle, unwilling to appear personally in court, put the dossier in the hands of his lawyers and left Paris to resume his tour of the schools in the South.

According to Blain, De La Salle's lawyers allowed the dossier to fall into the hands of those who were prosecuting the case. Even so, the judge in the case considered any defense irrelevant in the face of the undeniable fact that Clément was a minor. The Clément family had powerful friends in high places. De La Salle, by contrast, had none. In view of his long history of conflicts with Cardinal Noailles and Father De La Chétardie, he could hardly expect help from that quarter. He was on shaky legal grounds, besides, for trying to circumvent the court order forbidding him to engage in the training of teachers.

The condemnation came on May 31, 1712. In it the Châtelet formally annulled all the documents signed by the Abbé Clément. De La Salle was obliged to cancel the debt of 5,200 livres and to reimburse Clément for the 3,200 livres he had spent for the maintenance of the student teachers. By way of a criminal judgment, De La Salle was warned never again to enter into business negotiations with minors and to refrain for the future from trying to extort promises of money from such persons.

As soon as he realized that the case was hopeless, the lawyer Rogier dissociated himself from De La Salle to salvage what he could for himself. He put forth his claim as the titular owner of the house in Saint Denis. On June 15, the court assigned to him the 5,200 livres and title to the house on condition that the balance due to Mlle Poignant be paid or the house be sold. The Brothers had to vacate the house, and in this way the teacher-training program came to an end.

It may be that Rogier acted with the intention of repaying the 5,200 livres to De La Salle, but he never did so in his lifetime. It was only after Rogier's death that De La Salle learned that an equivalent sum had been left to him as legacy. In his will, Rogier specified that this bequest was intended as a matter of conscience.

Meanwhile, De La Salle was far away in the South and unaware of the distressing final scenes in this dismal drama. Betrayed by those whom he had every right to trust, in this matter as in all else he was willing to leave the outcome and the final judgment in the hands of Providence.

12

Seclusion in the South
(1712–1714)

Without waiting for the final judgment in the Clément affair, toward the end of February 1712 De La Salle had abruptly left Paris and headed once more for the foundations in the South. This second journey was to be rather prolonged — it lasted more than two years — and during most of this time the Brothers in Paris did not know where he was. This has raised many questions about the Founder's motives in leaving the Brothers in the North to their own devices at such a critical moment and for such an extended period of time.

There was no need for De La Salle to wait in Paris for the judgment in the Clément trial: it was a foregone conclusion. Without support or defense, betrayed by his own lawyers, already deprived of the right to teach and to train teachers, De La Salle knew well what the verdict would be. The failure of the pastors of Saint Sulpice and Saint Denis to come to his rescue was further evidence that some ecclesiastics in Paris wanted to bring the Society of the Brothers under clerical control. De La Salle himself may have begun to wonder whether his continued presence in the capital was doing more harm than good in the struggle to preserve intact the special character of his Institute.

According to Blain, the Founder's greatest suffering at the moment was caused by the impression he had, which later proved unfounded, that the majority of the Brothers in Paris were beginning to side with those who wanted to impose another form of government on the Society. This suspicion was strengthened when Brother Barthélemy thoughtlessly forwarded to him the court summons in which De La Salle was addressed as the "superior of the Brothers in Reims," not Paris. As Blain puts it: "With a feeling of abandonment by his Brothers, conscious of the silence of Jesus before his accusers, but also blaming no one but himself and thinking only of the good of the Institute, De La Salle left Paris for the South of France at the beginning of Lent in 1712."

Avignon

Toward the end of Lent, De La Salle had arrived in Avignon, where he remained for about a month. He devoted all his time to the Brothers, who received him graciously. His main concern was to encourage them in their vocation and in fidelity to their religious duties. On one occasion he took over the primary class as a replacement for a sick Brother. Each day he said Mass in the church of the Augustinians, only the tower of which still stands today.

There were opportunities to meet with Monsieur Château-Blanc, who had been instrumental in bringing the Brothers to Avignon, as well as with the clergy and the notables of the papal city. The Brothers had been so successful in their schools, founded almost a decade earlier, that De La Salle was well received everywhere in the city. Avignon always had a special meaning for the Founder. Not only was it the channel for communication with Rome, but it fostered in him the hope that he might himself some day make the journey to the eternal city. In his history of the Institute, Rigault remarks that the Founder left a piece of his heart in this papal city, which would one day become the center of the Institute in the South of France.

A Difficult and Dangerous Tour of the South

Once he had sufficiently recovered his spiritual and physical forces, and much encouraged by the friendly reception accorded him by the Brothers and the people of Avignon, De La Salle determined to resume the tour of the southern communities that had been interrupted the year before. The Brothers tried to dissuade him by pointing out the perils of such a journey. The terrain to the west was rugged: the steep mountains of the Cévennes were surrounded by high tableland and cut by deep canyons with overhanging cliffs that one had to descend and ascend continually — a journey that still today is difficult over paved roads that did not then exist — to say nothing of undertaking it on foot or even on horseback.

More dangerous still were the roving bands of Camisards, so called for the special shirts they wore identifying them as members of a militant Huguenot force of armed resistance. The route offered endless opportunities for ambush. Travelling priests were a special target for robbery, violence, and sometimes execution.

The first stop was the community at Alès, where Bishop De Saulx, happy at the progress Catholicism was making in his diocese, received the Founder most graciously and attributed the success in large measure to the work of the Brothers in the schools. To express his gratitude, the bishop had just recently provided a new and more comfortable house for the Brothers.

From Alès, De La Salle set out for Les Vans, some 30 miles to the north and deeper into the country of the Camisards. En route he stopped at Gravières, where he stayed at the house of the pastor, Father Pierre Meynier, who was in charge of the legacy left by Father Du Roure, the recently deceased founder of the school at Les Vans. At the time of De La Salle's visit, Father Meynier was the spiritual director for the Brothers in Les Vans. The pastor received the Founder with unusual signs of veneration and respect, for example, reserving for himself the honor of serving the Founder's Mass. This sort of treatment embarrassed De La Salle and, if anything, only served to shorten his visits and make them less frequent.

The stone church at Gravières still stands in the shadows of a high cliff of the Cévennes. In the sacristy there hangs a portrait of De La Salle, discovered in a granary in Les Vans in 1882. The portrait depicts a distinguished-looking person with a serene countenance and wearing secular clothes. When the church acquired the portrait, the pastor at the time, Father Canaud, had it cleaned only to discover at the bottom a legend identifying the subject as John Baptist de La Salle.

The fact that De La Salle was portrayed in secular clothes gave rise to two theories, repeated until recently by the modern biographers, but since proven to be without foundation. At first it was thought that the portrait was evidence that De La Salle travelled through the Cévennes and the Gévaudan disguised as a layman so as to avoid the Camisards. More recently, however, infrared photos reveal that the secular dress was in fact painted over at a later date; underneath, the Founder is visible in soutane and rabat. The other theory was that the portrait was one supposedly painted clandestinely by a retired soldier of the neighborhood during De La Salle's visit to the house of Monsieur Jauffret in Les Vans. However, studies have since shown that the portrait is not contemporary with the Founder but was made somewhat later. Subsequently, perhaps at the time of the French Revolution or even later still, it was apparently used as a base for a fresh portrait of some distinguished gentleman of the region.

The road westward toward Mende, the capital of the Gévaudan, was the longest — about 100 miles — the most difficult and perilous of all. Miraculously, De La Salle arrived safely at Mende, where Brother Timothée had replaced Brother Antoine, one of the founding Brothers in 1694, as Director. This Brother Timothée would prove to be a loyal supporter of the Founder in the difficult times ahead, and would himself one day become the second Superior General of the Institute. There was a new bishop at Mende as well, Bishop Baglion de La Salle, but no relation to the Founder.

The reception at Mende was so cordial, as it was everywhere on this tour of the cities where the schools were flourishing, that De La Salle felt it necessary to shorten his stay and to depart in semisecrecy lest he have more honors and accolades thrust upon him.

En route back eastward to Marseille, the Founder stopped briefly at Uzès to greet Bishop Michel Poncet de La Rivière, in whose diocese was the school at Les Vans. The bishop expressed his pleasure at the success of the Les Vans school. The bishop then asked that the Brothers there be given permanent assignments so as to assure the continued progress of the school. To this the Founder could not agree. When he explained his reasons in the light of the nature and purpose of the Institute, the bishop did not insist.

This sense of possessiveness on the part of sponsoring ecclesiastical authorities, a problem in Reims and Paris from the beginning, remained a continuing source of misunderstanding in many of the Lasallian foundations in the provinces. Not all bishops and pastors would be as obliging in the matter as Bishop De La Rivière. More than likely, even he found it difficult to understand how a Society of lay Brothers, without canonical or legal status, could demand such autonomy or even hope to survive in the church structure of the time. De La Salle, however, had always realized that his Institute could achieve its mission effectively only on condition that the association of the Brothers be independent of diocesan or parish control.

Reception in Marseille

Arriving in Marseille in late June or early July of 1712, De La Salle was as cordially received by Bishop Henri-François-Xavier Belsunce as he had been on his previous visit a year earlier. The Brothers' school in the parish of Saint Laurent had been functioning well from the time of its foundation in 1706. Now plans were under way to have the Brothers take over the schools in the parishes of Saint Martin and Notre Dame des Accoules.

Ever since he took possession of the see in 1709, Bishop Belsunce had been negotiating with De La Salle to open a novitiate of the Brothers in his diocese. If the Brothers were to be put in charge of the schools in the four quarters of the city—the "old city," as it is now called, surrounding the horseshoe-shaped harbor—it would be necessary to have a suitable number of Brothers recruited from the Marseille area. The language, culture, and lifestyle in Provence were so different from those in the North that it would be unrealistic to expect teachers from Reims, Rouen, or Paris to be effective in such a strange environment. It is not surprising then that the influential townspeople were generous in their support of the new novitiate project. When it opened in August or September of 1712 many candidates presented themselves for admission to the Society.

In a letter dated July 1712 and addressed to Brother Gabriel Drolin in Rome, De La Salle refers to the plans for the novitiate and his hopes to be able to send a Brother from the novitiate to join the lonely exile in Rome. Early that fall, De La Salle himself was preparing to leave for Rome when, in the act of saying good-bye to Bishop Belsunce, he was persuaded to stay to arrange for the opening of the school in the Accoules. That evening he returned to the Brothers' community where they had wished him a "bon voyage" only hours before. He is reported to have greeted them with the words: "God be blessed! Here I am back from Rome"—a rare bit of evidence that De La Salle had a sense of humor.

A Change in Attitude at Marseille

This atmosphere of support, of expansion, of great plans for the future, was suddenly dissipated as the mood of the clergy and the people of Marseille began to change. The school in the Accoules was never opened. The school proposed for the Brothers in the parish of Saint Martin was put in charge of a young seminarian. Financial support for the novitiate dried up and postulants no longer presented themselves. A wholly new attitude toward De La Salle had developed in the few months between September 1712 and March 1713. What had happened?

The traditional interpretation put forth by both the early and the modern biographers has been to blame the Jansenist party for instigating a whispering campaign against De La Salle because of his loyalty to the papal doctrine. More recent critical studies find this explanation too oversimplified. For one thing, the publication in France of the Bull *Unigenitus* condemning Jansenism was still a year away. The issue of Jansenism, although certainly in the air, was not that acute in the Marseille of 1712 and the early months of 1713. Additional reasons are needed to explain the sudden change in attitude.

Part of the explanation may lie in the expectation of the prominent townspeople of Marseille. They may have been willing to support a novitiate to supply native teachers for their own schools in their own city. When they heard that De La Salle was considering assigning some of the Marseille novices elsewhere, they began to withdraw their support. Once again, the issue was control as the price to be paid for patronage.

There were policy differences as well. The school board at Marseille was much under the influence of the catechetical center in Lyon, where the system, inherited from Charles Démia, favored the use of seminarians as the preferred catechists in the schools for the poor. Some seminarians had been so engaged in Marseille before the Brothers arrived there; it is altogether likely that these young ecclesiastics would have supported any movement to discredit the Brothers who had replaced them. There was, in fact, a legal technicality involved. Many of the legacies and foundations that provided the funds to support the Brothers and their novitiate stipulated that the monies be used to engage "ecclesiastics" for teaching the poor. When De La Salle refused to have the Brothers take the tonsure to cover this technicality, he was accused of obstinacy.

Little by little, the pastors of Saint Martin and the Accoules began to side with those who preferred the Lyon-Démia model that employed candidates for the priesthood as the ideal teachers for the parish schools. Although Bishop Belsunce made clear his personal preference for the Brothers, he had no legal control over the money that was made available for their support.

These policy differences might not have loomed so large if another more painful and embarrassing human factor had not entered the picture. It involved the two Brothers who had been conducting the school in the parish of Saint Laurent for six years before the Founder arrived in Marseille. During that time they had become accustomed to a great deal of independence and freedom. Many of the obligations of the Brothers' Common Rule and the practices of community life were impossible to maintain with only two together: such things as the accusation of faults, advertisement of defects, community recreation, reading at meals, and the like. In addition, these Brothers had developed a strong following among the people of the parish.

When De La Salle insisted that they join the novitiate community and resume the regular routine of community life, they objected strenuously. They complained to the people of the parish that they were being taken away from the center of parish life, forced twice daily to walk the long distance between the school and the novitiate, and thus less at the disposal of the parish that supported them. The parishioners sided with the two Brothers and made their representations to De La Salle. The Founder refused to yield, citing the central importance of community life in the vocation of the Brothers. Again, he was accused of intransigence.

When news of the dispute reached Avignon, even the nominal superior of the Brothers of the Region, Brother Ponce, who ought to have been more loyal, sided with the disgruntled Brothers. The Brothers were said to have challenged the Founder openly, saying in effect: "Everything here was going along fine until you came along. Why do you come here to destroy the whole enterprise instead of helping to make it grow?"

The Decision to Withdraw

In the face of all the opposition, De La Salle began to blame himself. Maillefer quotes him as saying: "I was convinced that my absence would calm my enemies and inspire them to think positively about my spiritual children." Taking the pilgrim's staff, he quietly left Marseille and climbed the steep 30 miles or so leading to the Sainte

Baume, the sacred grotto halfway up a vertical cliff where Mary Magdalen is said to have spent the last years of her life in repentance. Popes, kings, and saints had made the pilgrimage before De La Salle, and many of the great and not-so-great have done so since.

It was either there, in the hostel adjoining the grotto, or, more likely, in the monastery of Saint Maximin on the plateau beneath, that De La Salle experienced what the biographers have called "the dark night of the soul." Blain describes this as a time when the Founder saw himself at the crossroads, full of doubts as to which way to turn, seeking to find the will of God in solitude and prayer.

The withdrawal of De La Salle from the scene of controversy gave some credence to the rumors that began to circulate in Marseille that the Founder was about to abandon the Brothers and leave the Institute to the designs of Providence and its own fate. Even Blain admits that there was an element of truth in this: the Founder, he says, had indeed been thinking from time to time that he might someday retire to a remote parish and there work for the conversion of hardened sinners. But, as Blain hastens to add, these musings never came to anything in practice. It may well be, however, that the rumors that De La Salle was about to retire permanently only strengthened the resolve of the many Brothers who wanted to keep him at the head of the Institute he had founded.

Trouble at Mende

Whatever the state of the Founder's mind at the time, or however resolved or unresolved his doubts may have been after the weeks of retreat, De La Salle left the Sainte Baume, probably in June 1713, and headed for Mende, far to the west, where the community appeared to be in deep trouble. The sources are sometimes obscure and sometimes conflicting on the details of the situation, but there is a certain consistency in the accounts.

The villain of the piece seems to have been a certain Brother Médard. After being transferred from Calais to Marseille in 1708 and from there to Grenoble, he decided to leave the Institute. Welcomed back by De La Salle at Marseille in 1712, he again took the habit in the novitiate there and, quite possibly, became identified with the malcontents. Sent by Brother Ponce from Marseille to the school at Mende, he soon resumed his errant ways. He gradually won over his companion, Brother Isidore, to an easy lifestyle and the cultivation of extensive social contacts with the notables of the town. The errant Brothers resisted all attempts of the Director, Brother Henri, to bring them to order. To make matters worse, Brother Ponce, who as regional superior should have dealt with the situation, was on his way back to Rouen, where he soon left the Institute.

When news reached Mende that De La Salle was on his way, Brothers Médard and Isidore hurried to the bishop and the mayor to get their support for maintaining the status quo. Thus, when the Founder arrived on the scene, he was utterly frustrated in trying to deal effectively with the problem. He did not want to alienate the new bishop, Pierre Baglin de La Salle, by insisting on the Institute policy of assigning Brothers where they could do the most good. The bishop and the mayor, for their part, pointed out with some reason that in the six years since the school had been opened far too many Brothers had been transferred elsewhere or had left the Institute.

It was a further blow to the Founder to be told point blank that he could not be accommodated in the Brothers' house and that the community did not have the resources to provide his meals. Forced to seek hospitality with the Capuchins for a time, De La Salle was then invited to stay at the house of Mlle Lescure, Foundress of the Ladies of the Christian Union, a new congregation similar in many respects to that of the Brothers. De La Salle was happy to assist her in composing a Rule for these Sisters. Otherwise, during the two months that he stayed in Mende, De La Salle devoted himself to solitude and prayer, apart from the Brothers, and still undetermined about what it was God wanted of him.

During this time, Brother Timothée came from Marseille to Mende looking for his Superior. Turned away from the community of the Brothers as the Founder had been, he found De La Salle at the Lescure house. He brought the news that the Marseille novitiate, where he had been Director, was now completely empty of novices, and he asked for a new assignment for himself. Blain quotes the Founder's response: "Why do you come to me with all of this? Don't you know that I am not competent to give orders to others? Are you not aware that there are many Brothers who no longer want to have anything to do with me? They say they no longer want me as their Superior. And they are right. I am really incapable of that any more." There is good reason to accept the authenticity of the account and the substance of the quotation, since Blain was writing under the direction of the same Brother Timothée, who had by that time become Superior General.

Maillefer's version of this incident is even more forceful. He situates it in the context of the Founder's stay at Saint Maximin near the Sainte Baume rather than at Mende. In this version, the Founder says to Brother Timothée (who is not named but identified simply as the "superior of the novitiate at Marseille") that "he was surprised" that the Brothers were still thinking about him; that "he had hoped by leaving Marseille and retiring into solitude that people would soon get used to forgetting about him altogether;" that he found his hideaway so much to his liking that "he was resolved to stay hidden there and to condemn himself to perpetual silence."

Whether the interview with Timothée took place at Saint Maximin or Mende, the latter being the more likely since Blain was close to the source, it would seem that the Founder's sense of abandonment and betrayal carried from the one place to the other. The cool reception from the Brothers at Mende would have done nothing to dispel it. Mlle Lescure meanwhile was trying to induce De La Salle to settle permanently in Mende, promising to provide him with room and board for life and, after his death, to subsidize another Brother for the school.

Brother Timothée's visit came at a providential time. According to Blain, it took all of Timothée's powers of persuasion to convince De La Salle that the Brothers still needed him and wanted him to continue at the head of the Society. So encouraged, De La Salle refused the tempting offer of Mlle Lescure, yet he was still not entirely certain about what he eventually ought to do. When it came time for him to leave Mende, Mlle Lescure, though somewhat disappointed, graciously provided a horse for his long journey back to Avignon and Grenoble.

An Extended Stay in Grenoble

Arriving finally at Grenoble, sometime in August 1713, De La Salle was well received by the Brothers teaching there in the school of Saint Laurent. The house still stands at 40, Rue Saint Laurent in Grenoble, with an identifying plaque over the doorway. It is still possible to enter the inner courtyard and ascend the granite stairway leading to the upper floors. An even narrower stairway leads up to an isolated cubicle in the recess of the tower. This was the place that De La Salle selected to remain in solitude and in prayer and to work on the revision of his writings, especially the *Duties of a Christian,* which he soon had ready to send to the papal legate at Avignon for approval.

Maillefer again emphasizes the desire of the Founder to continue to remain aloof, but this time within the community of the Brothers. Thus he says:

> He withdrew to Grenoble where he found the Brothers very much at peace. He resolved to stay with them as long as he could. He chose the most remote and least accessible room in the house where he could devote himself to mental prayer. He remained there for several months, unknown and practically forgotten. He made no visits, received no visitors, and left his room only to be present at the appointed time for the usual exercises of the community.

This description conveys in a general way the attitude and the lifestyle adopted by the Founder during the months he spent in Grenoble.

Aware that he was only a short distance away from the monastery of the Grande Chartreuse, De La Salle decided to go to make a retreat there, probably during the school vacation period in September 1713. The Carthusians were important for De La Salle, not only for their austere life of solitude, but also because Saint Bruno, their Founder, had been like himself a canon of the cathedral chapter of Reims. Taking another Brother with him as a companion, De La Salle expressly forbade him to reveal their identity. The two pilgrims were graciously received by the monks, who were so impressed by this humble and self-effacing priest that they begged him to stay on indefinitely. The biographers seem to imply that De La Salle would have preferred to stay longer if his characteristic piety had not revealed his identity. Whether he was weighing the Chartreuse as a place to retire to definitively cannot be known for sure, but it remains a possibility.

There are indications, however, that he was actively seeking to keep in touch with what he had already undertaken and, at the same time, keep open the options for the future. Shortly after the opening of school late in September 1713, De La Salle became disturbed at the news that filtered through about the trouble that was brewing among the Brothers in the North. He sent Brother Jacques, the Director of the Grenoble school, to investigate. This Brother was a good man, dependable and discreet. During the Director's absence, De La Salle himself took over the classes in the school. During this time he also led the school children to the nearby church of Saint Laurent, where he celebrated Mass for them. For years the townspeople of Grenoble preserved the memory of the fervor with which he celebrated the Eucharistic liturgy.

What contacts there were with Paris, especially with Brother Barthélemy, who was nominally in charge, or what report was given by Brother Jacques on his return, remains uncertain through lack of evidence. But for the most part, as the sources seem to agree, the Founder remained isolated during the long winter of 1713 to 1714, devoting his time to prayer and to revising his written works for the schools and the Brothers.

Eventually the long hours of work and prayer in the drafty old "hole in the wall" at the top of the tower took their toll. In February 1714, De La Salle began to experience anew attacks of rheumatism so acute and so painful that it was thought he might die. At this news, the whole city of Grenoble became concerned about his recovery. Prayers were offered everywhere as if for an important matter of public interest, led especially by his two friends, Fathers Yse de Saléon and Claude Canel, the two canons of the church of Saint André who had been instrumental in bringing the Brothers to Grenoble. Once again De La Salle endured the remedy that had been used before in Paris whereby he was stretched over a grill beneath which were medicinal herbs steaming over burning coals. Torture though it was, the remedy was effective, and the Founder gradually began to recover.

Parménie and Sister Louise

As soon as he felt that he was regaining his strength, De La Salle began to think about making another spiritual retreat. His friend, Yse de Saléon, suggested that he might profit by an extended stay at Parménie, a hermitage that served as a retreat center atop a high hill not far from Grenoble. The hermitage had recently been rebuilt on the ruins of a medieval monastery through the efforts of a devout and determined visionary who was known as Sister Louise. She lived on the premises, and her advice was much sought after by reason of her exemplary prayerfulness and the clarity of her spiritual vision. Father De Saléon came there regularly as part-time chaplain and spiritual director.

De La Salle accepted the invitation eagerly. Even though it was still toward the end of the winter season, the stay at Parménie proved beneficial to his health. The early biographers of De La Salle speak of an initial sojourn at Parménie for a retreat that lasted 15 days, during which the Founder had extensive interviews with Sister Louise. There is reference also to subsequent exchanges, including even an exchange of letters or books, a strange arrangement since Sister Louise could neither read nor write.

The biographers of Sister Louise and the historians of Parménie, however, suggest that De La Salle either remained at or returned to Parménie, where he spent considerable time during the spring of 1714, even that he was seriously considering retiring there permanently. Both Sister Louise and Canon De Saléon were hoping that he might take over as resident spiritual director for the hermitage. When De Saléon had to leave for Provence on church business, he left De La Salle in charge of the retreats at Parménie for a period of at least a month.

While De La Salle was at Parménie, a young pilgrim arrived dressed in peasant clothes. He turned out to be a man of aristocratic origin and gentlemanly upbringing, the son of Claude-Lancelot Dulac de Montisambert, Claude-François Dulac by name. His earliest youth had been spent in the army, where he fell prey to a gambling habit and other excesses. Seriously wounded in the battle of Malplaquet in 1709, the young officer had time to reflect on the error of his ways. For the past two years, he had been travelling from one monastery to another seeking peace for his soul. After long conversations at Parménie to test the young man's virtue and determination, De La Salle brought him to the community at Grenoble where he gave him the religious habit and the name Brother Irenée. The date in the community register is June 6, 1714.

The Command to Return

Meanwhile, an event of the greatest significance had taken place. All during the time De La Salle was in the South the affairs of the

Parménie

Institute in Paris were going from bad to worse. Brother Barthélemy, whose mandate to act for the Superior was never entirely clear in the first place, had been less than forceful in resisting the efforts of the Sulpician pastors to control the internal affairs of the Society. There was no place for the Brothers to turn for guidance in even the simplest administrative matters. In desperation, the Directors and the principal Brothers of the Paris region drew up a joint letter in which they addressed De La Salle and ordered him to return in virtue of the vow he had made to obey the body of the Society. The text follows:

> Monsieur, our very dear Father: We, the principal Brothers of the Christian Schools, having in view the greater glory of God as well as the good of the Church and of our Society, consider that it is of the greatest importance that you return to the care and general direction of God's holy work, which is also your own, because it has pleased the Lord to make use of you to establish it and to guide it for so many years.
>
> We are all convinced that God himself has called you to this work and that he has given you the grace and talents necessary for the good government of this new Society so beneficial to the Church. We acknowledge in all justice that

you have always guided it with considerable success and edification. That is why, Monsieur, we very humbly beseech you, and we command you in the name and on the part of the body of the Society to which you have vowed obedience, to take up at once the general government of the Society.

The letter, dated April 1, 1714, was signed by all the Brothers present, and De La Salle could recognize the signatures of his sons. There was no longer any reason to hesitate or to consider other options for the future. When he explained the contents of the letter to Sister Louise, she pointed out that it was clearly God's will that he should not abandon the family God had given him, that he himself should now give an example of the obedience he had so often preached to others.

De La Salle did not return to Paris at once, however, since he had first to await the return of Yse de Saléon. The examination and reception of Claude Dulac may have caused further delay. There is some evidence, too, that he may have made one last tour of the communities in the South before heading for the capital, stopping en route at Lyon and Dijon. He arrived in Paris on August 10, 1714, greeting the Brothers with the words: "Well, here I am. What do you want of me?"

13

Return and Retirement
(1714–1718)

When John Baptist de La Salle reappeared at the house on the Rue de Barouillère in Paris in August 1714, he found the Brothers fully expecting that he would immediately begin to function again as Superior of the very troubled Society. Surprisingly, he did no such thing. He let it be known almost at once that he had no intention of assuming an active role in directing the day-to-day affairs of the Brothers. He was content to resume his sacramental ministry for them, give advice where it was needed and asked for, but otherwise to leave the details to Brother Barthélemy to work them out as best he could with the help of the senior Brothers. The presence of the Founder seemed itself to be enough to restore a semblance of stability and order where before there had been confusion and chaos.

A Backlog of Problems in Paris

During the two-year period that De La Salle was secluded in the South and out of contact with the center of the Institute, the situation of the Brothers, in Paris particularly, had degenerated to the point where the structure of the Society was threatened from within and from without. Although Brother Barthélemy had been appointed Director of Novices before De La Salle's sudden departure in 1712, it was only gradually and by default that he became more or less recognized as the lawful Superior to act in the place of De La Salle. Even then, several Brothers used this ambiguity as an excuse to go their independent way as Brothers, or to begin to look for a more stable situation outside the Institute.

Under these conditions, Brother Barthélemy could hardly be blamed if he was less than forceful in dealing with the pastor of Saint Sulpice, Father De La Chétardie, and his deputy, the nominal ecclesiastical superior appointed by the archdiocese, Father De Brou. Although not a Sulpician himself, De Brou worked closely with De

La Chétardie to help further the plans to bring the Brothers increasingly under clerical control.

One step at a time, and using pressure tactics that included withholding the Brothers' salaries (or restoring them insofar as the Brothers cooperated), these clerics had managed to get the Brothers to agree to a plan that would have totally destroyed the Society as the Founder had created it. They envisioned the separation of the Paris schools from the rest of the Institute and a federation of independent houses with Brothers assigned permanently to one house. The central novitiate was to be suppressed; novices would be recruited only as needed within each house.

Things got to the point where Brother Barthélemy was actually persuaded to arrange for the appointment of an ecclesiastical superior for each of the Brothers' communities. It was on this occasion that Canon Jean-Baptiste Blain became ecclesiastical superior of the Brothers in Rouen. Fortunately, most of those so appointed interpreted their role merely as intermediaries with the diocesan authorities. By and large they had the good sense to stay out of the way and not to interfere with the internal affairs of the communities or the schools.

By contrast, the more aggressive approach of men like De La Chétardie and De Brou constituted a genuine threat to the basic structure of the Lasallian foundation. De Brou went so far as to submit to the archdiocesan authorities for the approval of Cardinal Noailles a totally new set of rules for the Brothers, redesigning the Institute according to the ideas of De La Chétardie. Fortunately, the Brothers became aware of this maneuver and used what influence they had to counteract it. The vicar-general of the diocese, Father Vivant, wisely set the dossier aside and wrote to Father De Brou that it seemed best for the moment not to make any changes in the structure of the Society.

Meanwhile, all attempts to contact De La Salle in seclusion in the South proved to be in vain. No one in Paris knew for sure where he was. Most of the letters sent to him were never delivered; those that he did receive, he did not attempt to answer, whether by design or out of discouragement. It was this impasse that led the principal Brothers in Paris, in April 1714, to order the Founder to return in virtue of the vow he had made to obey the body of the Society.

While De La Salle was trying to decide how to respond to this command, the news arrived that Father de La Chétardie, the pastor of Saint Sulpice, had died on June 29, 1714. Commenting on this event, Blain remarks: "His great enemy no longer lived; God had called him while the servant of God was still at Grenoble. The news of the former's death which he had received there had hastened his return to Paris, for he would not have dared to come back if that man had still been alive. De La Salle himself stated this to some of the Brothers he trusted."

The Situation at Mende

One concrete example of the ambiguity that prevailed during the absence of the Founder was the degenerating situation of the community at Mende. It may be recalled that during his last visit to Mende De La Salle was thwarted in his attempt to transfer the two malcontents, Brothers Médard and Isidore. They had so won over both the mayor and the bishop that neither De La Salle nor the Director, Brother Henri, could effectively challenge them in any way. Within a short time, however, Brother Médard left Mende without authorization to go to Avignon, but he died en route in the community at Alès. Brother Isidore went off to Paris, where he reported to Brother Barthélemy his version of the events, with special emphasis on his complaints against Brother Henri, the Director. Brother Barthélemy evidently believed him. Meanwhile Brother Henri was left alone in Mende.

In this crisis, Father Martineau, the pastor at Mende, passing over Brother Barthélemy altogether, wrote instead to Father De Brou at Saint Sulpice to get replacements for the Brothers who had abandoned the school. Fortunately, by this time De La Salle had returned to Paris and was able personally to deal with the situation. Two more Brothers were sent to Mende to work with Brother Henri in the school. Eventually, Brother Henri and one of his companions, Brother Nicolas, gave their lives working heroically with the victims of the plague that devastated Mende in 1721.

One Year in Paris

De La Salle resided with the Brothers at the Rue de Barouillère in Paris for just about a year, remaining as much as possible in the background, avoiding direct confrontation with Father De Brou, whose ascendancy over the Brothers was rapidly eroding in the presence of the Founder, and allowing Brother Barthélemy to continue to function for all practical purposes as the Superior.

On one quite dramatic occasion during this period De La Salle conducted an exorcism on a former officer in the German army, a convert from Lutheranism named Armestad, who had presented himself for admission to the novitiate. The young man had a history of dealing with satanic forces that apparently were unwilling to loosen their grip on the poor fellow. Old war wounds that had completely healed were reopened, the blood flowed freely, he went into contortions; paralyzed with fear and pain he lapsed into unconsciousness only to be assaulted with dreadful visions.

The Brothers feared for his life and had the last sacraments administered. This helped for a time, as did the occasional invocation of Our Lady, but then the phenomena would recur. When he was given the habit of the Brothers in the hope that this would provide permanent relief, the demons seemed to redouble their fury. Finally, De La Salle, convinced that these were manifestations of diabolic power, quietly and without fanfare performed the ritual of exorcism prescribed by the Church. This left the young novice in peace at last, but shortly thereafter he decided to leave the Institute.

The Return of the Center to Saint Yon

In 1715 the situation in Paris was becoming increasingly complicated: King Louis XIV died on September 1; Cardinal Noailles and the Jansenist party were gathering support to protest the Bull *Unigenitus,* which had finally been promulgated in France; Father De Brou continued his efforts to preserve a measure of control over the Brothers in the Paris schools; the cost of living in Paris, especially of food, was making it increasingly difficult to support the novitiate financially. In October De La Salle decided it was time that Brother Barthélemy should return to Saint Yon with the three or four novices that still remained.

De La Salle himself returned to Saint Yon a month later, after being detained by Father De Brou, who still counted on his presence to stabilize the situation of the Brothers in the capital. Having arrived in Rouen, De La Salle presented himself to Archbishop D'Aubigné, who, ever since the encounters at Chartres, had remained cool to the Brothers in general and the Founder in particular. When the archbishop dismissed him summarily, the Founder accepted the humiliation with characteristic equanimity.

Although De La Salle had hoped to spend his remaining days in solitude and prayer, assisting as best he could with the formation of the novices, he soon found himself in continual demand as a confessor and spiritual director. Parish priests in particular sought his advice in dealing with hardened sinners, such was the reputation of De La Salle for ministering effectively to persons of this kind.

Visit to Calais and Boulogne

Among those who came to pay their respects to De La Salle at Saint Yon were two laymen who had been instrumental in bringing the Brothers to the channel ports, Monsieur Gense of Calais and Monsieur De La Cocherie of Boulogne. Both were known for their religious devotedness and their zeal for orthodoxy. At Calais, Gense had become a veritable watchdog defending the orthodox faith; at Boulogne, De La Cocherie followed a routine of spiritual exercises that was all but monastic in duration and rigor. Blain tells us that De La Salle received them at Saint Yon and took them to a remote bower in the garden where he had a meal served to them. Their conversation lasted through the greater part of the day. It would not be idle to speculate that the problem of Jansenism, which was spreading in the channel cities, might have been one of the principal topics discussed.

The Jansenism question, as well as respect for the obligations of mutual hospitality, may have been part of the reason why these gentlemen were able to persuade De La Salle to come north and return the visit. He could then see for himself the work of the Brothers in the schools at Calais and Boulogne. Encouraged by Brother Barthélemy, the Founder agreed to make the trip.

At Boulogne De La Salle was received enthusiastically by the people of the town and by the dignitaries as well, including the Marquis de Colembert who had been so instrumental in providing the labor and the materials for building the school. The Founder might have stayed longer had not De La Cocherie prepared an elaborate reception and banquet in his honor, which only caused the humble priest acute suffering and embarrassment.

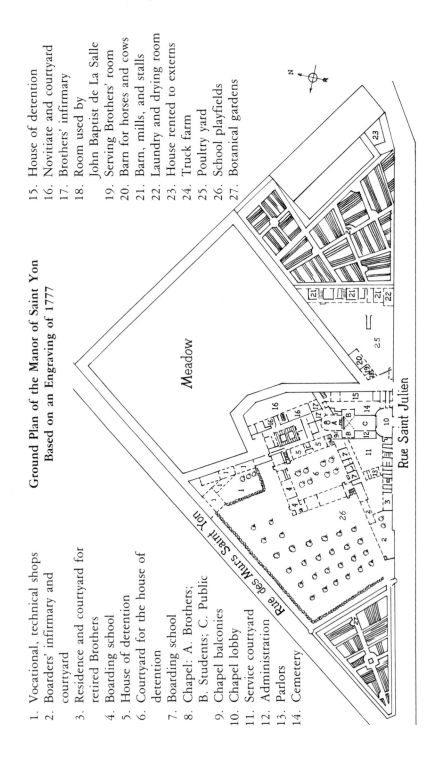

Ground Plan of the Manor of Saint Yon
Based on an Engraving of 1777

1. Vocational, technical shops
2. Boarders' infirmary and courtyard
3. Residence and courtyard for retired Brothers
4. Boarding school
5. House of detention
6. Courtyard for the house of detention
7. Boarding school
8. Chapel: A. Brothers; B. Students; C. Public
9. Chapel balconies
10. Chapel lobby
11. Service courtyard
12. Administration
13. Parlors
14. Cemetery
15. House of detention
16. Novitiate and courtyard
17. Brothers' infirmary
18. Room used by John Baptist de La Salle
19. Serving Brothers' room
20. Barn for horses and cows
21. Barn, mills, and stalls
22. Laundry and drying room
23. House rented to externs
24. Truck farm
25. Poultry yard
26. School playfields
27. Botanical gardens

Meadow

Rue des Murs Saint Yon

Rue Saint Julien

At Calais, he found that the schools were flourishing again. There had been a brief period following the death of Louis XIV in 1715 when public funds were withheld, and it seemed doubtful whether private funding would be adequate to keep the schools going. But the royal grants had meanwhile been restored, and the classes designed especially for the seafaring population were assured of a promising future.

Contrary to his usual custom, De La Salle agreed on more than one occasion to take meals at the home of M. Gense. He might have visited more often if that gentleman had not engaged an artist to try to paint the Founder's portrait from behind a screen. Once De La Salle became aware of what was happening, he made a hasty departure and did not return again.

Since De La Salle was still in Calais on August 15, 1716, he was invited by the Dean of Calais to officiate at the solemn High Mass. The dean himself preached the sermon, but made no mention of the Blessed Virgin Mary, whose feast it was. De La Salle was astonished at this omission and did not hesitate to make his displeasure known to the dean after the service. The dean promised to make amends at the evening Vespers and did so to the great surprise of the congregation. They were not accustomed to hearing their pastor speak so devoutly of Our Lady. The fact is that the dean was inclined to the Jansenist view that tended to belittle the role of Mary in the plan of salvation.

Jansenism continued to be a problem for the Brothers in the channel cities. The Bishop of Boulogne, Pierre de Langle, whose diocese also included Calais, was one of four French bishops—another was Cardinal Noailles—who publicly appealed against the papal bull *Unigenitus* condemning Jansenism. He tried to win the Brothers over to his cause, at first by flattery and then by threats, but the Brothers remained staunchly faithful to the directives of the Founder to avoid theological controversy and to adhere to the official papal teaching.

Preparation for the Succession

Even though De La Salle did not concern himself directly with administrative affairs, his presence among the Brothers was sufficient to dissipate once and for all any thought of a basic reorganization of the Institute into a series of federated units under ecclesiastical control. All that was needed was to provide for an orderly succession to the superiority, which, according to the solemn agreement of 1694, could go only to a Brother who had been vowed by association to the Society.

By this time De La Salle was 65 years old, but already physically weakened by chronic illness, arduous travel, and heroic austerities. In his last letter to Gabriel Drolin, dated December 5, 1716, he wrote:

> I have had many disappointments during this time. At present I am living in a house in a suburb of Rouen. It is called Saint Yon and we have our novitiate here. . . . For nearly ten months now, I have been ill in this house where I have been living for a year. The vacillations of the Archbishop of Paris are causing concern among the bishops. I don't know what is thought of this in Rome. . . .

The Brothers had learned from hard experience that in the absence of De La Salle they would not be able to keep the Institute intact unless the succession had been fully provided for beforehand.

Brother Barthélemy

The obvious choice for a successor was Brother Barthélemy. During the long absence of the Founder in the South, despite the lack of a clear mandate and the importunities of the ecclesiastics who were trying to gain control, Brother Barthélemy had managed somehow to hold the Institute together. Ever since the return of the Founder, he had continued to handle the administrative details that De La Salle left completely to his care.

At this particular time, in 1716, Brother Barthélemy, born Joseph Truffet, was just 38 years old. His father had been a schoolteacher, and Joseph himself attended the Jesuit college in his native Douai. After his brief period in the seminary, his love for retirement and meditation led him to seek admission to the Trappists, but his delicate constitution proved incapable of sustaining the rigors of Cistercian life. In 1703 the 25-year-old Truffet came to Paris, where he met the Founder, who accepted him into the novitiate which was still at the Grande Maison. He was assigned

to the primary class at Chartres, but both his rather advanced education and his physical limitations made teaching at this level difficult
for him. Nevertheless he persevered with dogged determination to
do his best for the education of the young boys entrusted to his care.

In 1705 De La Salle, who knew how to place his disciples where
they could do the most good, recalled Brother Barthélemy to Paris
and put him in charge of the six or seven novices who had just been
displaced from the Rue de Charonne to the Rue Princesse. Later
that year the novitiate was moved to Saint Yon, where the number
of novices doubled. It was when the novitiate had been brought
back to Paris in the famine of 1709 that Brother Barthélemy con-
tracted the case of scurvy, so debilitating that the Brothers tried to
have him sent away. After an entire night spent in prayer the Founder
decided instead that he should stay and be allowed to take his vows.
When two years later the Founder suddenly decided to leave Paris,
Brother Barthélemy was forced by circumstances and his position
as head of the novitiate to assume the functions of Superior.

It was only natural, then, that De La Salle should now turn
to this man as the likely successor. Years before, the Founder had
been gravely disappointed when his first choice, Brother Henri
L'Heureux, had suddenly died. Of the two associates of the Founder
who had made with him the "heroic vow" of 1691 to found the
Society, Nicolas Vuyart had returned to secular life, and Gabriel
Drolin was far away in Rome and out of touch with the situation
in France. Brother Ponce, who had certain administrative skills, had
been guilty of imprudence on more than one occasion and ended
up leaving the Institute. The only other possible candidate might
have been Brother Timothée, but he was needed to keep things
together in the South. All indications were that the Brothers generally
were prepared to go along with Brother Barthélemy as the man to
succeed De La Salle.

Preparation for the General Assembly

Toward the end of 1716, De La Salle suggested to the Brothers at
Saint Yon that the best way to assure the success of the upcoming
assembly and election was to involve all the Brothers of the Institute
in the preparations, to alert them to the problems that had to be
solved, and to obtain their agreement beforehand to abide by what

might ultimately be decided. For this purpose, they decided to send
Brother Barthélemy to visit all the houses of the Institute.

In a meeting held at Saint Yon on December 4, 1716, the
following declaration, formulated in classic style in one long French
sentence, was agreed upon:

> We, the undersigned Brothers of the Christian Schools, being
> assembled in the house at Saint Yon, in order to make provi-
> sion for those matters that are most pressing in what concerns
> the good of our Institute; and aware that for more than a year,
> Father De La Salle, our Founder, has been ill during all this
> time and in no condition to attend to its affairs; have therefore
> judged it fitting and even believe it necessary that Brother Bar-
> thélemy, to whom the guidance of our Institute has been en-
> trusted for several years, should go immediately to visit all the
> houses that pertain to the Institute to learn what is going on
> in each of them and how they are being directed, in order that
> we will be able afterwards to discover, with the principal Brothers
> of the Society, the means to establish, to preserve, and to main-
> tain union and uniformity in the Institute, to fix by decree the
> regulations to be observed and, at the same time, to provide
> for the general administration of our Institute, in an assembly
> which, as he will indicate, is to be held in the house at Saint
> Yon, from the feast of the Ascension until Pentecost.

The document was signed by the Director of the boarding school
at Saint Yon, the Director of the schools in Rouen, the Director
of the house of detention, and two of the teachers at Saint Yon.
After the signatures of the participants, De La Salle himself added:
"I believe that what the Brothers have decided in the above statement is appropriate." Then Canon Blain, acting in his capacity as
ecclesiastical superior for Rouen, added his approval and gave Brother
Barthélemy leave to be absent for several months to accomplish "what
Father De La Salle and the Brothers considered necessary."

Brother Barthélemy set out at once. In each house the Brothers
were asked to sign a statement agreeing in principle to the idea of
a general assembly for the purposes stated in the declaration from
Saint Yon. Since these signed and dated documents have been
preserved, they enable us to follow Brother Barthélemy as he made
his rounds of the Brothers' communities. To follow him in his
itinerary gives an idea of the possibilities of travel and communication available at the time, the spread of the Institute throughout

France, and the number of the Brothers in the schools in 1716–1717. Some 100 signatures were appended to the documents.

Thus, Brother Barthélemy was already in Chartres on December 9, 1716. By December 16 he had gone as far as Moulins in the Bourbon country to the south. Travelling by horseback as winter was settling in, he fell from his horse on the slippery road en route to Mende. Although he was dragged for a considerable distance and was terribly frightened, he suffered no serious injury. He was at Les Vans on December 31. From there he went to Alès, where he waited out a storm until January 7, 1717. He was in Avignon by January 10, then went to Marseille, and from there to Grenoble, where the Brothers signed the formula on January 26.

Making his way back north, Brother Barthélemy was at Dijon on February 8, and Troyes on February 15. En route to Rethel, he was accosted by some highwaymen who followed him for a while, but they were somehow unable to force him to yield either his money or his life. Blain tells us, "They seemed to be restrained by an invisible hand." From Rethel he went to Reims, where the Brothers signed the declaration on February 28, and then to Laon. He made his way back to Saint Yon by way of Guise, Calais, and Boulogne, arriving home in time for Easter, which that year fell on March 28. After Easter the indefatigable emissary took off again for Versailles, Paris, and Saint Denis. By May 7, 1717, the tour was complete and the register closed with the signatures of 99 Brothers, not including De La Salle, Drolin, and Barthélemy himself.

The General Assembly of 1717: The Elections

The assembly opened, not on the feast of the Ascension as originally planned, but on Pentecost Sunday, May 16, 1717. There were 16 delegates altogether, all of them Directors of the various houses. The oldest was Brother Dosithée, 46 years old, Director at Rouen; the youngest was Brother Cosme, 29 years old, Director at Versailles. Unable to attend were the Directors of the communities in Moulins, Mende, Les Vans, Marseille, Dijon, and Troyes. Thus the Brothers in the South had to be represented by the Directors of Avignon, Alès, and Grenoble.

The election of the new Superior went smoothly after a day or two of prayer and preparation. The probable date would be Tuesday, May 18, 1717. De La Salle himself remained aloof from the discussion and the voting. When he was informed that Brother Bar-thélemy had been elected to succeed him, he only remarked that the new Superior had been already acting in that capacity for some time. Brother Barthélemy, after expressing his unworthiness, ac-cepted the election as an expression of the will of God.

It is worth noting that in the subsequent history of the Institute, Brother Barthélemy is counted as the first Superior General of the Brothers. The purpose was to emphasize the special role of De La Salle as Founder while, at the same time, affirming the principle established in 1694 that his election as Superior on that occasion was a special case, that thenceforward no cleric should be accepted as Superior.

Brother Barthélemy let it be known at once that he would need help to carry out the duties imposed upon him. Accordingly, the assembly agreed to elect two aides with the title of "Assistant," pro-vided that they continue to reside and to function in their former communities. The two chosen were Brother Jean (Jacot), one of the survivors of Vaugirard and Director of the Brothers in Paris, and Brother Joseph (Le Roux), who had entered the Institute in 1697 and was serving as Director in Reims.

Discussion of the Rule

Once the elections were over, the delegates turned their attention to a discussion of the Common Rule of the Brothers. Strange as it may seem, the topic that took the longest time and caused the greatest disagreement was the matter of the community recreations. Blain devotes ten full pages to summarizing the various points of view. It was the custom of the Brothers to take recreation together twice daily, after the noon and the evening meals. The recreation was restricted to conversation on pious topics, beginning with the subject matter of the book read during the meal. Frivolous topics were forbidden, as were references to personal matters, gossip of any kind, or even friendly banter, to say nothing of criticism or uncharitable talk.

Over the years abuses had crept in. Some Brothers easily ex-cused themselves when they thought they had something better to do. Others thought that if it were to be recreation, it should not be so restricted, that greater freedom and relaxation should be al-lowed. This was the point of view defended by some of the delegates, citing with approval the fact that in some communities games such as bowling, tenpins, and quoits had been introduced.

The matter was considered serious enough for the assembly to send some of the delegates around to the religious houses in the neighborhood of Saint Yon to seek advice. Apparently this topic was much discussed in religious communities at the time, stimulated in part by a spate of writings deploring the abuses that had become common in the recreation periods of certain monasteries of men and of women. The final conclusion was that the Rule of the Brothers as it had been practiced from the beginning should remain in force.

There was not sufficient time for the assembly to come to definitive decisions on all the details of the Rule. Instead, it was decided that De La Salle himself should prepare a revised version based on the discussions held in the assembly, which he attended, and in which each delegate was free to express his opinions openly. To the original Rule De La Salle added three new chapters: one on the serving Brothers; one on regularity, drawing on the Rule of Saint Augustine; and one on modesty, taken in large measure from the Rule of Saint Ignatius. De La Salle completed this work in the following year, 1718. A copy of the revised Rule, authenticated and signed by Brother Barthélemy, was sent to all the communities. It was this Rule with only minor adaptations that guided the Institute for 250 years until the thorough revision of 1967, mandated by Vatican Council II.

Brother Irenée, Director of Novices

To replace Brother Barthélemy as Director of Novices, it was decided to appoint Brother Irenée, Claude Dulac de Montisambert, the aristocratic soldier of fortune who, after mending his ways, had come to De La Salle while he was still at Parménie. After several unsuccessful attempts at teaching assignments in Avignon, Paris, and Laon, Brother Irenée had been brought by De La Salle to Saint Yon to assist with the novices. In addition to his responsibilities as Director of Novices, he was appointed Director General at Saint Yon, and eventually was elected as Assistant to the second Superior General, Brother Timothée. He continued as Director of Novices as well, a position he held until his death in 1747. By reason of his ascetical and contemplative spirit, the influence of his position at Saint Yon, and the fact that he had been personally close to De

La Salle, he would be a major influence on all the candidates in formation during the first half of the eighteenth century.

De La Salle in Retirement

From the moment Brother Barthélemy was elected Superior, De La Salle took the lead in showing him all the marks of submission and deference. When Brothers continued to come to him seeking advice or permissions, De La Salle would say, "I am nothing; go to the Superior." At first he refused even to answer letters addressed to him. When Brother Barthélemy insisted that he reply, according to Blain, De La Salle would add at the end: "Take care not to address yourself to me on such topics again. You have a Superior; you should lay your difficulties before him. As for myself, I do not wish to interfere any more in anything; I want only to think of death and bewail my sins."

Brother Barthélemy, for his part, did not hesitate to turn to the Founder when he felt the need of his advice. One such notable instance was occasioned by a visit of a zealous layman from Canada, Monsieur Charon by name, who asked for four Brothers to be sent to Canada to take over the schools. Brother Barthélemy was favorable to the project, and De La Salle himself at first seemed to agree. Brother Joseph, the Assistant, came from Reims to help choose the Brothers for the mission. All the arrangements were complete, and even the tickets for the voyage had been purchased. It was only at the last minute De La Salle intervened. "What do you think you are doing?" he asked. This was stated so strongly that the Brothers decided to back away from the project. Soon thereafter Charon admitted that he had planned all along to put the Brothers in separate localities, each under the direction of a different parish priest, an arrangement totally opposed to Institute policy.

The Purchase of Saint Yon

The peace and isolation that De La Salle so eagerly sought at Saint Yon was interrupted in October, 1717, when he had to go to Paris to deal with the legacy left by Rogier as restitution for the 5,200 livres that this lawyer had acquired as part of the judgment in the Clément affair. De La Salle discovered that he was described in Rogier's will as the "Superior of the Brothers of the Christian

Schools," and the lawyer insisted that he so sign himself. De La Salle refused, preferring to renounce the legacy rather than employ a title that was no longer his. After a delay of three months, the lawyer finally agreed to accept his signature without the title.

The legacy came at an opportune time. The Marquise of Louvois, who owned Saint Yon and had rented it to the Brothers for a rather reasonable sum, died. Her heirs were anxious to sell the property at its true value, a price the Brothers could not afford. But the Brothers were anxious to hold title to the property. The Rogier legacy proved to be the providential source for part of the down payment. A few smaller legacies, and the sale of some other assets from investments that De La Salle had made over the years, provided the rest. The Abbé Louvois, the son and executor of his mother's will and the nephew of Archbishop Le Tellier, aware of the work of De La Salle and the Brothers, proved to be helpful in obtaining for them the best possible terms.

Sojourn at Saint Nicolas du Chardonnet

De La Salle remained in Paris from October 1717 until March 1718. During all this time he lived in seclusion at the Seminary of Saint Nicolas du Chardonnet, a vibrant center for clerical renewal and reform. In this way it would be easier for the Founder to keep from being involved in Institute business and to avoid marks of honor and deference from the Brothers. His presence made a profound impression on the priests and seminarians studying at Saint Nicolas, as attested in a long letter that the superior of the seminary wrote to Brother Barthélemy after the Founder's death.

One paragraph from that letter gives an idea of the daily routine of De La Salle during the five months that he spent at Saint Nicolas du Chardonnet:

> He made at least three hours of meditation every day. He was more faithful to the house regulations than the lowliest of seminarians, obeying with admirable promptness the first sound of the bell which announced the exercises. He was so submissive that he wearied the prefect by coming to ask him for permissions, even for those which are not required of the seminarians themselves, as for instance to speak with persons who came asking to see him; to bring them to his room, as you yourself noticed more than once; to go out on free days; and even to write

letters, for he never wrote a single one without express permission. He was so willing to accede to the requests made to him to take part in a funeral procession without a stipend, or to conduct the funerals of children, that it seemed as if that was something he valued very much. In a word, retirement, prayer, charity, humility, mortification, a poor and hard life seemed to be what delighted him.

Evidently, if De La Salle had his way, he would have remained at the seminary until his death. He felt that his work for the Institute was finished. The Brothers had one of their own as Superior, and now they owned a commodious center at Saint Yon. There was nothing more that he could do for the Society. If he were to go back to Saint Yon, he felt that he would be occupying a place uselessly. At least that is what Blain tells us the Founder replied to the Brothers who begged him to return. In response to one such request he went so far as to say, "After serious reflection, I am much inclined to end my days here."

Neither the Brothers generally nor Brother Barthélemy were prepared to allow this to happen. The only recourse they had was, once again, the command of obedience. In this, they had the collaboration of the superior at the seminary. Once he received the formal order, De La Salle reluctantly agreed to leave the place he had apparently chosen to end his days. He went from the seminary to stop over briefly at the Brothers' community at the Rue de la Barouillère, where Brother Barthélemy awaited him. After giving the Brothers in Paris his last blessing, he left with the Superior for Saint Yon, where he arrived on March 7, 1718. He had little more than a year to live.

14

Faithful to the End
(1718–1719)

It is easy to understand De La Salle's reluctance to return to Saint Yon and to the Brothers. He thought of his life's work as finished and wanted only time to prepare himself for death in peace, solitude, and union with God. Despite his claim that he could no longer be of any use to the Brothers, the last months of his life were as full of activity, service, controversy, and opposition every bit as much as any other period in his life.

The activity that gave him the most satisfaction was training the novices in the practice of meditation. Each day before the noon meal he would give them instruction on the various methods of prayer. Each novice in turn would then express his prayer aloud. The Founder would point out mistakes in the use of the method, suggest a better approach, and gradually lead the novice to be able to pray for long periods of time on his own. Out of these lessons De La Salle developed his treatise on prayer, entitled *Explication de la méthode d'oraison.* Over the years, he had been composing meditations for the Brothers which he now gathered into his collections of meditations for Sundays, feasts, and the time of retreat.

During this period the Founder was also kept busy in the exercise of his sacramental ministry for the Brothers at Saint Yon, as well as for the boarding students and the inmates of the house of detention. He celebrated Mass regularly and gave extended homilies on Sundays and feasts. He heard the confessions of all the Brothers once and sometimes twice a week. He took a particular interest in the hardened adults in the house of detention, winning many of them over by his kindly manner with them, and in some cases effecting permanent conversions to a better way of life.

Not all the Brothers appreciated what it meant to have the Founder in their midst. Blain tells of one insolent serving Brother who chided De La Salle for having dinner in a rectory in Rouen after celebrating High Mass in the parish church. The same Brother, on another occasion, told him that he was being lodged and fed at Saint

Yon out of charity, that he was a penniless priest who was no longer good for anything. At this, Blain tells us, the Founder could not help laughing. Occasions such as this show that De La Salle had a sense of humor.

Of somewhat greater importance during this period were the legal matters that had to be attended to. Since the Institute had no corporate legal status, all the property had to be in the name either of De La Salle himself or one of the Brothers. It was time now to put all the assets of the Brothers under the control of Brother Barthélemy. Accordingly, on August 11, 1718, De La Salle had his personal library brought from Paris to Saint Yon and the title transferred to the new Superior. On September 18, he did the same for all the legal documents pertaining to the houses of the Society. On November 14, he handed over to Brother Barthélemy title to the furnishings at Saint Yon. In this way the financial stability of the Institute was assured until such time as letters patent, giving legal corporate status, could be obtained.

Family Problems

Ever since the publication of the Bull *Unigenitus* there had been a falling out between John Baptist and his blood brother, Jean-Louis, now a doctor of theology and canon of the cathedral at Reims. It distressed the Founder terribly that Jean-Louis had aligned himself with the Jansenist party appealing the Bull. After all entreaties to side with the Roman view had failed, John Baptist cut off all further relationships with his brother and, if Blain's account can be trusted, he neither spoke of him any further nor would allow him to be spoken of.

A reconciliation of sorts was effected when their youngest brother, Jean-Remy, became seriously ill. After a career in the army, Jean-Remy had become an official in the royal monetary exchange at Reims. In 1711 he married Madeleine Bertin du Rocheret, but the marriage seems never to have been a happy one. Three of the children born to the union survived. By 1715 Jean-Remy began to show signs of a mental breakdown, and consequently had to resign his position at the exchange. In 1717, as his condition grew worse, he was deprived of all civil rights and confined to a mental institution in Paris, where he died in 1732.

This tragic situation was compounded by the reluctance of the Du Rocheret family to provide adequately for the three children. The concern of the De La Salle family for their nephews is manifest in an exchange of letters between John Baptist and Jean-Louis. In a letter addressed to Jean-Louis in March 1718, the Founder agreed to make over to the children of Jean-Remy the income from some properties to which he had personal title.

For many years, in fact, Jean-Louis had been at the head of a group of trustees that had founded at Reims a civic association to acquire property for the Institute and otherwise deal with financial matters in the name of John Baptist de La Salle and the Brothers. As news of the precarious condition of the Founder's health reached Reims, Jean-Louis wrote to his brother on January 3, 1719, to remind him that there was urgent business involving both the family and the Institute that needed attention. The letter begins as follows:

> Reims, January 3
>
> My very dear brother,
>
> Although it would appear that you are determined to forget this part of the country completely and that you have decided to cut off all communication with us for a year or even several years—so that I have only with great difficulty been able to get a reply from you in matters of great importance—I do not consider myself free from my obligations. So I take it upon myself to write to you once more, not only to pay my respects to you at the beginning of this new year and to wish you a very happy one, insofar as there can be a happy one in this life, but mainly to remind you once more of some matters of importance to your Institute, which I have already had the honor to speak and write to you about on several occasions.

The letter goes on to speak of the need to replace some members of the group of trustees, and the importance of making a will so that the in-laws of Jean-Remy will not be in a position to claim title to properties destined for the use of the Institute. De La Salle did get around to making such a will, but only on his deathbed.

Jansenism Again

Just about this time, De La Salle learned from the Brothers in Calais that his name was on a list, published by the Dean of Calais, of those who were appealing the Bull *Unigenitus* in which the pope had condemned the Jansenist doctrine. In a letter to the Brother Director at Calais, dated January 28, 1719, De La Salle stated in no uncertain terms:

> I do not think, my very dear Brother, that I have given the Very Reverend Dean of Calais any reason for saying that I am one of the appellants. It has never been my intention to appeal any more than it has been to embrace the doctrines of those who appeal to a future council. I have too much respect for our Holy Father the Pope and too great a submission to the decisions of the Holy See not to give my assent to any of them.

The letter goes on to support his position by arguments from Saint Jerome and Saint Augustine. De La Salle concludes with the words: "Such are my sentiments and such are my dispositions, which have never been different and which I will never change."

It is quite obvious that De La Salle's name appeared on the list by being confused with that of his brother, Jean-Louis, who indeed was among the appellants. It is also possible that the Dean of Calais used this ploy to try to win the Brothers over to the Jansenist party. In the year following, the Brothers would have much to suffer at the hands of the Dean and his partisans at Calais for their resistance to this kind of pressure.

The Final Illness

As the season of Lent approached in 1719, it became increasingly difficult for De La Salle to conceal the fact that he was seriously ill. The rheumatism which had plagued him for many years became chronic and would not yield to even the most potent remedies. To this were added attacks of asthma, which were aggravated as he began to observe the penitential season of Lent with his usual rigor. As breathing became more and more difficult for him, the Brothers urged him to mitigate his penances, but to no avail. He only replied that the victim was ready to be immolated and needed to be purified. Even Brother Barthélemy, returning from a trip to Paris, was unable to convince him to go easy on himself. Finally the Brothers persuaded his confessor to forbid the Founder to continue a fast that was putting his life in danger.

A series of mishaps only aggravated his condition. One Brother, trying to be helpful, pulled back a chair as De La Salle was about to sit down. The Founder lost his balance and fell on his face. This opened a gash in his head and later caused pain in his ear. Although he tried to conceal the extent of the injury, he admitted to the infirmarian one day that he had such a headache that he felt as if his head were split in two. What bothered him most was that he found it increasingly difficult to concentrate so as to be able to read or write.

Shortly thereafter he was struck again on the head by a falling door. Then pains in his side became so unbearable that he finally had to take to his bed. The doctor who attended him made no secret of the fact that the illness was terminal. De La Salle received the news with equanimity, and even joy. Since the remedies prescribed proved to be quite useless, the Founder asked the Brothers not to waste any more money on him, but to leave all in the hands of the divine Physician.

After the medication was discontinued, De La Salle was able to say Mass daily and to hear confessions regularly for another week or two. But even this proved to be beyond his strength, and he was obliged to remain in bed. He expressed the hope that he would soon "be delivered from Egypt and brought into the true promised land."

As March 19, the feast of Saint Joseph, was drawing near, De La Salle expressed a great desire to celebrate Mass in honor of this special patron and protector of the Institute. So weak was his condition and so intense the pain, that any such idea seemed to be out of the question. However, on the eve of the feast, he felt all of a sudden that the pain was subsiding and that his strength had returned. At first he thought he was dreaming, but in the morning he was well enough to get up and celebrate Mass for the Brothers. They were overjoyed at the prospect that a miraculous cure had returned their Father to them. But almost immediately thereafter he relapsed into his former condition. It became clearer than ever that the end was near and that it was in honor of Saint Joseph that he had celebrated Mass for the last time.

One Final Humiliation

While De La Salle was thus hovering between life and death, a vicious campaign was being waged behind his back in the chancery office of the archdiocese of Rouen. The vicar-general, Father Bernard Couët, was engaged in the last stages of a long-standing vendetta against the Founder and the Brothers.

The trouble had its origins in the arrangements made under Archbishop Colbert in 1706, shortly after the Brothers had moved into Saint Yon. Although Archbishop Colbert was a supporter of the Brothers in many ways, and had given extensive faculties to De La Salle to exercise his priestly ministry in the archdiocese of Rouen, he also had supported the vicar-general in affirming the rights of the pastor of the church of Saint Sever, in whose parish Saint Yon was located. The pastor had insisted that the Brothers and the boarding students at Saint Yon attend Sunday Mass in the parish church. The chaplain at Saint Yon had to be approved by the pastor and was allowed to say Mass in the chapel there only for the Brothers and their students, but not for outsiders.

When Colbert died in 1708 and Claude-Maur d'Aubigné succeeded as Archbishop of Rouen, the claims of the Brothers at Saint Yon for autonomy in their internal affairs became a continual source of annoyance to the ecclesiastical authorities. When De La Salle himself first came to pay his respects to D'Aubigné, he was rudely rebuffed. On another occasion, D'Aubigné berated him unmercifully. The Founder simply fell to his knees and uttered not a word in his own defense.

The sticking point seemed to be the requirement that the boarders attend the Sunday Mass in the parish. Once the house of detention was opened, this proved to be impossible. The prisoners confined under the *lettres de cachet* would only take advantage of this opportunity to escape. Accordingly, De La Salle had Sunday Mass said for the Brothers and the boarders in the Saint Yon chapel.

The vicar-general interpreted this as defiance and a violation of the rights of the pastor of Saint Sever. When called in to answer this charge, De La Salle had explained that he and the Brothers were not violating any of the articles of the agreement except those that had proven from experience to be impossible to keep. The vicar-general was unconvinced. In the spring of 1719 he reported the affair to the archbishop, and in the process declared that De La Salle was a liar. Canon Blain happened to be present at the time and tried to speak up in the Founder's defense, but he was not listened to. As a result, the archbishop suspended De La Salle's faculties to exercise his priestly functions. Canon Blain was commissioned to communicate the decision to the Founder, who by then was on his deathbed.

Blain said nothing at first and could not bring himself to communicate the decision to the Founder. Conscious that if he himself did not soon do so someone else would be sent, Blain warned the Founder that serious trouble was brewing at the chancery and that he had been unable to do anything to avert it. When Blain went to visit De La Salle on April 5 he learned from the Founder's lips that someone indeed had come to inform him that his faculties had been revoked. "They had asked me to bring you the news myself," Blain told him, "but I was in no hurry to carry out such an unpleasant task." "I suspected as much," the Founder replied, "after what you told me the last time you were here." He accepted the decision, this final and ignominious blow, with the same serenity and equanimity with which he had received so many others. "God be blessed!" was all he would say.

Last Will and Testament

Meanwhile, aware that death was imminent, on April 3 De La Salle revised his handwritten will to provide for the concerns that had been expressed by his brother. The text begins as follows:

> In the name of the Father, and of the Son, and of the Holy Spirit. Amen. I, the undersigned John Baptist de La Salle, priest, being sick in a room near the chapel of the house of Saint Yon, in the faubourg of Saint Sever in the city of Rouen, wishing to make a testament to conclude all the matters which still remain to my charge, I recommend to God first of all my own soul, and then all the Brothers of the Society of the Christian Schools with whom he has united me.
>
> I urge them above all else always to have entire submission to the Church, especially in these evil times and, in order to give proof of this, never to separate themselves from the Church of Rome, always remembering that I sent two Brothers to Rome to ask God for the grace that their Society be always entirely submissive to it.

> I also recommend to them to have a great devotion to Our
> Lord, to have a great love for Holy Communion and the prac-
> tice of meditation, to have a special devotion to the Most Blessed
> Virgin and to Saint Joseph, the patron and protector of their
> Society, and to fulfill their assignments with great zeal and
> without self-interest, to have a close union among themselves
> and blind obedience toward their superiors, which is the foun-
> dation and support of all perfection in a community.

There then follow several clauses in which the Founder con-
firms the transfer of his library and other properties to Brother Barthélemy made the previous year. Finally, as requested by Jean-Louis,
he clarifies the status of the properties occupied by the Brothers in
Reims and Rethel, and the provisions he made earlier for the welfare
of the children of his younger brother, Jean-Remy.

The Death of a Saint

Early in Holy Week, the pastor of Saint Sever, having heard that
De La Salle was near death, came to visit him and to reconcile their
differences over the role of the Brothers in the parish. De La Salle
then asked to receive the Holy Viaticum, which was arranged for
the next day. The Brothers were asked to prepare the house and
the sick room so as to make it a suitable place to receive the Blessed
Sacrament. De La Salle, weak as he was, insisted on getting out of
bed and vesting in his surplice and stole. In this way, seated in a
chair, he awaited the coming of his Lord. When he heard the bell
announcing the arrival of the priest, he fell on his knees to adore
Christ in the sacrament. He received the sacred host with what Blain
called "seraphic devotion," and so transformed did his face become
that some wondered why Viaticum was being given to such a healthy-
looking person.

The following day was Holy Thursday, and it was arranged to
have him receive the sacrament of the sick, at that time called the
"last anointing." He received it in the full possession of his faculties,
responding to all the prayers. When the ceremony was over, he remained in repose for many hours, giving thanks for the final graces
that the last sacraments had bestowed upon him.

Later that day, as the Brothers gathered around him, he began
to have difficulty speaking. Brother Barthélemy asked him for a final
blessing for those present and for all the Brothers of the Institute.

Engraving of a portrait painted during the wake prior to burial of the
Founder's body.

Reluctantly, and with great effort, he lifted his eyes to heaven and said simply, "May the Lord bless all of you."

Toward evening, as his speech became erratic and he began to lose consciousness, the Brothers began to recite the prayers for the dying. Blain tells us that he regained consciousness long enough to give the Brothers his last bit of advice:

> If you wish to persevere in your state and to die in it, never have familiar dealings with people of the world. Little by little you will acquire a liking for their way of acting, and you will be drawn into conversation with them so that out of politeness you will not be able to avoid their way of speaking, no matter how objectionable it may be. This will cause you to become unfaithful, and once you are no longer faithful to the observance of your Rule, you will become disenchanted with your state, and finally you will abandon it.

At about midnight De La Salle broke into a cold sweat and entered into an agony which lasted until half past two the next morning. He then recovered slightly and, at the suggestion of one of the Brothers, invoked the Virgin Mary in the concluding verse of the night prayer: *Maria, Mater gratiae . . . in mortis hora suscipe.* (Mary, Mother of grace . . . receive us at the hour of our death.) When asked by Brother Barthélemy whether he accepted his sufferings, the Founder replied, "Yes, I adore in all things the will of God in my regard." These were his last words.

At three o'clock in the morning, he fell into agony again and, although much agitated in body, his face appeared tranquil and reassured. At about four o'clock, he made an effort to rise from bed as though to greet someone. He then joined his hands, raised his eyes to heaven, and breathed his last. It was Good Friday, April 7, 1719. He was just a few weeks short of being 68 years old.

He was buried the next day in a side chapel of the church of Saint Sever. Because of the celebrations of Easter week, the solemn obsequies were not held until a week later. Throughout all Rouen, and soon throughout the Institute, the word spread: "The Saint is dead!" But saints do not die. They live on in eternity in the blessed vision and experience of God. John Baptist de La Salle, in particular, lives on in time and history in the Institute he founded, the Lord's work as he liked to call it, that he left as his legacy to the Church and the world.

15

The Enduring Legacy

John Baptist de La Salle did not die intestate. In his testament, signed only four days before his death, he provided for his needy nephews from what little he possessed by way of property, and then turned title to the rest over to the Brothers in the person of Brother Barthélemy. He also left to the Brothers some words of advice: be loyal to the Church, have a love for prayer and Holy Communion, be zealous and generous in service, and be obedient to superiors as a support for the community.

In the normal course of events, the material elements of such legacies are dissipated or transferred, the dying recommendations of the testator quickly forgotten. Such might have been the fate of the testament of De La Salle had he not left behind a more enduring legacy whose value and effectiveness would only increase with the passing of time, namely, his Institute. If the Brothers were the beneficiaries specified in his will, the Brothers themselves were to become De La Salle's legacy for the benefit of the Church and the world for generations to come.

His Portrait

It is customary on the death of a loved one for the survivors to treasure any available physical images that might help keep the memory of the deceased alive. No painted portrait of De La Salle made during his lifetime has survived, if indeed there ever were such a thing. A portrait made while his body was being waked survives only in a poor photographic reproduction and an engraved copy. Several attempts at portraits were made shortly after his death with varying degrees of success. Both Blain and Maillefer provide toward the end of their biographies descriptive portraits that are almost verbally identical. Here is Blain's version:

> De La Salle stood a little above average in height; his frame was well proportioned and solidly built. A wide forehead, prominent nose, and two large beautiful eyes, nearly blue, made up

an arresting countenance. His features were gentle and agreeable; his voice was strong and distinct. Exteriorly he appeared cheerful, serene, modest, and pious. His skin, somewhat tanned by his long travels, usually appeared slightly flushed. His manners were simple, gracious, and inviting, without affectation. His hair, chestnut and curly in his youth, had with the years become gray or white, and made him look venerable. Finally, grace enthroned, so to speak, on his countenance made him amiable and inspired piety.

It is understandable that any artist might find it difficult to capture all of these qualities in a portrait to serve as an adequate memorial of such a personality.

Succession

When De La Salle died on Good Friday, 1719, the institutional embodiment of his spiritual and educational vision was all but complete. The Institute had a governmental structure headed by a Brother Superior elected from among the Brothers. The Founder had left behind a detailed Rule that had been formulated in collaboration with the Brothers on the basis of their experience and reflection. The other writings of the Founder, some still in manuscript form, would help to preserve and interpret his charism. There was a growing body of oral and written policies and practices to guide the conduct of the schools. All that remained was to obtain the necessary papal and royal approvals for this new form of consecrated ministry within the Church and the kingdom of France.

Brother Barthélemy was called to his eternal reward early in 1720, a little more than a year after the Founder's death. That was time enough for the new Superior to demonstrate that the Institute could operate on its own. A new foundation was opened in Saint Omer on the basis of negotiations begun by De La Salle on his trip to Calais in 1716. Encouraged by their new Superior, the Brothers resisted mightily the pressures put upon them by the bishop and the Jansenist party in Boulogne. With an eye to the future, Brother Barthélemy gave orders to collect documents and personal reminiscences to serve as the basis for a projected biography of the Founder.

In a General Chapter convened for the purpose in 1720, Brother Timothée (Guillaume-Samson Bazin) was elected to succeed Brother

Barthélemy. The new Superior General was 38 years old at the time and had been a member of the Institute since 1700. He had served as the Director of the community and the novitiate in Avignon and had been in charge of all the communities in the South after the departure of Brother Ponce. It was he who had come to Mende after the demise of the Marseille novitiate to ask the Founder for a new assignment and to persuade him that the Brothers wanted him to return.

In a thinly disguised reference to himself, Canon Blain relates how "a canon, a friend of the Institute," had taken care to ask Brother Barthélemy on his deathbed "which of the Brothers he considered the best qualified to replace him:"

> The dying Superior had indicated Brother Timothée, at that time Director of the house in Avignon, and had added that Brother Timothée was the one who, also in De La Salle's opinion, deserved to be chosen, and that the saintly Founder might have picked him to take his place, even during his life, if the Brother had been a little longer in the Society. . . .
>
> Such was the testimony that this canon gave in his favor, relating the statement of the late Brother Barthélemy to some of the principal Brothers who had come for the election. They did not need to be persuaded on this point, for either because of a divine inspiration or a prepossession in favor of Brother Timothée, they were nearly unanimous in choosing him.

The choice proved to be a good one. Brother Timothée guided the Institute with vigor and imagination for 31 years until his death in 1751.

Letters Patent

The most pressing problem for the new Superior in 1720 concerned the title to the property at Saint Yon. Because the Institute had no legal corporate status, which could be conferred only by letters patent from the king, the property was held in the name of Brother Barthélemy and the ever-available and financially shrewd Brother Thomas (Charles Frappet). The death of Brother Barthélemy left Brother Thomas as the sole proprietor, and he was beginning to show the wear and tear of his 50 years. If anything were to happen to him, without the letters patent the title to the property would revert to the original feudal owners. To dramatize the urgency of the situation, Blain describes Brother Thomas as a "sick and infirm Brother," whose death might come at any moment. In fact, Brother Thomas lived another 20 years, dying in 1742 at the age of 72.

The first application for letters patent was made in 1721 with the support of De Pontcarré, president of the Rouen parliament, and the new archbishop, Armand de Bezons. The petition was forwarded to the royal Minister of Justice, Chancellor Henri d' Aguesseau, who in turn, it was hoped, would obtain the approval of Philip of Orleans, the regent during the minority of Louis XV. Unfortunately, the chancellor's secretary, perhaps for reasons relating to the Jansenist crisis, opposed the petition on the grounds that it was unnecessary: the Brothers had already been authorized to teach. Teaching was not the issue, however; it was the right to own property. In any case, the regent accepted the secretary's view, and the petition was rejected.

When D'Aguesseau was replaced as chancellor, a new attempt was made and the process had to be gone through all over again, beginning with the authorities in Rouen. This time the petition was supported by powerful friends at court, including the Marquis de La Vrillière and Cardinal Du Bois. Still the regent temporized, and the death of the archbishop in Rouen provided an excuse for further delay in granting the letters patent.

The regent, Philip of Orleans, died in 1723. Once a new archbishop had been appointed for Rouen, and Louis XV became of age, there was reason to hope that a new try might succeed. Blain attributes much of the success to the role of Brother Thomas:

> Tall, well-built, with a venerable air which won respect, he looked like one of the patriarchs of old, although his pallor and emaciation caused him to resemble one of the ancient desert abbots. His candor and simplicity won the favor of those whom he approached. So it was decided to send him in person to promote the affair in the hope that the sight of him might touch those responsible and hasten its conclusion.
>
> Although he was not feeling well, Brother [Thomas] left for Fontainebleau, where the court was, and he did all that could be expected of him. His pale and drawn countenance, which seemed to warn those he spoke to that his death could not be far off, pleaded more eloquently than his words and gave visible testimony that it was urgent to guarantee the possession of Saint Yon to the Institute by letters patent, or else consent to the loss of the property and the death of the Brother.

There was surely more to it than that, but in time King Louis XV was won over and the letters patent were granted on September 28, 1724. After some opposition from the pastor of Saint Sever, who was reluctant to lose control over any source of revenue in his parish, the letters patent were registered by the parliament of Rouen on March 2, 1725.

The Bull of Approbation

While the complex negotiations for the letters patent were going on, a parallel process was under way to have the Institute approved by papal authority. The intermediary for Brother Timothée in this instance was a serving Brother named Honoré who had once worked as a menial in the household of the Prince of Soubise. In 1721 Cardinal Armand-Gaston de Rohan, a son of that prince, was appointed ambassador of France to the court of Rome. Brother Timothée, accompanied by Brother Honoré, paid a courtesy visit to the cardinal, who received the two Brothers graciously, expressed his pleasure at seeing the former family servant in the Brothers' habit, and promised to aid the Institute in any way he could.

On the eve of the cardinal's departure for Rome, Brother Timothée sent Brother Honoré and a companion to the cardinal with a formal petition seeking papal approval for the Rule and the Institute of the Brothers. The Brothers were received cordially by Father Jean Vivant, the cardinal's secretary, who promised to make the cause of the Brothers his own. Father Vivant's brother, François, as the vicar-general of Cardinal Noailles, had earlier come to the help of the Brothers by rejecting the proposal of Father De Brou to have the Rule changed during the absence of De La Salle. Brother Honoré died shortly thereafter, having faithfully played his part in providing access to the persons in the best position to assure the success of the enterprise.

Cardinal De Rohan and his entourage arrived in Rome only to find that Pope Clement XI had just died. After taking part in the election of Innocent XIII the cardinal returned to France. But there was enough time for Father Vivant to place the Brothers' petition into the hands of the important people in Rome. Negotiations were carried on over the next few years, as the Brothers were asked to explain the nature and purpose of their Institute, the vows they would take, and the principal rules by which they would be bound.

In March 1724 Pope Innocent XIII died, and Cardinal De Rohan and Father Vivant returned to Rome for the conclave that elected the 75-year-old Dominican, Cardinal Orsini, as Pope Benedict XIII. On July 28 of that same year, the Brothers' petition was ready to be sent to the Congregation of the Council, whose prefect was Cardinal Corsini, the future Clement XII. Shortly thereafter the authorities in Rome were notified that the letters patent had been granted. That fact, plus the favorable report of Cardinal Corsini to the Congregation of the Council in November 1724, was a guarantee of success, and the signature of the pope a foregone conclusion.

Shortly after the opening of the Holy Year, on January 26, 1725, the Bull of Approbation, known by its opening Latin words *In apostolicae dignitatis solio,* was promulgated *in forma gratiosa perpetua,* the most solemn form of a papal bull. The news came as a surprise to most of the Brothers, since the negotiations had been conducted in great secrecy, and only four or five of them were aware that they were going on.

In August of that year the principal Brothers assembled at Saint Yon in a General Chapter for the solemn reception of the Bull of Approbation. On August 15, the feast of the Assumption of Mary into heaven, the Brother capitulants, beginning with Brother Timothée, made their vows for the first time in accordance with the bull. The ceremony was presided over by the vicar-general of Rouen as the representative of the Holy Father.

In this way, within six years of the Founder's death, the Institute to which he had already given its definitive form achieved its corporate and legal status in the kingdom of France and its canonical status as a lay institute of pontifical right in the Catholic Church. This did not, however, constitute the Brothers as a religious "order" in the technical sense. It was not until the Code of Canon Law of 1917 created the category of a religious "congregation" with simple vows that the term "religious" could properly be applied to the Brothers' Institute. The revised Code of Canon Law of 1983 uses the word "institute" to refer to all forms of consecrated life whose members live in community under vows or similar sacred bonds.

The Mortal Remains and Immortal Glory

Almost immediately after the Founder's death, precautions were taken to preserve as much of his writings as possible, to obtain written recollections of the Brothers who had known him, and to commission a biography to make the vision and achievement of De La Salle more widely known. Part IV of Blain's biography, entitled *Spirit and Virtues,* is actually organized according to the list of questions that have to be answered for the Vatican authorities in presenting a candidate for canonization, a sure clue as to what the Brothers had in mind from the beginning. They were also well aware that one matter of special concern in such cases was the identification of the mortal remains of the saintly deceased.

The body of John Baptist de La Salle had been buried in the chapel of Saint Suzanne in the parish church of Saint Sever in Rouen on Holy Saturday, the day after his death in 1719. At the time there were no facilities for burial at Saint Yon. But once an expanded building program was under way on their property, the Brothers decided to erect a separate chapel that could also serve as a more suitable place to house the relics of the Founder. The work on the building was done for the most part by the Brothers themselves with the help of the inmates of the house of correction under the direction of Brother Irenée.

The building was going up as Canon Blain was completing his biography of the Founder. He devotes the last paragraph to a description of how construction was progressing, ending with a nasty remark on the stinginess of his fellow Rouenians:

> The Brothers do most of the work themselves. They extract the sand, transport the materials, shape the stones, and do just about everything else. They live mostly on the produce of their garden, a dry and not very fertile spot, situated in a sandy bottom which they water with their sweat, and which they force by their hard and assiduous labor to reward its owners. Moreover, they drink only weak beer and eat only coarse bread. In this way they economize enough on food to be able to build, and their own work represents over half the building costs. The rest comes from the endowment of divine Providence, causing their work to progress only a little at a time. Up until now, public charity, which they serve in Rouen with such unexampled disinterestedness and generosity, has not helped them in any way.

With these words, Blain concludes the biographical section of his study on the Founder.

By the middle of 1734 most of the work on the chapel was finished. The solemn transfer of the relics of De La Salle from the church of Saint Sever to the new chapel at Saint Yon took place on July 16 of that year. The ceremony lasted from three in the afternoon until nine in the evening. Once the relics were exhumed and formally identified, they were placed in a new lead coffin that was then enclosed in another of wood. The procession to Saint Yon was led by 80 Brothers carrying lighted torches, followed by the priests and seminarians of the diocese. The coffin was carried by 16 priests under the covering of a huge canopy. In the new chapel the reburial was presided over by the vicar-general and the eulogy preached by the pastor of Saint Sever. On the following day the Archbishop of Rouen came to bless the chapel and to celebrate the Eucharist.

During the French Revolution in December 1792, the house at Saint Yon was taken over by the revolutionary forces. For their refusal to take the oath of the Civil Constitution of the Clergy, the Brothers were dispersed and the furnishings of the house confiscated or sold. Some months later, at the height of the anti-religious fervor, a gang of bloodthirsty ruffians invaded the chapel, demolished the altars, and broke open the graves. The stone slab covering the tomb of the Founder was smashed in pieces and the lead coffin taken away, probably to be turned into bullets. Fortunately the bones were not scattered, but were left buried in a recess in the cellar of the chapel where they remained hidden for 42 years.

It was not until 1835 that the mortal remains of De La Salle were rediscovered, exhumed, identified, and placed under the seal of the Archbishop of Rouen. The reliquary was kept for many years in the chapel of the Brothers' normal school in Rouen on the Rue Saint Lo. At one point the Brothers hoped that the relics might be brought to the generalate, which was then in Paris, but the archdiocesan authorities in Rouen flatly refused to release them.

By this time enough preliminary documentation had been prepared so that the cause for the canonization of John Baptist de La Salle could be introduced into the court of Rome in May 1840. The signed writings of the Founder were submitted for examination, and on January 12, 1852, they were officially declared to be in conformity with the doctrine of the Church. Another 20 years passed before the decree was promulgated acknowledging, to the surprise of no one who knew the story, that De La Salle had practiced virtue in a heroic degree. Finally, on November 1, 1887, three miracles attributed to the intercession of De La Salle were formally approved, and the way was clear for the beatification to proceed.

The ceremony of beatification took place in the large hall above the portico of Saint Peter's basilica in Rome on February 19, 1888, in the presence of cardinals, bishops, the Superior General and six of his Assistants, and representatives of the Brothers from around the world. Pope Leo XIII himself did not preside, but he appeared in the afternoon to receive the customary gifts and homage of the Superior and his entourage. Among those present was Brother Miguel Febres Cordero from Ecuador, who would one day himself be raised to the honors of the altar. The celebration in Rome was echoed by similar events throughout the Lasallian world as the Founder of the Brothers was offered to the veneration of the universal Church.

The two additional miracles needed for canonization were not long in coming. One concerned the cure of a young student in the boarding school at Rodez in France who was dying from complications associated with pneumonia; the other was the sudden and dramatic cure at Communion time during Mass of a paralyzed Brother in Montreal. On May 24, 1900, in Saint Peter's basilica, the aging Pope Leo XIII canonized John Baptist de La Salle, declaring him forever after to be numbered among the saints of the Roman Catholic Church.

In 1875, the relics of De La Salle had been moved to a large chapel, built especially for the purpose in the style of a Roman basilica, attached to the newly opened boarding school on the Rue Saint Gervais in Rouen. In 1904 the religious teaching congregations in France were suppressed, and the relics had to be moved again to the relocated generalate in Lembecq near Brussels in Belgium. In 1936 the generalate of the Brothers was moved to Rome. After a sometimes furtive and sometimes triumphal journey, the precious remains of De La Salle were brought to the Eternal City and were enshrined in the chapel of the generalate on January 26, 1937. There, with some variation in their surroundings, the bones of De La Salle have, it is hoped, found at last their place of rest.

The Writings

An important part of the legacy of De La Salle that is more significant, perhaps, than his corporeal remains, and certainly more available for dissemination, is the body of writings that he produced in his lifetime. Of the manuscripts in the Founder's own hand that have survived, the most valuable are the draft of the *Memoir on the Habit,* written in 1689 or 1690 in response to the objections of Father Baudrand, the pastor of Saint Sulpice; the signed vow formula of 1694, and the collection of 53 manuscript letters that have survived out of the thousands that De La Salle must have written.

Among the texts that De La Salle composed for the use of the schools, the earliest seems to have been the *Rules of Christian Politeness,* dating from Vaugirard in 1695. The longest of the school texts is entitled *The Duties of a Christian.* Published for the first time in Paris in 1703, it was extensively revised by the Founder while he was staying at Grenoble during the winter of 1713–14. In its final form this work comprises three volumes: a doctrinal treatise in story form, a catechism in the form of question and answer, and an explanation of public worship in the form of a dialogue. In 1703 De La Salle also published for the use of the schools a short, three-part manual entitled *Instructions and Prayers for Holy Mass, Confession, and Communion.*

The treatise entitled *The Conduct of the Schools* was developed over the years by the Founder in collaboration with the Brothers to serve as a guide for the policies and practices to be observed in the schools. It was progressively modified to conform to the experience of the Brothers and the need to experiment with new pedagogical methods. The oldest extant copy dates from 1706. The first printed edition appeared in 1720, a year after the death of the Founder.

Also in collaboration with the Brothers, De La Salle composed the book of *Common Rules* to guide the Brothers in their community and apostolic life. The oldest manuscript dates from 1705, but probably reflects the redaction made by De La Salle at Vaugirard in 1695. A copy has survived of the revision undertaken by De La Salle in 1718 and circulated to the Brothers with an introductory letter by Brother Barthélemy. The Founder's *Rule of the Brother Director* also dates from 1718 and served as the basis for what would eventually become the Rule of Government for the Institute.

The spiritual writings intended for the Brothers were written relatively late in the Founder's lifetime. Except for the short *Collection of Various Treatises for the Use of the Brothers,* published in 1711, most of the others were published only after the Founder's death: the *Meditations for the Time of Retreat,* published in 1730; the *Meditations for Sundays and the Principal Feasts,* published in Rouen at an unknown date; and the *Explanation of the Method of Mental Prayer,* published in 1739.

The original French editions of all the writings of De La Salle have been republished in anastatic copies by the Brothers' generalate in Rome in volumes 10 through 25 of the *Cahiers lasalliens.* A ten-year project is currently under way to produce new English translations, some for the first time, of all the writings of De La Salle. Known as Lasallian Publications, this project is sponsored by the Christian Brothers Conference, based in Romeoville, Illinois.

The Legacy of the Schools

The legacy that is the Institute of the Brothers, and that includes the entire Lasallian family, assumes its most concrete form in the schools and other educational enterprises conducted by the Brothers and their colleagues. It should not be surprising that the schools of the Brothers assume a distinctive quality, one that is often re-marked but difficult to define, a quality derived from a long tradition of religious consecration to a specific apostolic mission carried on in association and brotherhood. What is said here about the Brothers' schools extends as well to other educational works in which the Brothers are involved.

Religious and value-centered education has always been a high priority in the Brothers' schools. In the contemporary context, with due respect for religious freedom, the Brothers take into account the needs and experiences of their students to open them to gospel values and to bring to maturity their personal faith commitment. The Brothers continue to do this, as they did in the Founder's day, not only by effective religious instruction, but also by the witness of their personal and community life and that of their associated colleagues.

Sensitivity to social issues is an important aspect of the Brothers' school. That is what brought the Institute into being in the first place. The Brothers continue to give priority to direct educational service to the poor where that is still possible. Where it is not, the Brothers try in all their educational endeavors to show special concern for the disadvantaged, and to make education for peace and social justice an important element in the curriculum and in extracurricular activities. That is why the Brothers still take a special vow of "association for the service of the poor through education."

Since the ideal of brotherhood is such a dominant theme in the Lasallian tradition, it is to be expected that the Brothers' schools would be noted for the quality of the relationships between the teachers and the students. De La Salle himself urged the Brothers to be with the students from morning to night, to be like an elder brother to them. On a deeper level he encouraged the Brothers to have a regard for each pupil as a person, to see in the students before them the person of Jesus Christ.

The fact that the Brothers renounce the possibility of entering the clerical state, and the title "Father" that goes with it, makes it easier for them to avoid the clericalism associated with ecclesiastical pomp and privilege. The exclusively lay character of De La Salle's Institute demonstrates the authenticity and effectiveness of a lay ministry and a lay spirituality in the Church.

Finally, the Lasallian schools feature quality teaching with a practical orientation. One of the principal achievements of De La Salle was to elevate the despised function of the schoolteacher to the status of a vocation worthy of the dedication of a lifetime. Devoted exclusively to the work of education, the Brothers bring to the school a sense of permanence, commitment, and competence that they share with the teachers associated with them. The result is a quality school. The Brothers are justly proud of the reputation they enjoy for conducting good schools.

This is not to say that many of these qualities are not to be found in educational institutions directed under other auspices. But somehow, all of them taken together seem to describe that elusive something that people everywhere who benefit from this aspect of the Lasallian legacy can recognize as the Brothers' school.

The Spiritual Legacy of De La Salle

Although he authored a series of meditations, an introduction to the method of meditation, and a collection of short spiritual treatises, De La Salle did not develop what might be called a system, much less a school, of spirituality. The spiritual doctrine found in these writings, all intended for the use of the Brothers, was drawn from a variety of sources: the founders of ancient orders as well as the more recent ones; the classic spiritual writers current in seventeenth-century France; and, above all, the authors of the New Testament, especially Saint Paul.

There are, however, distinctive and enduring elements in the synthesis that De La Salle produced from these varied sources: the emphasis on the presence and the Providence of God, for example; the importance given to obedience and self-abnegation in union with the mystery of the incarnate Word; the reliance—unusual for its time—on the guidance of the Holy Spirit; the centrality of the gospel message and its maxims; sensitivity to the divine voice to be discerned in the crying needs of the poor; the call to an apostolic mission and Christian ministry on behalf of young persons "far from salvation."

All of De La Salle's spiritual writings were composed for and with the Brothers in the context of the life he daily shared with them. He wanted to give them a religious vision, a sense of vocation and mission, to sustain them in the often thankless and disagreeable tasks they were called upon to perform each day in the schools. In such a context, the spiritual message had to be specific and practical while, at the same time, opening the minds of the Brothers outwards and upwards toward the reality and infinity of the Triune God.

The closest De La Salle comes to providing the framework for an organized system of spirituality is to be found in the Rule, where he speaks of the spirit, in other words, the spirituality of the Institute. Thus he writes:

> That which is of the utmost importance, and to which the greatest attention should be given in an Institute, is that all who compose it possess the spirit peculiar to it; that the novices apply themselves to acquire it; that those who are already members make it their first care to preserve and increase it in themselves; for it is this spirit that should animate all their actions, and be the motive of their whole conduct. . . .

De La Salle identifies the spirit of his Institute in three distinct passages in his Rule. In chapter two he writes: "The spirit of this

Institute is, first, a spirit of faith," and "Secondly, the spirit of this Institute consists in an ardent zeal for the instruction of children. . . ." Then in chapter three he writes: "A true spirit of community shall always be evident and preserved in this Institute."

Faith, zeal, and community are not three separate entities attached to the word spirit. In the thought of the Founder, faith overflows into zeal for the spread of the Gospel and is lived in a faith community. That is why the most recent revision of the Rule insists on the integration of the three essential constituents of the Lasallian vocation: consecration as an expression of faith, ministry as an expression of zeal, and community life.

The spirit of faith is the core of Lasallian spirituality. It is the spirit of radical faith in the Providence of God that leads the Brothers "not to look upon anything but with the eyes of faith, not to do anything but in view of God, and to attribute all to God." This God is the one, true, real, and Triune God, Father, Son, and Holy Spirit, prostrate before whose "infinite and adorable majesty" the Brothers "consecrate themselves entirely to procure the glory of God as far they are able and as God will require of them." De La Salle urges the Brothers to nourish this spirit of faith by sensitivity to the presence of God, recalled frequently during the day; by fidelity to the practice of meditation; by self-discipline; and by serious doctrinal study and spiritual reading, especially in the Sacred Scriptures.

If the spirit of faith were to remain fixed on these mostly otherworldly elements, Lasallian spirituality would be suitable only for contemplatives. De La Salle envisioned the energy that constitutes the spirit of faith as overflowing into a spirit of zeal for a specific mission: the overpowering urge to bring the good news of salvation in Jesus Christ to the educational world, specifically to those whose poverty in one form or another places them "far from salvation." Thus faith and zeal are two aspects of the same spirit or spirituality: faith overflows into zeal; zeal is rooted in faith.

The same is true of the relationship in Lasallian spirituality between the spirit of faith and the spirit of community. The spirit of community unites the Brothers among themselves, and the Brothers in association with their colleagues, in a faith community fired by a missionary zeal in an educational enterprise. The mutual brotherhood that builds the Lasallian community has its foundation in faith. Thus the Rule of the Brothers says: "The distinctive character of the Brothers' community is to be a community of faith where the experience of God is shared."

The spirituality that results is thus apostolic and not monastic, a lay rather than a clerical way of seeking the perfection demanded by the Gospel, a spirituality accessible to beginners as well as beneficial to the spiritually mature. The effectiveness of this approach to spirituality is seen in the person of De La Salle himself and the number of saintly Brothers, many of them candidates for formal canonization. Lasallian spirituality has had a significant effect as well in transforming the lives of the generations of students who have been exposed to its influence.

More recently, the distinctive features of Lasallian spirituality have proven useful and attractive to the professional colleagues of the Brothers and other adults who constitute the Lasallian family. As the 1987 Rule puts it:

> The spiritual gifts which the Church has received in Saint John Baptist de La Salle go far beyond the confines of the Institute which he founded. . . . The Institute can associate itself with lay people who want to lead the life of perfection that the Gospel demands, by living according to the spirit of the Institute and by participating in its mission.

The Institute of Brothers as Legacy

The spiritual vision of De La Salle could never have survived to enrich future generations of Brothers, students, and colleagues, if the Community had not achieved institutional form. Its formally approved and clearly defined juridical character is a necessary and important guarantee that the legacy of De La Salle will have stability and permanence, that the spirituality and the charism of the Founder can be kept alive, developed, and transmitted from one generation to the next. Thus it is the Institute itself that constitutes the total legacy of John Baptist de La Salle.

At the same time, it might be said that the language of institute and institutionalization is not the best way to describe the totality of the legacy left by De La Salle. It is not even the language that the Brothers used from the beginning to describe themselves. The corporate term that they preferred was Society or Community rather than Institute.

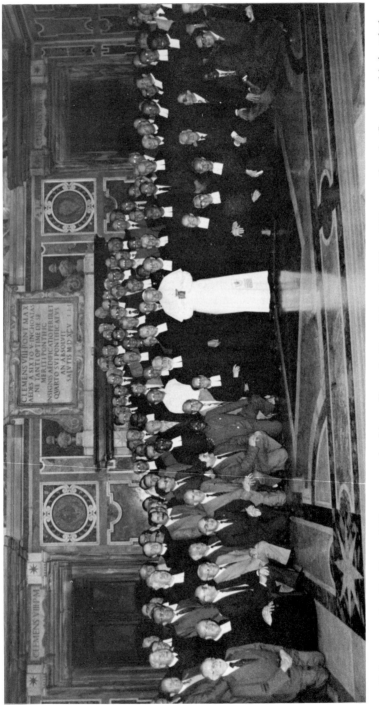

Delegates to the 41st General Chapter, received in audience by Pope John Paul II just 300 years after the first assembly in 1686

Implicit in the words society and community is the fact that the Institute is an association of persons, of persons who call themselves Brothers. It was in 1682, at the moment when the small band of schoolteachers moved with De La Salle into the Rue Neuve and formed themselves into a community, that they began to call themselves Brothers. It soon became their custom to post a wooden placard over the door of their schools announcing for all to see that they were the Brothers of the Christian Schools: not a school, not an institution or an institute, but Brothers, Brothers to one another and elder brothers to the young lads they would serve. It was this same sign over the door at the Rue de Charonne in Paris that was interpreted as a challenge to the educational establishment of the day.

The Brothers are not only the sons and heirs of De La Salle, but they are themselves part of the legacy. Thus the *Declaration on the Brother in the World Today,* issued by the 39th General Chapter in 1967, affirms that "the wealth of the Institute is nothing less than the Brothers who compose it."

This awareness that the Brothers are at the same time part of the legacy and entrusted with it is expressed in the same document in these terms:

> The charism of the Founder involves institutions only through the mediation of persons. Saint John Baptist de La Salle founded a living community of Brothers with whom he shared his apostolic ideal and who in turn passed on this ideal to their successors. Fidelity to the specific intentions of the Founder and to the tradition of the Institute is confided to us as living persons. It is we who carry on the task of discovering how fidelity to his charism can be lived in the present time.

More recent general chapters have come to realize that the brotherhood lived in the Institute is an open concept: that brotherhood implies relationships that transcend canonical categories. More and more the concept of the Institute extends beyond the Brothers to include all the members of the Lasallian family. The legacy of association, community, and brotherhood is to be shared not only with colleagues but with students, parents, and former students as well. Thus the Institute that De La Salle left as his legacy becomes an inheritance available to the Church and the world through an ever-widening association of legitimate heirs.

The testamentary document of the legacy of De La Salle in this wider sense is the Rule, revised in the post-Vatican II General Chapter and approved by church authority in 1987. A superficial comparison with the Rule written by De La Salle in 1718, looked at from the point of view of external practices and obligations, would reveal striking discontinuities, as if the testament had been changed after the death of the testator. Looked at in terms of an enduring legacy, however, all of the essential elements are still there: the spirit of faith and zeal, apostolic mission, consecration, community life, prayer, formation, government, and the vitality of the Institute itself.

With that in mind, this Rule can say of itself: "The Rule defines the meaning of the Brothers' life. It translates into modern terms and reaffirms what Saint John Baptist de La Salle intended in his Rule." There can be no better way to conclude this study of the life and the enduring legacy of John Baptist de La Salle than to quote the final article of the Rule:

> The Brothers bear witness to their love for Saint John Baptist de La Salle as their Founder. They imitate him in his abandonment to God, his loyalty to the Church, his creative apostolic spirit, and his definitive commitment to the evangelization of young people.
>
> The life of an Institute is a continual challenge to be creative while remaining faithful to its origins. It can sometimes call for difficult commitments, as John Baptist de La Salle discovered at various points in his life. Today, as in the past, he challenges the Brothers, not only as the one who established the Institute but as the Founder who continues to inspire and sustain it.
>
> Filled with the spirit which he left them as their legacy, the Brothers grow in the living tradition of the Institute. In communion with those who have gone before them, they continue to respond with ardent zeal to the appeals of the Lord, the Church, and the world, in order to procure the glory of God.

In these words, the life of a man who lived more than 300 years ago, and left as his legacy an Institute that has been a force for good ever since, becomes a challenge for the future. That future is in the hands of God, the God whom De La Salle himself often addressed in these words: *Domine, opus tuum* — Lord, the work is yours.

Index